The Moonlighter's
Short-Term
Trading
Bible

Ten Commandments
for Making Money Trading Stocks
While Keeping Your Day Job

David Rye

EP
Entrepreneur.
Press

Managing Editor: Jere Calmes
Cover Design: Debra Valencia
Composition and Production: Eliot House Productions

This publication is designed to provide accurate and authoritative information in
regard to the subject matter covered. It is sold with the understanding that the publisher is not engaged in rendering legal, accounting, or other professional services. If
legal advice or other expert assistance is required, the services of a competent professional person should be sought.

—From a Declaration of Principles jointly adopted by a
Committee of the American Bar Association and
a Committee of Publishers and Associations

Library of Congress Cataloging-in-Publication
Rye, David E.
    The moonlighter's short-term trading bible: ten commandments for making
money trading stocks while keeping our day job/by David Rye.
        p. cm.
    Includes bibliographical references and index.
    ISBN 1-891984-52-7
        1. Stocks—United States. 2. Electronic trading of securities—United States. 3.
Investments—United States. 4. Finance, Personal—United States. I. Title.
    HG4910.R94 2002
    332.6'0285—dc21   2002019156

Printed in Canada

09 08 07 06 05 04 03 02 01   10 9 8 7 6 5 4 3 2 1

Preface

THE START-UP OF THE NEW MILLENNIUM WAS NOT FOR THE FAINT OF heart who were investing in the stock market. It was laced with dramatic changes and events such as the destruction of the World Trade Center in which astute investors were forced to surf swelling waves of volatility to achieve financial success. Although many of them made lots of mistakes and consequently didn't make it back to shore, more millionaires have been created in this past decade than ever before in spite of the fact that the Lord giveth and the Lord taketh away. The stealth economy of the '90s suddenly turned into a bear in early 2000 that literally gobbled up billions of investors' dollars. The stock market soared, then plummeted, then soared again, forcing investors to tear up and reconstruct their financial strategies.

Add the international economic crisis that spread like a contagion throughout much of the world after the terrorist attacks in September of 2001 and you had near panic on Wall Street. For companies in Asia and much of the developing world, the mixture of plummeting currencies and depressed economies put pressure on the earnings of U.S. firms whose export markets were virtually shut down. Throw in rising wages, a huge increase in unemployment, a significant drop in consumer spending and consumer confidence, and it was a chaotic picture for all of us.

Despite radically different ages, races, and backgrounds, thousands discovered how to make money trading stocks online. What's so profound is that they were just average people like you and me. Most of them didn't have a silver spoon stuck in their mouth when they were born. And yet, they've become wealthy or are well on their way to being wealthy because they learned what commandments to obey when they invested in the stock market. It's not complicated if you're willing to spend a few hours reading this book and learning how to play the game. Then, you too will be rewarded with unprecedented wealth.

Introduction

WELCOME TO THE EXCITING WORLD OF ONLINE TRADING. HANG ON
tight because if you jump aboard, it will be the most exhilarating
ride you'll ever take. The stock market is the mother of all roller
coasters that's capable of lifting investors to hair-raising heights
and then dropping them to new lows without regard for their
screams. Adrenaline junkies become addicted to the excitement
while the more timid simply quit.

Online trading, or the art of buying and selling stocks over the
Internet is exploding as a home-based business for moonlighters
and many are making big bucks doing it. The Dow Jones
Industrial Average (Dow) has doubled since 1995. In earlier years,
the most boisterous stocks might have added one or two points
(dollars) a share per day. Today, some stocks rocket five or more
points in a day yielding huge profits to those who have the intes-
tinal fortitude to hang on for the ride. As a result, the market's
volatility has encouraged a growing number of people to forsake
the "buy and hold" rule of investing. Instead, they're turning their

portfolios over quickly and trading in and out of the market to take advantage of wide price swings.

The mighty Internet allows average investors to get in on the action. Never before have they been able to access so much information to make informed buying and selling decisions. Facts known only to stockbrokers a few years ago are now at investor's fingertips. Want to know the price of Microsoft? Type "nasdaq.com" in your URL address space, enter "MSFT" for Microsoft, and zap! The Nasdaq Stock Exchange Web site appears with more information about Microsoft than you can imagine.

And, God bless the online brokers who have helped make this all possible. They have popped up like mushrooms offering cheap trading fees. While full-service brokers charge up to $250 commission per trade, an online broker's commission can be as low as $5. Although most online brokers don't offer the personal services of full-service brokers, the majority offer online "help yourself" research tools to help you get whatever information you need to make intelligent decisions.

Their highly sophisticated trading software also gives online investors the ability to route their trading orders to "the floor" in seconds. All you have to do is jump onto the Internet, pull up a chart, review the news and what analysts have to say about a stock that interests you, make your decision, and press a button to instantly buy a stock in nearly any publicly traded companies in the world. We'll cover each of the steps you need to go through to become a successful online trader. Here's are four easy steps to get you started:

1. *Create an investment plan.* Visit Quicken's Web site (www.quicken.com) to get ideas on what you need to do to create a plan.

2. *Select on online broker.* Etrade (www.etrade.com) offers a variety of services to their customers.

3. *Find great stocks and mutual funds to invest in. Smart Money* magazine offers an excellent Web site (www.smartmoney.com) where you can find the movers and the shakers in the market.

4. *Track you portfolio and know when to buy and sell.* Stock Point, a company that offers on-line financial applications (www.stock point.com) offers a free portfolio-tracking program.

WHO ARE THE MOONLIGHTERS?

Moonlighters are what you get when you combine a traditional long-term investor who has got a full-time job with someone who makes a living day trading stocks full-time online. They're interested in making extra bucks on the side (moonlighting) by trading stocks and many would ultimately like to become full-time traders if they could develop a winning system. Moonlighters hold stocks longer than most day traders, actively watch their portfolio, and if the conditions are right, sell faster than traditional buy-and-hold investors. They like using short-term trading strategies to improve their long-term returns and they all have a burning desire to become financially independent.

Although moonlighters don't dislike the corporate world, they would much rather be working for themselves than someone else. They're fiercely independent in their thinking and will go to great lengths to learn about new ways to become financially independent. They also have specific goals that they're driven to accomplish. Risk is a word they're not afraid of and know they must accept risk to get ahead.

THE ODDS FAVOR YOU

Betting on stocks bears little resemblance to gambling at a casino, in spite of what your friends may have told you. Casino odds always favor the house. But in the stock market, the odds favor the investor.

Over time, the vast majority of quality stocks increase in value. In fact, the overall stock market tends to move up over the years. From 1983 through 2001, the Dow set new highs 15 out of 19 years. That's not to say there won't be some ups and downs as we saw in 2000 and 2001. There will be slow, volatile periods, and even dramatic declines in stock prices from time to time. Experienced investors like to refer to those periods as "buying opportunities." Those who invest for the long term clearly have the odds in their favor.

Since 1900, there have been four years when the market dropped more than 20 percent, which is considered bear territory. There have also been 27 years when the market rose by more than 20 percent, which is considered bull territory. And, as profits climb, the value of the company increases, which in turn boosts the value of its stock. One key to beating the market is finding companies that are growing the fastest. We'll show you where to find them later in the book. When you invest in their stock, you become a part owner in a corporation that is serious about making a profit.

BENEFITS OF TRADING ONLINE

Trading online is a made-to-order opportunity for moonlighters. You can trade when and where you want to, structure your days as you choose, and work from your regular or home office, or even when traveling. If you think of online trading as a home-based business, your initial investment in equipment (i.e., a good personal computer setup) is relatively inexpensive or "no cost" if you already have one. You're independent and answer to no one but yourself. Forget about reporting to a boss since you are your own boss. You don't have to wear a tie that chokes you or high heels that dislocate your back. You can trade in a torn T-shirt and bare feet whenever you want.

When you start-up an online trading business, you'll develop your own trading style based on what you'll learn in this book. It could be a fast-paced-high-return style or an easy-going-low-risk style. When the market is highly volatile, you might be content to sit on the sidelines and watch the action until you spot a good opportunity. All the while, you're learning everything you can to improve your odds of picking winning stocks and making money.

WHAT MAKES ONLINE TRADERS SUCCESSFUL?

Successful traders are not afraid to make decisions that may affect their accounts by thousands of dollars. They can easily handle multiple tasks to get the most out of their limited free time. They may scan charts while listening to CNBC. If they're watching a list of market indicators, they will mentally compute the indicator's relationship to one another, while keeping an eye on one or more stock positions. These traders rely on intuition and experience that's backed up with "gut feel" when they buy or sell a stock.

Traders know that sticking to a bad decision is the worst thing they can do. Emotional discipline is a must and the best traders constantly monitor their emotions. In *Trading for a Living*, Dr. Henry Elder says, "Your feelings have a direct impact on trade decisions. You may have a brilliant trading system, but if you feel frightened, arrogant, or upset, you'll make bad decisions and your portfolio will suffer. I've traded while feeling scared, smug, and sad. During those times, I've always lost money. One emotion I still allow myself is pure self-congratulation. After I close a great trade, I punch the air with my fist, and whap myself on the back."

WHAT THIS BOOK WILL DO FOR YOU

During the height of the great bull market in the Roaring '20s, Will Rogers was asked what he thought of the returns in the stock market. "To tell you the truth," he said, "I'm more concerned about the return of my money than the return on my money." As you will see, I'm not promising you high returns without any risk. However, I will show you how many investment risks can be systematically avoided or minimized so that you can enjoy the benefits of high return rates on your money. You will learn how to avoid common mistakes that people make when investing in stocks. If you follow my advice, you'll make more money than you ever dreamed possible. And, once you set-up your investment program, you won't need to spend a lot of time managing it.

Your investment program should be based upon common sense. Review the facts and ideas that I present and apply common sense to every investment decision you make. Here's how my common sense philosophy works. Let's suppose you've been invited to participate in a 20-mile race down a wide, straight road with no traffic. You're racing against Lance Armstrong, the winner of the Tour de France, the Super Bowl of bicycle races, and the best bicycle racer on earth. He'll be riding the most sophisticated racing bike ever built.

You're going to be racing him in your vintage 1961 Volkswagen Beetle. Even though it has some rust spots on it, the engine still runs and the gear box works. Who do you think will win the race? No matter how good Lance is, there is no way he's going to beat a car. Although he'll probably get off to a faster start than your VW, you will eventually overtake him and win the race.

This analogy forms the basis of the investment approach that I take throughout the book. Over the long haul, stocks have historically outperformed bonds, savings accounts, certificates of deposit, and just about any other available investment option. The only thing you have to do to make it happen is invest in the right stocks and avoid making stupid mistakes.

I discourage you from buying one of those "hot" initial public offerings (IPOs) or stocks that your buddy told you about on the golf course. Why? It's simple. It would be a stupid mistake! If you want to control your risk, don't buy highly speculative stocks under the illusion that you'll enjoy high rates of return. And, don't buy "cheap" stocks just because they're cheap. They are cheap because they aren't worth much. Instead, invest in value stocks that are financially solid, have proven track records, and are consistently earning high rates of returns. That's how you make the real money in the market while minimizing your risk. I will show you how easy it is to find winning stocks.

REMEMBER THE TITANIC

I like to remind people of how the investors who owned the Titanic must have felt just before it set sail. They probably felt pretty good. After all, they had just invested in something that could not sink. The next time you get excited about a "cannot lose" investment, remember the Titanic.

DON'T PROCRASTINATE

Investing in the stock market does not require a degree in rocket science. What trips most people up is that initial hurdle, the act of actually putting money into the market. Millions of would-be investors never succeed because they don't take that first step. They don't take money out of their bank accounts and put it into the stock market, citing a litany of excuses like "the market is down right now" or "the market is too high."

If you're caught in this trap, you will never know anything about investing in the stock market. Years later, those that had the courage to take the plunge and invest in the market will look back on a lifetime of successful investing, not because they were lucky, and not necessarily because they were good. They succeeded in large part because over the long term, the stock market has produced an average rate of return of 12 percent.

THERE'S A FORTUNE TO BE MADE

There's a fortune in your future that's not pie in the sky if you know how to avoid the common mistakes most investors make and have a desire to make it happen by investing in today's dynamic stock market. Americans are retiring with more money today than at any time in our nation's history. And, they're doing it by investing wisely in stocks and mutual funds. A couple of years ago, investors were satisfied with just a 10 percent return on their money. If you were 30-years-old, all you had to do to become a millionaire at age 65 was to save $3,500 a year. In today's market, you can cut that time at least in half because smart investors are demanding and getting at least 20 percent or more out of their investments in the stock market.

The Ten Commandments cover the ten strategic steps you need to take to start-up a successful online stock trading business. The beauty of this business is that start-up costs are minimal since all you need is a PC with an Internet connection. You can open an online account for as little as $500, start buying and selling stocks as a moonlighter, and let it grow into a full-time venture.

WATCH FOR ICONS ALONG THE WAY

Icons are used throughout *The Moonlighter's Online Trading Bible* to help guide you through all of the book's great ideas. These icons include:

- *Insights.* These give you another perspective on the principles and practices covered in the chapter. They also define less familiar terms and provide you with meaningful information to consider.
- *Buzzwords.* Although we explain all "buzzwords" in the text, certain ones demand and require immediate and additional definition. You'll find expanded definitions under this icon.

- *Warnings.* Mistakes are always possible when you invest in the stock market. Each warning tells you to how to avoid common mistakes that could cost you thousands of dollars so that you stay head of the investment game.
- *Pointers.* These direct you to specific steps you may want to take to achieve your financial goals.
- *Sidebars.* These are short paragraphs that elaborate on key topics that are covered in the various chapters.

Each chapter ends with a "Putting It All Together" section covering chapter highlights and important steps readers should take before reading further. Chapter-related Web sites are also featured after this section so that you'll know where to go if you need additional information.

A comprehensive appendix in the back of the book is filled with information to help you successfully invest in the stock market. The appendix is divided into two parts. Appendix I includes the questions for the quiz that we cover in Commandment #1. Appendix II lists publications to check out, associations to consider joining, a glossary of terms, and great Web sites to visit. Investing in the stock market is a high-energy game so pull up a chair and read on: you'll learn how to do it, have fun while doing it, and make a fortune all at the same time.

Do Not Think You Know Everything

*Investors who tell me they already know
everything there is to know about
investing are fools. I don't pretend to
know everything and I'm not a fool.*

—PETER LYNCH

WELCOME TO THE STOCK MARKET GAME AND PLEASE DON'T TELL ME you already know everything there is to know about how to play it. Nobody does! Although anyone can play by simply turning on their computer and using a few keystrokes to instantly buy a piece of a company or mutual fund, only a few moonlighters know how to make real money trading stocks online. And, even they are not afraid to admit they don't know everything about the market. That's why they constantly strive to learn everything they can. Before you get started, take the "What Do You Know?" quiz in the back of this book. It will help you determine how much you know about the market and determine what investment areas you may need to work on to improve your overall knowledge of the market.

> Anyone can improve upon their investment knowledge now that the Internet makes learning as easy as trading stocks online. For a crash course, review the interactive "Money 101" seminar at www.money.com. You can also learn a lot by visiting Morningstar University (morningstar.com) and the Motley Fool's School (www.fool.com). Also, check out resources like the Road Map to Investing, sponsored by the Securities and Exchange Commission (www.sec.gov).

MARKET BASICS

Every day you hear that the market is either up or down. Usually, the phrase refers to the U.S. stock market as measured by the Dow Jones Industrial Average (DJIA) better known as the Dow. However, the Dow is not the entire market, but just an average of 30 well-known companies like IBM, Merck, McDonald's, and Sears that are chosen by the editors of The Wall Street Journal. The list changes occasionally as companies merge, lose prominence, or rise to the top of their industry.

The Dow is an index you can use to judge the trend of the overall market by looking at a piece of it. It's the most widely cited index, but is not the best gauge of the market. A more popular index among investors is S&P's 500 (S&P 500) that tracks 500 leading companies across four industries. It accounts for 80 percent of the value in the New York Stock Exchange (NYSE). The Russell 2000 tracks 2,000 small companies across several industries while the Wilshire 5000 tracks about 6,000 stocks of all sizes. The Morgan Stanley EAFE (EAFE stands for Europe, Australia, and Far East) tracks foreign stocks. There are dozens of other indexes that you will encounter as you dig deeper into the market. Each index attempts to monitor the progress of a market by looking at a sliver of it.

TABLE 1-1 Components of the Major Market Indexes

Market Index	Companies Tracked
The Dow Jones Industrial Average (Dow)	30 Large U.S. Companies
S&P's 500 (S&P 500)	500 Large U.S. Companies
Russell 2000	2,000 Small U.S. Companies
Wilshire 5000	6,000 U.S. Companies of All Sizes
Morgan Stanley (EAFE)	1,100 Companies in 20 Countries
Nasdaq	100 Top Companies in the Nasdaq

PRICE/EARNINGS (PE) RATIO

A common tool investors use to evaluate a stock is its Price/Earnings or PE ratio. This is determined by dividing a company's stock price by its annual earnings per share. For example, a company with earnings of $2 per share over the last 12 months and a stock price of $30 per share, would have a PE ratio of 15. In many respects, a PE ratio is similar to a popularity index. Stocks that are popular with investors sport high PE ratios, while those that are in the doldrums usually carry lower PE ratios. A company experiencing rapid earnings growth usually has a much higher PE ratio than a company in a cyclical industry with volatile earnings.

Several studies suggest that stocks with low PE ratios often outperform the market. The logic is that low PE stocks are already discounted and any positive increase in earnings should drive them higher. Conversely, stocks with high PE ratios reflect high expectations and are vulnerable to sharp sell-offs should results come in below Wall Street's expectations. One of the best ways to use a PE ratio is relative to the market and its historical range. For example, a stock with a PE ratio that is usually above the market average but that has recently dipped below the market average may signal a buying opportunity.

Companies that are expected to have fast-growing profits generally have higher PE ratios than stocks with modest growth prospects. Why?

INSIGHT

One investment rule of thumb is to never invest in an issue whose earnings growth rate does not match or exceed the PE ratio. A company with a 40 percent earnings growth rate could support a stock with a PE ratio of up to 40.

Because a PE ratio reflects expectations for future earnings growth and investors are willing to pay a premium for that growth. The better the expected earnings growth, the higher the PE ratio.

If the value of future earnings is expected to be affected adversely by inflation, then investors will not be willing to pay as much today for a company's future earnings.

Investors will not want to pay as much for stocks with high PE ratios since the value of the growth is discounted by inflation. The upshot is that PE ratios contract during periods of high inflation. During periods of low inflation, the future value of earnings remains the same and investors may be more willing to pay a premium for growth stocks.

BOOK VALUE

Book value is one of those terms that few investors understand or know how to use it when evaluating a stock. It is determined by subtracting a company's liabilities from its assets, and then dividing the result by the number of shares outstanding. A company with balance sheet assets of $5 million and liabilities of $3 million has a "net worth" of $2 million. If there are one million common shares outstanding, the book value is $2 per share ($2 million net worth divided by one million shares). Many investors use book value as a benchmark of the company's underlying worth and compare book value with the stock price to determine whether the stock is over or under priced.

TOTAL RETURN

In order to evaluate the performance of a stock in your portfolio, you must understand the concept of "total return." A stock's total return measures the entire gain or loss that it generates over some specified period of time. Total return is the sum of a stock's price appreciation plus the stock's yield. Let's say you own a stock that's trading for $50 at the beginning of the year. At the end of the year, the stock is trading for $75 per share and over the course of the year, you receive $2 per share in dividends.

What's the stock's total return?

First, add up the stock's capital gains, and convert that to a percentage. In this example, the stock rose 25 points during the year, which translates to a 50 percent price appreciation (25 divided by 50 equals 50 percent). You also received $2 in dividends on your $25 investment, which translates to a yield of 8 percent. Add the yield to the price appreciation and the stock's total return is 58 percent.

You can use a similar computation to figure out your portfolio's return. Let's say the value of your portfolio at the beginning of the year is $25,000 and you add no new money during the year. At the end of the year, it has increased to $35,000. The increase includes dividends paid on your stocks that totaled $1,000. Thus, your portfolio's total return is 40 percent ($9,000 in capital gains plus $1,000 in dividends divided by $25,000).

How do you know if your portfolio's yearly performance was good or bad? One way is to compare it against a benchmark, such as the S&P 500 index. If your portfolio's total return for the year was 10 percent, but the S&P 500's total return was 25 percent, your portfolio dramatically trailed the market. What's a reasonable expectation for a stock portfolio's annual total return? Obviously, total return will vary greatly from one year to the next. However, it's useful to know that the average annual total return of the S&P since 1926 has been about 11 percent.

RULE OF 72

The rule of 72 provides an easy way to determine average annual return of any investment you make. If your portfolio doubled in value over the past four years, what was your average annual return? To find out, divide 72 by the number of years it took your portfolio to double (assuming you invested no new money). What if your portfolio doubles every 10 years? Dividing 72 by ten gives you an annual return of 7.2 percent.

The rule of 72 provides an easy way to gauge the value of boosting a portfolio's return an extra 1 or 2 percent each year. A portfolio that earns 9 percent a year doubles in eight years, whereas a portfolio that earns 10 percent annually doubles in a little over seven years. The rule also makes it easy to put the stock market's long-term performance in perspective. Recall that the stock market's average annual return since 1926 was 11 percent. Dividing 72 by 11 means that since 1926, the stock market has doubled every 6.6 years.

MARKET CAPITALIZATION

If you had deep pockets and wanted to buy a publicly traded company, the first thing you'd want to know is the company's price tag. To determine the price, you need to know the company's market capitalization. A firm's market capitalization is determined by multiplying the stock price by the number of outstanding common shares. For example, the market capitalization of a company with a stock price of $50 per share and 10 million outstanding common shares is $500 million ($50 times 10 million).

Remember that the value of a publicly traded company is ultimately determined by Wall Street. A good way to view a stock's market capitalization is to look at how Wall Street is pricing the entire company. A company with a market capitalization of $500 million means Wall Street believes the price tag for the entire firm is $500 million.

STOCK YIELDS

A stock's yield is determined by dividing its annual dividend per share by its price. Yield is like the interest earned in a savings account. For example, if you have $200 in a savings account earning 5 percent interest, you will receive $10 in interest for the year. Similarly, if you own a stock priced at $50 per share with a yield of 5 percent, you will receive $2.50 per share in annual dividends. If a stock you own is trading at $25 per share and pays $1 per share in annual dividends, the yield is 4 percent (1 divided by 25 equals 0.04 or 4 percent).

Some investors use yield to pick stocks, while others ignore yield and focus on a company's capital-gains potential. Capital gains represent the rise in the stock price over time. One reason an investor may trade a higher yield for capital-gains potential is that long-term capital gains are taxed at a lower rate than dividend income for individuals in high tax brackets. Conversely, an investor who needs dividend income to supplement other forms of income may focus their investments in higher-yielding stocks.

WHY DIVIDENDS ARE IMPORTANT

A number of studies breaking down stocks' total return over time show that investors should give more than a passing thought to dividends. For example, for the 15-year period ending in 1995, the S&P 500 achieved a total return of 694 percent. If the dividends in the S&P stocks had not been reinvested, the gain would have only been 354 percent. Investing in good dividend-paying stocks is especially important during rocky market periods. An issue paying good dividends does not depend solely on capital gains to reward shareholders and acts as a buffer during weak markets.

BID, ASK, AND SPREAD

The bid is the highest quoted price that buyers are willing to pay for a stock at any given moment, the ask is the lowest price that sellers are willing to accept for a stock. The bid is the price you get when you sell the stock. The ask is the price you pay to buy the stock. The spread is the difference between the two numbers and is kept by a dealer who's called a market maker. Market makers maintain fair and orderly trading by keeping an inventory of stock to satisfy demand when buyers and sellers can't be matched up. They're the middlemen who purchase inventory at a price lower than they sell it. Spreads are generally larger for stocks that are thinly traded because it takes fewer dealers to satisfy demand.

Take a closer look at how the system works. If the bid for XYZ Corporation's stock is $15½ and its ask is $15, the spread is $.50. If you place a market order, you could buy shares at $15½. The instant after you buy, your shares are only worth $15 because that's the price other sellers are asking. You might wonder if you could ask for the extra $.50 to recoup your purchase price. Even if you could ask for a higher price, nobody would pay it since everybody but you are selling at $15. Why would they pay $15½ to buy from you?

The spread can translate into a serious investment cost if you sell right away. In our example, a 50-cent spread represents 3.2 percent of the $15½ bid price. A flat brokerage commission of $18 on a 100-share trade is only a 1.2 percent cost. The spread is more than 2½ times the expense of the commission. However, you don't actually suffer the burden of the spread unless you sell right away. Hopefully, your stock will appreciate far beyond the spread and make it irrelevant. However, always be aware of the spread because your stock must move beyond the combined spread and commission costs to break even.

Placing an order to buy stock is a thrilling experience. It means you've done your research and are ready to take action. Placing a stock order online is delightfully simple and we'll cover some of the "how-to" details later in the book. For now, you should be familiar with the different types of online orders you can make.

MARKET ORDERS

A market order instructs your online broker to buy a security at the current ask price. Your buy price is whatever the stock is trading for when your order reaches the floor. With today's fast communications, that price is going to be close to where it was when you placed the order, if not the exact same price. For instance, if XYZ Corporation is trading at $15½ per share and you place a market order for 100 shares, you'll probably pick them up somewhere between $15¼ and $15¾ a share.

LIMIT ORDERS

A limit order instructs your online broker to buy or sell a security at a price that's equal to or higher than a price you specify. If you want to sell a stock at $10, your stock will be sold for $10 or higher. If you say to buy a stock at $20, you will buy at $20 or lower. Limit orders have a time period associated with them (see example in figure 1-1). When you place a limit order, it is either a day order or a good-'til-cancelled

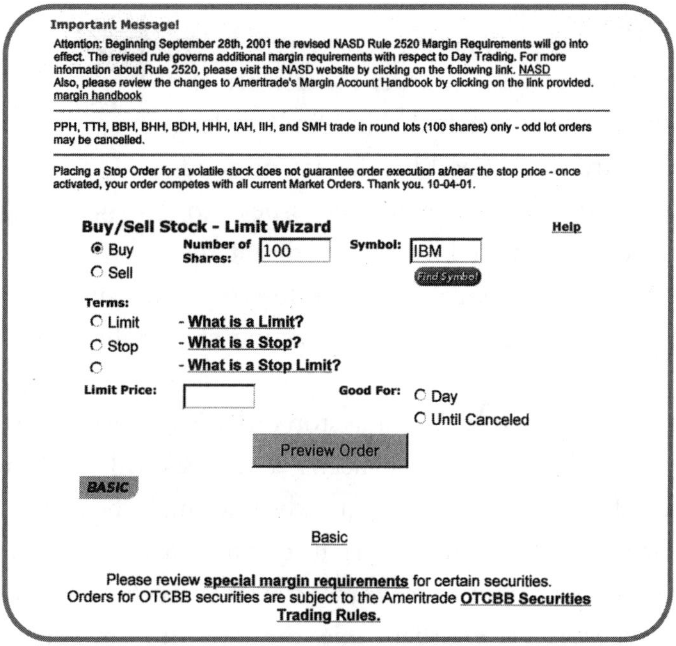

Important Message!

Attention: Beginning September 28th, 2001 the revised NASD Rule 2520 Margin Requirements will go into effect. The revised rule governs additional margin requirements with respect to Day Trading. For more information about Rule 2520, please visit the NASD website by clicking on the following link. NASD Also, please review the changes to Ameritrade's Margin Account Handbook by clicking on the link provided. margin handbook

PPH, TTH, BBH, BHH, BDH, HHH, IAH, IIH, and SMH trade in round lots (100 shares) only - odd lot orders may be cancelled.

Placing a Stop Order for a volatile stock does not guarantee order execution at/near the stop price - once activated, your order competes with all current Market Orders. Thank you. 10-04-01.

Buy/Sell Stock - Limit Wizard   Help

⦿ Buy   **Number of** 100   **Symbol:** IBM
○ Sell   **Shares:**   Find Symbol

Terms:
○ Limit   - **What is a Limit?**
○ Stop   - **What is a Stop?**
○   - **What is a Stop Limit?**

Limit Price: **Good For:** ○ Day
                                      ○ Until Canceled

Preview Order

BASIC

Basic

Please review **special margin requirements** for certain securities.
Orders for OTCBB securities are subject to the Ameritrade **OTCBB Securities Trading Rules.**

FIGURE 1-1   Screen Example of a Limit Order

(GTC) order. A day order expires at the end of the current trading day regardless of whether or not its conditions were met. A GTC order remains open until its conditions are met, which might never happen.

I love limit orders and use them almost exclusively. There's no better way to remain calm about the markets than to evaluate a company, decide on a fair price to pay for its stock, specify the price you're willing to pay, and forget about it. If the stock hits your buy price, you end up owning the stock at that price. If not, you never hear about it. It works the same way when you sell. If a stock you own is bouncing around what you consider to be a good sell price, just specify your sell price and number of shares to sell. Then forget about it. A few days later, perhaps, the stock will spike up for a brief moment, hit your price, and sell at the price you wanted.

> **WARNING**
>
> Monitor your limit orders after you place them. The last thing you want is for a stock to hit its buy limit when you don't have enough money sitting in your account to cover the transaction.

STOP ORDERS

A stop order becomes a market order when the price you specify is reached. Like limit orders, stop orders are either good for the day or good-'til-cancelled. If you own a stock and issue a stop order to sell it at a price lower than what it currently trades for, that's called a stop-loss order because you're either limiting your potential loss or protecting the profit you've already gained.

When the price you specify in a stop order is reached, the stop order becomes a market order. That means your stock will trade at its current price. If the price is moving quickly, that might be higher or lower than your stop. This is an important distinction between limit orders and stop orders. A limit order trades the stock at the price you specify or better, whereas a stop order trades the stock at its current price after it touches the price you specify. Thus, with a stop order your trade might occur at a price better or worse than the stop price.

To get around this problem, you can use a stop limit order. As its name implies, it combines the features of a stop order and a limit order. First, you specify the price at which you want the stop order to kick in. Then you specify the price at which you want the limit order to trade. If the price you specify in the limit order isn't reached, your stop limit order never executes.

For example, let's say you want to buy 100 shares of XYZ Corporation that are trading at $15 per share if the price starts to move up consistently. You could place a stop order at $17. That means that if XYZ Corporation suddenly spikes up to $19, your stop order will become a market order to buy 100 shares at $17. If the price is moving quickly, the order might not go through until XYZ Corporation's asking price is $18. Perhaps that's fine with you because you just want to pick up your shares when the stock breaks out.

On the other hand, suppose you don't want to pay more for XYZ Corporation than you think it's worth. You still want to buy 100 shares if it starts moving up. You could place a stop limit order with the stop at $17 and the limit at $17½. If the stock hits $17, your stop order becomes a limit order to buy 100 shares at $17½ or better.

Now, let's assume you bought 100 shares at $17 and the stock rises to $30 a share. You don't want to lose the profits you've already gained, so you place a stop-loss order at $28. If XYZ Corporation hits the skids and plummets back down to $17, your stop-loss order will kick in at $28 and sell at the next opportunity. That really bugs you, so on further consideration you decide to cancel the stop order and replace it with a stop limit order with a stop at $28 and a limit at $28 as well. Now, if XYZ Corporation plummets to $17, you might go with it. Why? Because your limit order to sell at $28 or better won't kick in if the price hits $28 and immediately falls lower without ever coming back up. Know what you want to do and place the right kind of order.

LARGE-, MID-, AND SMALL-CAP COMPANIES

The capitalization of a company is figured by multiplying its stock price by the number of shares it has issued. A company with ten million shares outstanding whose stock price is $25 has a market cap of $250 million. Though the definition varies widely among experts, large-cap stocks are generally thought of as companies whose market values top $1 billion. The blue-chip stocks found in the Dow have market caps far exceeding that amount. By contrast, small-cap stocks are generally those companies with market capitalization of less than $500 million. In between are the mid-cap companies with capitalization ranging from $500 million to $1 billion.

Investing in small-caps is generally considered riskier than mid- and large-caps. By their nature, smaller companies have less proven records, sometimes lack adequate financing and managerial expertise, or can be vulnerable if larger competitors target their market niche. But small companies should not be discounted. Because of their size, they can deliver results many other companies can't deliver. Those with the most promising products or services have potential for explosive growth and their management teams are often more entrepreneurial and visionary. Remember that today's large-caps including giants like Microsoft and Intel were once small-caps.

Small-caps are more volatile than large-company stocks in the short term. But over long periods they deliver superior returns. The compound average annual return on the large-cap S&Ps 500 index from 1926 through September 1995 was 10 percent. But the return on small-caps during that period was 13 percent. Small-cap stocks have tended to perform strongly for periods ranging from five to seven years.

WHERE TO FIND ANSWERS TO YOUR QUESTIONS

If you're looking for answers to questions like "What is a stock PE ration?" or "Why does a company issue stock?" or "What do investors look for in value stocks?" or "How are stocks rated?" visit Investor FAQ's (Frequently Asked Questions) Web site at www.invest-aq.com/articles/stock-a-basics.html.

KEEPING TRACK OF THE MARKET

All great companies with outstanding long-term financial track records have a tendency to hit an occasional lull in the market due to cyclical Wall Street trends. A study by *Investment Business Daily* found that 90 of the best 100 stocks had periods over the past decade when they traded below their two-years-low price. When stocks are down simply because their industry sector is out of favor on Wall Street, bargains are readily available.

If you've ever followed a particular stock closely, you probably had a good idea of its trading range and a lowball price you'd like to pay for the stock. But stocks don't always cooperate. Sometimes they unexpectedly move up a few dollars before you have a chance to buy in at the price you want. If the price continues to climb, you might do better to forget that stock and move on to another one. There's a good chance that if you wait, your patience will be rewarded. All stocks go through periodic lulls and nothing goes straight up. Wait for the stock you want to drop back into your target price range.

GET RID OF YOUR LOSERS

Some people get emotionally attached to a particular stock. If you love a stock because it's made you a lot of money, that's makes sense as long as the situation doesn't change. Some people bond with a stock because they inherited it from a relative and are subsequently reluctant to sell it. Perhaps it's because they or their relatives worked for the company or they've held the stock for many years and have grown attached to it. They'll often hold onto stocks for sentimental reasons even though the stocks are poor performers.

If there's a poor performing stock in your portfolio that you won't sell for sentimental reasons, then here are the facts of life: The stock doesn't know you own it. It doesn't care about you and it has no emotional attachment to you. It doesn't have any opinion one way or another about whether you hold or sell it. So, if it's not performing, get it out of your portfolio, and put your money into a stock with more potential.

Weed out your losers as quickly as possible. If it turns out your "past" judgment was incorrect and a company comes out with an unexpectedly low earnings report, get out of the stock. Sell out a portion of your holdings in a stock if the PE ratio gets too high or if the stock grows so quickly that it ultimately accounts for more than 20 percent of your portfolio. Watch your stocks closely to make sure they stay on track. If there's a negative change in the business or the industry, or if a stock can't meet its earning projections, sell it and move on. Be willing to take lots of little losses, but never ride a stock down for a big loss.

Sell signs include changes in management strategy and failure to execute. For example, if profit margins are down, key personnel are leaving, products are coming out late, costs are out of control and earnings are lower than projected, then you have all the signs that management is not executing a viable plan. Your goal should be to accumulate a portfolio of winners.

KEEP YOUR HEAD ON STRAIGHT

If you can keep your head on straight when everyone else is losing theirs, you'll win every time. Success in the stock market requires a combination of many traits including intelligence, patience, persistence, and luck. But nothing is more important to successful investing than the ability to balance your emotions through good and bad times. Buy when stocks are down and investors are fleeing the market. Sell when market euphoria has pushed prices up beyond reason.

Fear, greed, and other emotional extremes will only get in your way. If you can keep your cool and make investment decisions based on solid research and long-term market trends rather than on emotion, you'll be way ahead of the game. You may not be able to put as much time and effort into your portfolio as mutual fund managers put into theirs, but then you don't need to maintain a portfolio of 100 to 200 stocks, as they do. Before you buy any stock, learn as much as possible about the company to determine if it's likely to perform well over the long term. Take advantage of volatility in the frenzied markets to build positions in the stocks when they're down.

BE A DISCIPLINED TRADER

In *The Disciplined Trader*, Mark Douglas says, "When winning traders were asked for their secrets of success, they categorically stated they didn't achieve any measure of consistency in accumulating wealth from trading until they learned self-discipline, how to control their emotions, and how to change their minds to flow with the markets." I can say, without hesitation, that the first day I traded with composure as my only emotion was the day I became a winning trader. By trading from my head and not my heart, I started making money consistently, trade after winning trade.

DON'T GET CONFUSED

Fortunately, experience will diminish much of your confusion, but catastrophes can occur before experience calms you down. To save time and money, take steps early on to avoid unnecessary confusion. Here's how:

1. When you start trading, buy small lots of 100 to 300 shares per trade. That way, if the stock tanks, you won't swallow a big loss.

2. Complete one trade before you enter another. Keeping up with one stock in a fast-moving market is enough of a job. If you feel like you're missing out on other opportunities, rest assured that more will come along.

3. Paper trade until you feel comfortable placing real trades. Paper trading is when you buy and sell stocks with "play money" until you feel comfortable with the market strategies you have developed.

4. Learn one trading strategy at a time. If it works, stick with that strategy and refine it over time. If it doesn't work, replace it with a new strategy.

DON'T TRY TO ALWAYS BE RIGHT

The need to always be right in trading can cause enormous losses. For example, let's suppose you decide to buy 500 shares of IGOTU.COM for $50 a share. The stock promptly falls to $45, hitting its stop-loss sell price. Instead of selling without hesitation, you grit your teeth and shout, "I'm not selling at a loss because IGOTU.COM is a good company. This will end up being a great trade. I know I'm right."

IGOTU.COM continues to fall, sinking to $40, then $30 a share, but you hold your position. Now if you sell, the loss will seriously dent your trading account, as well as your ego. You're no longer a trader. You're an "investor," as traders joke when they see other traders knowingly hold onto a losing position. When people ask you why you're still holding, you aggressively respond with, "It's a good company. It'll come back."

Maybe it will and maybe it won't. Meanwhile, the loss is very real, and even if IGOTU.COM struggles back to $50, it may take months for that to happen. During that time, you could have used that money to make profitable trades. The need to always be right can become an expensive proposition. Even the best investors are not always right. Here are several ideas to help you avoid getting caught up in the "always be right" syndrome:

- When you make a trade, don't get emotionally attached to the outcome.

- Plan your trade with exact entry points, exit points, and a protective stop-loss order. It's one of the most efficient ways to cure "the need to be right." Following your plan assures you limit your risk, and keeps your losses small and your profits big.

- Never beat yourself up for making "dumb mistakes. Berating yourself cripples your trading career by paralyzing you when a good opportunity comes up.

DON'T GET GREEDY

Bulls make money, bears make money, and pigs get slaughtered. Greed motivates new and even experienced traders. It also comes into play when you "chase" a stock, or pay too high a price for one. When you chase a stock, odds are good you'll buy at the top of the move and sell at the bottom. As a new trader, limit your risk by trading small lot sizes and don't compromise. This alone will temper any notions that "more is better."

When you see a stock screaming straight up on your quote screen and get the urge to join in the fun, sit on your hands. Go get a soda and play with the dog or walk away from your computer if you have to. If you insist on staying to watch, notice how fast the stock drops when the buyers leave and the sellers rush in.

WATCH OUT FOR FEAR

Fear, which can range from mild anxiety to gut-wrenching terror, causes more havoc in a trader's life than any other emotion. As a child, do you remember those dark nights when you believed a monster lurked under your bed? Recall the feelings? Your heart pounded, your mouth went dry, and your hands sweated. You curled into a quivering ball and waited for the monster to come and get you. Of course, no monster lurked under your bed but the sensation of fear was real. When you realized that monsters didn't exist, the fear went away.

WARNING

Don't be afraid to admit when you make an investment mistake; we all do it and that's the best way to learn. Even the Peter Lynches of the investment world make mistakes and are not afraid to admit it.

For new online traders, fear takes on many faces, from mild to severe. Dismay happens when you enter a trade and watch the S&P futures dive. Will your stock follow? Alarm and frustration arise when your Internet server goes down just when you have open positions. Fright occurs when your stock is falling a point every five seconds and you can't sell it to anyone. Outright panic comes when you hold a stock overnight, and in the morning, it opens down 13 points. Fear of losing money can cause you to exit good trades too early and stay in bad ones too long. It may also make you ignore information that's telling you what the real situation is, not how you want it to be.

How do you conquer fear? You don't. You displace it. Just as a rock displaces water in a bucket, you displace fear with a positive foundation of knowledge, experience, and self-trust. Most new traders gain a

DISPLACE FEAR WITH EXPERIENCE

As your knowledge and experience expand, they will present you with a priceless gift: self-trust. When you finally evolve to the point that self-trust guides all of your trades, your fear will disappear. You'll start trading with a calm, controlled attitude. Self-trust will give you a new sense of inner assurance and the confidence that now you're a "real" trader.

little knowledge, and then stop studying. Yet they continue to trade, repeating the same mistakes over and over, until they blow away their trading accounts.

ASK YOURSELF QUESTIONS

As an online trader, you'll meet every personality trait you own. Some traits will aid your quest for success while others will need to be reined in. It's best to identify all these characteristics early on. The more you know about yourself, the more it will benefit your trading career. When you make a questionable trading move, ask "Why did I do that? Which one of my personality traits caused that to happen?" Then consider your possible answers:

> **INSIGHT**
>
> Trading on a gut feeling that's merely a whim usually gets you into trouble. Trading on a gut feeling that's honed by knowledge and experience can save you money and fatten your wallet.

- *"I was impulsive."* Do you feel and act first, then think last? That can get you into trouble. Replace impulsive urges with thoroughly planned trades. Refrain from trading on whippy or choppy market days.

- *"I was too optimistic."* Did you hope for the best? Optimism is a cousin of faith and hope. Rose-colored glasses distort market reality.

- *"I was stubborn."* Stubbornness is a cohort of "the need to be right" and will cost you a fortune in losses.

- *"I wasn't concentrating."* A scattered mind leads to losses. Replace it with razor-sharp concentration. Practice makes profits.

- *"I was impatient."* New traders are famous for their impatience. Impatience adds to stress. Whenever possible, temper impatience by striving to stay unattached to the outcome of your trades.

LEARN TO SWIM WITH THE CURRENT

Americans are taught to be proactive rather than reactive, and we constantly think of ways to alter our relationships and environments. If you're dissatisfied with the color of your living room, you paint it. If you disagree with your partner, you take action to change things for the better. If your children misbehave, you ask them to redirect their actions.

The stock market flows like a river. Unfortunately, you cannot push it in the other direction or paint it a different color. You can disagree with it but you cannot demand that it behave differently. Once you have this concept firmly in place, your goal is to come to the market each day and regard it with positive objectivity. Learn to observe and interact with the market as it truly is, not as you wish it was. Feel no pressure to do anything except follow your plan. When the market gives you a signal to act according to your plan, execute your trades.

Assume full responsibility for every action you take during the trading day. Blame is destructive and should not be part of your trading life. Never blame anyone, not even yourself for bad trades. You made choices and must live with the results of those choices. If you follow a "hot tip" from a taxi driver and get creamed, don't blame the taxi driver. You pushed the button.

GETTING STARTED

Now that you know more than you did when you started reading this chapter, let's review some of the basic start-up principles that will help assure your success as an investor.

- *Time is the great equalizer.* Time is the great equalizer for investors and best of all, it's free and available to everyone. If time is the most influential factor in the performance of your portfolio, it follows that the most important thing you can do is to get started on an investor program as soon as possible. I know what some of you are thinking. In the 1990s, the stock market soared to record levels, but as we entered into the new millennium, the market began making huge corrections. At the time, you probably thought, "Why should I be investing now?" The problem with this thinking is that determining whether the market is too volatile is a loser's game. Many people refused to buy stocks in 1994 because they thought the market was too high, only to see it skyrocket in 1995. Those who refused to get started in 1997 because they felt that after the strong 1995 and 1996 markets, stock prices had to come down, lost out on huge gains that followed.

- *Stay in the game.* If the market is down and you pull your dollars out and walk way from it with the attitude that you'll come back when things improve, you're pulling yourself out of the game. What's the biggest risk of investing? You probably think it's being in the market when the market crashes. Wrong! The biggest risk of investing is being out of the market when the market advances. Money that's out of the market sitting on the sidelines is often a recipe for disaster. Since 1926, stocks have risen more than two out of every three years. Anytime you pull money out of the market, you are bucking strong historical upward trends. Nobody knows for sure if the market is too high or too low. What we do know is that corporate earnings will drive stock prices higher over the next 5, 10, or 15 years. If you stay in the game, you'll benefit from that trend.

- *Invest regularly.* A critical aspect of staying in the game is investing regularly, in good markets and especially in bad ones. It's the investor who maintains a regular investment program during all of the market cycles who wins big over time. If you are a long-term investor, you have to buy when the market falls if you want to maximize your long-term profit potential. Because the market's long-term trend is up, view down markets as opportunities rather than tragedies. You may have to wait several years before the market's long-term upward trend kicks back in, but there's a strong probability you will eventually be rewarded for buying when the market was down.

- *Keep your game plan simple.* Having a simple investment strategy has a variety of benefits. First, it is easier to implement and monitor over time. Many investment programs get bogged down needlessly by investors making the process more complicated than it needs to be. Make sure you have diversity in your plan. Successful investors understand the importance of diversification when constructing an investment program. Proper diversification does not mean owning 50 stocks and mutual funds. You can achieve adequate diversification in your portfolio by owning just a few stocks and funds. Diversification strategies are covered in detail in Chapter 9.

- *Play to your strengths.* Apply whatever advantages you might have when you invest in the market. For example, if you have a special expertise in a particular industry that you've worked in, consider investing in stocks within that industry.

- *Take advantage of opportunities.* Successful sport teams often maximize their score based on opportunities their opponents give them, like turning over the football at their ten-yard line. In the investment world, taking advantage of huge price declines when the market is down or when a company misses their earnings estimates can prove to be a profitable play. When a company's quarterly earnings results are just a shade below Wall Street expectations, does the fact that the company missed its earnings forecast by a couple of pennies mean that its long-term prospects are in danger? Probably not. Sure, bad news may lead to further bad news in subsequent quarters. However, I've seen Wall Street myopia shave billions of dollars in value from a quality company in a single day because they missed projected earnings by a few pennies. When Wall Street's nearsightedness hands you a great stock at a discounted price, take it.

- *Watch analysts carefully.* Wall Street is one of the few market-places where merchandise is more popular as it gets more expensive. That's because Wall Street says that if a stock's price is rising, it must be worth buying. Investors who have the courage to act on their own convictions that run counter to Wall Street's can find substantial rewards. One reason to stick with your convictions is that they're unbiased. You can't say the same for a Wall Street analyst's view of companies because their role has changed radically in recent years. Their main role today is to bring equity deals into the analyst's firm. If an analyst aggressively recommends a "strong buy" for a company's stock, their brokerage firm has a much better chance of doing underwriting and merger work for the company. Therefore, be wary of most analyst recommendations because they're probably biased.

- *Engage in foreign investment.* As an astute investor, you must be willing to go wherever value can be found. That may mean investing beyond the borders of the U.S. In the past, foreign stocks under-performed the U.S. market, which caused a number of market pundits

---

THREE DEVELOPMENT STEPS TO SUCCESSFUL INVESTING

1. Develop buy selection rules that will help you determine when it's the right time to buy.
2. Develop a set of sell rules that will tell you when it's time to take a profit or minimize your losses.
3. Develop a method for following general market averages and indicators so that you can project when the market is going into an uptrend or downtrend.

---

to jump on the "stay out of the foreign market" bandwagon. Today, many foreign stock prices are the best they have been in decades and are rising faster than U.S. stocks. If you want to be a successful investor, don't ignore overseas investment opportunities.

BUZZWORD

Growth Versus Value Investing: Growth stock investors want companies to show consistent earnings and sales growth, usually 20 percent or more each year for the past three to five years. Typically, growth stocks have high quality repeat type products or services that generate superior profit margins and return on equity. Value investors, on the other hand, search for stocks they believe are undervalued. They evaluate a company's balance sheet and profit-and-loss statements, looking for signs of hidden value such as large amounts of cash or valuable real property carried on the books below current market values.

PUTTING IT ALL TOGETHER

Don't confuse the new millennium with the past decade because it's not going to be just more of the same. Ten years ago, eBay, Cisco, and Dell weren't even around and no Federal Reserve chairman had ever warned about "irrational exuberance" in the stock market. In the old days (i.e., just a few years ago), individual investors focused more on real estate when home prices were skyrocketing throughout most of the 1980s and 1990s. In 1998, *Business Week* reported that the individual investor "has become as rare on Wall Street as a short-nosed sturgeon in the Hudson River."

A decade ago, only 50 million Americans owned stocks either directly or through mutual funds. Now that number is over 100 million and the passion with which individual investors are tracking the market on the Internet has exploded. In 1990, there were about 8,000 investment clubs. Today, there are over 40 thousand. In 1990, Nasdaq trading volume averaged 91 million shares a day. Today, Nasdaq averages 1.5 billion shares a day.

There's no question the stock market has dished out its share of pain over the past few years, but many of the problems investors endure are of their own making. To succeed in today's market, the first thing you need is common sense and the ability to make prudent, educated investment decisions rather than ones based on hot tips and emotion. You also need the patience and persistence to hold on to good stocks through down times. And, you must be calculating and confident, drawing on the knowledge that no matter how bad things look, the market will ultimately move back up. The more you put into your buy and sell decisions, the more you'll get out of them.

CHAPTER-RELATED WEB SITES

The National Association of Investors Corporation (NAIC) has local chapters throughout the country. Their goal is to help investors develop a disciplined approach to successful investing. For more information, visit their Web site at www.investing.org.

Smart Money magazine (www.smartmoney.com) offers free charts and quotes on all U.S. stocks and most funds. The Web site features company profile articles and timely comments on market trends.

Legg Mason's Web site (www.leggmason.com) provides an online questionnaire to help you develop your expertise in investing.

Invest Wisely (www.sec.gov/consumer/inws.htm) is a feature educational article for new investors from the Securities and Exchange Commission (SEC).

Investing Basics (www.aaii.com/invbas) offers feature articles about how to start successful investment programs, pick winning stocks, and how to evaluate your options.

CHAPTER-RELATED WEB SITES, continued

 If you're interested in testing your skills as an online trader with Monopoly money, checkout Hedge Hog Competition (www.market-player.com). It allows participants to build on a $1 million stock portfolio as they compete against other contestants.

 First Capital Corporation (www.firstcap.com) offers two free newsletters. *Market Timing* presents a short-term technical approach for the stock and bond markets. *Global Viewpoint* provides a weekly technical analysis of world markets.

Thou Shall Have an Investment Plan

"If you don't have a good plan, your investment program will be like a ship without a rudder, floating wherever the tide takes it."

—DAN RYE

ACCORDING TO WEBSTER'S DICTIONARY, A PLAN IS AN ORGANIZED way of methodically applying ideas and principles to make favorable events happen. Think about it. If you could consistently apply a set of ideas and principles when investing in the stock market that rewarded you with high rates of return, you'd have a winning game plan. If you don't have a plan, you won't know where you're going, let alone where you have been when you invest in stocks. You'll make countless errors in judgment and timing that will cost you thousands of dollars. You'll buy stocks that suddenly go down and continue to go down after you buy them and sell stocks that suddenly go up after you sell them. Here you will learn how to create a plan that will work for you. We'll show you how to determine your investment objectives and financial goals and put your ideas together in a financial plan.

CREATING A PLAN

Some people believe that if they're not wealthy, they don't need to do any financial planning. To do no financial planning or to allow a friend or financial advisor to do it for you is flirting with disaster. Always remember that no one cares more about your financial well-being than you do. If you don't have a solid, well thought out investment plan, then forget about investing in the stock market. If you think you have a good plan and don't need to write it down because it's all in your head, then it can't be much of a plan.

Step #1: Get in the Game ASAP

The worst excuse I've ever heard for refusing to invest in the market is the old line, "Well, the market's kind of down right now, isn't it? I'd rather wait until things turn around." That's like saying; "I'd really like to buy a new suit, but Macy's has that ridiculous 50 percent off sale going on right now, so I think I'll wait. When prices get back to normal, I'll buy the suit." The stock market is one of the only venues of commerce in which consumers actually shrink away from bargains. When stocks are on sale, that's the time to buy.

> **POINTER**
>
> Charles Schwab helps you develop a financial plan with his online calculators, tools, and advice. Go to Schwab's home page (www. schwab.com) and click "Planning" and then "General Investing." The next screen shows financial tools that include a primer on the principles of investing, a general goal planner with an online savings calculator, and an asset diversification tool.

There is always uncertainty in the market with every stock and every sector. In one of my talk show appearances, I was asked what was my top stock pick. It was a bank stock that had done very well over the past ten years. But the interviewer questioned the timeliness of the pick, suggesting that if interest rates should take a sudden upward turn that could hurt the banking industry. I answered, "Yes, that could happen. The wolf is always at the door. Every day, every week, every month, every year, interest rates could go up and bank stocks could go down. And with every stock and every sector, you could find a similar wolf at the door ready to spoil a stock's peaceful ascent."

But if you worry about every possible negative element that could affect the market, you'll never invest in stocks. At some point, if you're going to make it in the stock market, you have to get over your fears and put your money on the table. You wouldn't get far in poker if you assumed your opponent always had four aces. You'd never bet, no matter how strong your hand.

Professional gamblers know how to play the averages and so should you. Assume you will lose some hands, just as you assume some stocks will occasionally drop. But most of the time, quality stocks in your portfolio will provide solid returns. The greater evil is to let your fears keep you out of the market. If you want to make money, you've got to ante up and play the game. Over time, you will win. Just for fun, visit the Financial Center at www.financialcenter.com and click on the "Savings" icon. Then click the calculator titled, "What will it take to become a millionaire?" Enter the required data and click "Calculate." The results show how much you need to invest today to be a millionaire in the future.

As you can see, if you save a little money each month, you'll be surprised at how little you have at the end of the year. You can't make big money in stocks by throwing nickels and dimes at the market. To reach your financial goals, you need to invest substantial sums along the way. And, the older you are when you begin, the more you will need to invest each year. For instance, to reach $1 million by age 65 (assuming

WARNING

Eliminate all of your excuses. You can't do anything about "should-have-dones" like "I should have sold" or "I should have bought" because they pertain to events that happened in the past. Unless you've figured out how to build a time machine, get on with the future of your investment life.

an average annual return of 11 percent per year), a 19-year-old needs to invest just $1,000 a year. But a 40-year-old would have to invest nearly $10,000 a year to reach $1 million by retirement.

Is there an easy way to get started without losing your shirt? Yes! There's a method called "dollar cost averaging" that is simple to implement. Most Wall Street investment managers tend to trail the overall market average over the long term, despite devoting long hours every day researching companies and tracking the ups and downs of the Dow before they buy or sell. So how can small investors outperform the gurus on Wall Street? Use dollar cost averaging.

The system relies on the volatility of the market to ensure that dollar cost averaging investors automatically buy more shares when stocks are down and fewer shares when stocks are up. For example, let's say that you invest $100 a month in shares of an index mutual fund that holds a broad selection of stocks in the overall market. When the market is high and shares are trading at $25, your $100 buys four shares. When the market is down, and shares are trading at $20, your $100 buys five shares. So you're buying the most shares when stocks are low and the fewest when stocks are high.

You can implement a dollar cost averaging program automatically through a checking account deduction plan that's tied into companies that offer direct stock purchase plans; these include most of the Fortune 500 companies. Here's how the plan works. Let's say you want to open a dollar averaging account with IBM. You contact IBM's public relations office and authorize them to deduct $100 a month from your checking account to purchase whatever number of shares or partial shares that money will buy. You sign a bank authorization form to make this all happen. In this example, you start accumulating IBM stock every month until you submit written notice to end the process.

As you build up your equity position and trading experience over time, you can begin to make more aggressive trades online using the money you've accumulated in your dollar cost averaging account to increase your rate of return. Here's how. Let's assume you're purchasing IBM stock on a monthly basis and have accumulated $5,000 of stock. You simply call IBM and instruct them to sell your shares and they'll send you the check, which you can use to fund your online account. You'll learn more about dollar cost averaging in Chapter 6.

Step #2: Set Goals

The second step in the financial planning process involves setting strategic and tactical goals. Strategic goals are long term and tend to be general such as, "I want to be a millionaire by the time I'm 50." Tactical goals are short term and more specific like; "I want to save and invest $5,000 this year." Your financial plan needs to include both strategic and tactical goals. Write them down and periodically check on your progress. Update your goals to reflect changes in your life.

POINTER

Successful investing doesn't require a lot of effort or expertise. It does take commitment and perseverance. The more you put into it, the more you'll get out of it.

You don't have to follow the market every day and you don't have to take big risks. You do have to maintain an ongoing investment program with solid financial goals since success for most investors occurs over a long period of time.

INSIGHT

According to Franklin Resource Fund Manager Michael Price, "Everyone's goal should be patience and risk avoidance. Then, let time make you money. Our theme is slow and steady wins the race and hence our logo is a turtle. Our newsletter is called *The Patient Investor*, since patience is very important in successful stock market investing."

Most investors share a common goal: They want to make money investing in the market. The ones that are successful establish investment plans that cover the essential money-making steps that support their goals. First, they develop buying selection rules that help them pick the best stocks. They rely on stock charts to determine the right time to buy. Second, they develop a set of selling rules so that they know when to sell to make a profit and when to sell to avoid major losses. They rely on stock charts to help them determine the right time to buy and sell. In other words, they have a specific method that tells them when the market averages are topping or falling, and subsequently, when to buy or sell. We'll show you how to do that later in the book.

Your investment program will determine how you achieve your financial goals. Stop and evaluate your financial situation before you start investing. You want to be certain you're financially ready to be an investor. You don't want to pay penalties on early withdrawals made because you needed the cash to cover unexpected expenses. Make sure you have the following categories covered:

- *Emergency funds.* The first thing on your planning list should be to create an emergency fund. Unexpected expenses can include uninsured medical costs, auto repairs, and unemployment.

- *Adequate insurance.* Make sure you have insurance to cover disability, health, life, automobiles, and property.

- *Monthly bills.* Your goal here is to pay your monthly bills without relying on future cash sources like a bonus or credit.

- *Credit cards.* If you use credit cards to pay for everyday expenses and can't pay off monthly card balances, you aren't ready to become an investor. You need to change your spending habits and pay off credit cards before you begin investing.

- *Retirement accounts.* If you have one, make sure you continue making your full independent retirement contributions (i.e., TDSP, IRA, etc.).

Step #3: Determine Your Net Worth

The next step in getting to where you want to go financially is figuring out where you are today. Although calculating your net worth may not be exciting, it's the starting line for your investment program. Later, you can compare your increased net worth to where you started to see how well you're doing. One of the tasks that makes calculating net worth difficult is sorting personal finance data into the right asset classifications. The following suggestions will help you organize your data for the categories needed to calculate your net worth:

- *Liquid assets.* Refer to your most recent bank and brokerage statements to determine the cash value of liquid assets.

- *Property assets.* For real estate assets, use your most recent property appraisal or check with a realtor who knows your neighborhood.

BUZZWORD

Net worth is the amount of money you would have if you liquidated all of your assets and paid off all of your debts. It's determined by adding up the value of all your assets and subtracting all of your liabilities (debts). Hopefully your net worth is a positive number, which means you own more than you owe.

- *Vehicles.* Remember to deduct depreciation from the original cost of each vehicle.

- *Jewelry, art, and collectibles.* Use your insurer's appraised value or your best estimate of what you could realistically get for your collectibles.

- *Other assets.* Use your best estimate of each asset's resale value.

The Internet offers several online calculators that can assist you in determining your net worth. For example, the Altamira Resource Center's Net Worth Calculator (www.altamira.com) helps you determine your current net worth and track changes over time. You can also determine your net worth with a pencil and paper by following the format in figure 2-1.

Property Assets		Fixed Assets		Liabilities	
Residence	$	Gov. Bonds	$	Home Mortgage	$
Real Property	$	Municipal Bonds	$	Other Mortgage	$
Furnishings	$	Corporate Bonds	$	Bank Loans	$
Jewelry/Art	$	Certificates	$	Auto Loans	$
Automobiles	$	Other Fixed	$	Charge Accounts	$
Other Assets	$	Other Fixed	$	Other Debts	$
				Total Liabilities	$_____
Equity Assets		**Cash Assets**		**Net Worth**	
Real Estate	$	Checking Account	$		
Stocks	$	Savings Account	$	Total Assets	$_____
Mutual Funds	$	Credit Union	$		
Annuities	$	Other	$		
Gold/Silver	$	Other	$	Total Liabilities	$_____
Other	$	Other	$		
		Total Assets	$_____	Net Worth	$_____

FIGURE 2-1   Net Worth Form

SAVINGS VERSUS INVESTING

Saving and investing are different, although savings are often the source of funds for investing. Savings are a set level of funds that you put aside regularly in an account (i.e., savings account) that usually earns interest at a fixed rate. Investment funds are used to buy securities that can increase or decrease in value and they may earn interest or dividends, but you have no guarantee of increased value or future income.

After you've determined your net worth, test your financial fitness by visiting Quicken's Web site (www.quicken.com) which offers a variety of financial fitness tools and a questionnaire (see figure 2-2). After you answer a series of questions covering key areas such as investments, debt management, and retirement planning, you get a summary of ideas to will help reinforce your financial goals.

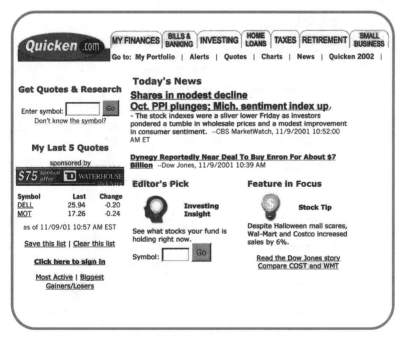

FIGURE 2-2   Quicken's Main Menu

Step #4: Create a Portfolio

Actively managing your portfolio will help you squeeze profits from your investments and realize your financial goals. You'll need to keep current on what's happening in the market, study analytical techniques, and update your financial plan on a regular basis. The Internet provides several portfolio-management tools such as the one offered on Morningstar's portfolio set-up menu (www.morningstar.com) in figure 2-3.

You can create a portfolio on the Morningstar Web site by simply entering ticker symbols for stocks, the number of shares you own, and the purchase price you paid for each stock. When you click the "Save Portfolio" button on the menu, your portfolio is saved under the name you've assigned to it. Portfolio updates are handled using the same

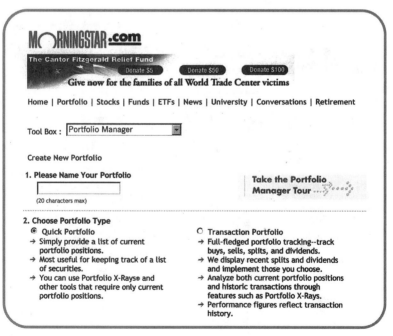

FIGURE 2-3   Morningstar's Portfolio Creator

FIGURE 2-4   Morningstar Portfolio

procedure. Now, the next time you assess your portfolio, it will appear in a format like the one shown in figure 2-4.

To keep your investment plan on track, you'll need to know how to calculate the returns on the investments in your portfolio. Start with the ending investment balance and subtract the beginning balance. Divide this number by the beginning balance and then multiply by 100 to determine the percentage of your return. For example, suppose that you invest $10,000 in stocks on January 1 and at the end of the year (December 31) your account has a value of $12,175. Here's the formula for calculating your return:

$$\text{Total Return} =$$
$$[(\text{Ending Balance} - \text{Beginning Balance}) \div \text{Beginning Balance}]$$
$$\times 100$$

Start with the ending balance and deduct the beginning balance.
$$\$12,175 - \$10,000 = \$2,175$$

Divided the result by the beginning balance:
$$\$2,175 / \$10.000 = 0.2175$$

Multiply the result by 100 to calculate your percentage
rate of return: $0.2175 \times 100 = 21.75\%$
(your return is 21.75% or 22%)

A return of 22 percent in one year by anyone's standard is pretty good. This rate means that for each dollar invested, you earned $.22 annually. Choosing the right investments to reach your annual rate of return goal is just one of many elements you need to consider when you enter the investment game. Others include:

- *Know where you stand.* Gain a good understanding of what your financial commitments are now and will be in the future. Make sure you have emergency funds set aside to cover unexpected expenses like car repairs.

- *Your financial goals.* How much do you want to make over what period of time? How much risk can you tolerate? If you lost all of your investments in the stock market, could you recover mentally and invest again?

- *How you want to allocate your investments.* What's the appropriate diversification of your personal assets for your age group (young adult, middle aged, retiree, etc.)?

POINTER

For more information about the investment process and bulletproofing your portfolio, check out Investor Home at (www.investor home.com).

Step #5: Create a Watch List

Monitor your investment alternatives on a regular basis by using what is know as a "watch list" similar to the one shown in figure 2-5. Online

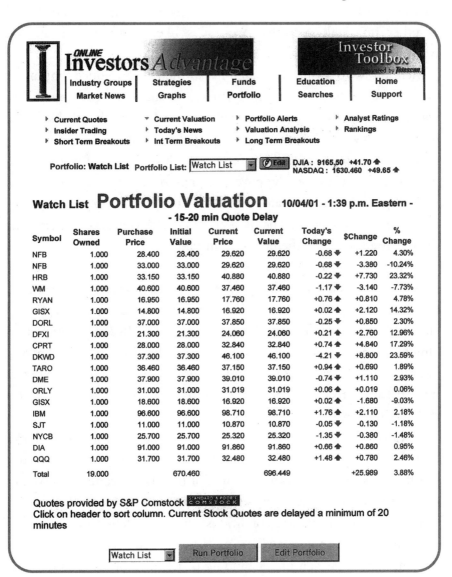

FIGURE 2-5   Investor's Watch List

tools available at several Web site locations (See Appendix) allow you to set-up and maintain watch lists. The watch list shown in figure 2-5 (www.investortoolbox.com) is offered to members who pay a monthly fee to Invest Online (801-229-3966). Free watch list tools can be found at other financially oriented Web sites like www.morningstar.com, www.money.com, and www.smartmoney.com.

Here's how to set-up the watch list in figure 2-5. Notice that under the "Shares Owned" column, I entered 1 share for each stock I'm watching even though I don't actually own it. I watch the stocks on the list to see how they perform before I buy them. You need to enter some number of shares to get a watch list to track changes in a stock's price over time. Next, I enter the purchase price of the stock on the day in which I placed it on my watch list. That's all the data you need to enter to create any watch list. The data entry process is exactly the same as the one used to create the portfolio in figure 2-3.

Now, every time I review my watch list, it tells me how well or poorly each stock on my list performed in the market. For example, GISX on the list in figure 2-5 is down 9 percent from the time I entered it. However, the third stock on the list (HRB) has jumped up almost 23 percent since it was placed on the list. That catches my attention and I may decide to conduct some research on HRB to determine if I want to buy stock in the company. I'll show you how to do that in Chapter 4.

A watch list allows you to track the performance of up to 30 stocks that you're considering for your portfolio. Use your watch list to constantly check on the performance of your investment candidates so that you can make appropriate buy decisions over time. You can expect that changes in general market conditions, the introduction of new products, and new technology will change how businesses operate. Use this information to gain an understanding of when to buy stocks on your watch list.

In order for a new company to get a space on your watch list, it must satisfy specific selection criteria that you'll set-up in chapter 4. Everybody has their own system for selecting stocks that go on their watch lists. Here's a quick outline of what I look for in a stock before I'll put it on my list. In general, I am only interested in investing in stocks that are in the top ten percentile of their respective industries. And, I only follow stocks that are on either the Nasdaq or New York stock exchanges. Since there are approximately ten thousand stocks listed on these two exchanges, that gives me a list of 1,000 stocks to consider (i.e., 10 percent of 10,000 stocks is 1000). I'm

> **WARNING**
>
> Be wary of harvesting stocks from investment grapevines. Always be careful of stories that sound too good to be true. It's human nature to talk about our triumphs and to build them up bigger than they really are.

constantly scouting to find the top 30 out of those 1,000 stocks to place on my watch list.

If I replace a stock that's on my watch list, it must be better than the stock it's replacing. By structuring your list in this manner, it improves over time. When you invest in a stock that's on the list, transfer it from your watch list to your portfolio. When you sell a stock that you want to continue following, remove it from your portfolio and put it back on your watch list.

LOOK BEYOND FIRST IMPRESSIONS

As Peter Lynch points out, a product that is a tiny part of a company's business can't move the stock very much. So no matter how much your kids love the lunar ball you bought for them, if it's one of 800 toys made by Wacky Whimsical, you don't have much reason to invest. Always, always look beyond your first impressions.

Step #6: Diversify, Diversify, Diversify

Before you buy anything, decide how you want to diversify your portfolio. Much like a recipe for a pie, your diversification plan should be in place before you make your first stock purchase. The key to a good portfolio is diversity and balance. Some people believe in buying only

FIGURE 2-6   Graphic Display of Motorola Stock

a few stocks and watching them closely. You can do that, but if one of your chosen stocks had been Motorola in the spring of 2001, you would have watched it drop 26 points in one day and continue to drop to 25 percent of its 52-week high (see figure 2-6).

However, if Motorola had been less than 5 percent of your portfolio, and even if it had gone to zero, your life still would be unaffected except for the emotional wrench that large declines elicit. Realistically, you can afford to lose 5 percent of your portfolio. However, if you have only three or four stocks sharing equal funds in your portfolio and one crashes, you could potentially lose 25 to 33 percent of your investments. That would be an emotionally disturbing exercise to go through.

Diversify your portfolio across industries as well as stocks. Have at least five to ten industries and never let any one be more than 20 percent of your total investment. If you own stock in the company you work for, make sure you include it in your industry groupings. Many people have a disproportionate amount of their portfolio in their employer's stock. I did when I worked for IBM several years ago.

Trust me on this because really nasty things can happen. Don't believe everything management tells you or that the company's stock can go nowhere but up. IBM's stock fell 50 percent in 1993 and it took several years for it to recover. Count your company stock like any other, no matter how attractive it may seem. You may find you're over-weighted in that one investment. Sell some to balance your portfolio.

Your company also has to be counted in its industry group. Too many people think they know their own industry and therefore have a competitive advantage over other investors. However, no matter how well you know your company or industry, exogenous shocks will hit either or both of them. No one industry should be more than 20 percent of your portfolio.

Limit yourself to no more than 10 percent of your investing in any one stock, no matter how great it sounds. This is one of the hardest rules to follow, especially if a stock has deteriorated in price for no apparent reason, and you just know it's going to rebound since it seems it can't go any lower. It's such a bargain. The fact of the matter is the stock can go lower for reasons you are not aware of. Again, look what happened to Motorola. Each stock that's in your portfolio should be tied to your goals. How you choose to diversify (e.g., mutual funds, stocks, bonds, etc.) depends on the following:

- Your rate of return goals
- How much risk you can tolerate
- How long you can invest your capital
- Your personal tax liability
- Your need for quick access to cash

If You're Under 30

- If you have a high-risk profile, your portfolio should be made up of 20 percent fixed income investments and 80 percent stocks.
- If you have a medium-risk profile, 30 percent of your funds should be in fixed income investments and 70 percent in stocks.

THE IBM STORY

Everyone knows this stock, and most investors presume it means safety because it's so large. Being large does not make an investment safe. IBM went from $120 to $46 a share in 1993. The collapse came mostly from a shift in the way computers were purchased. Instead of buying large mainframe computers, a market in which IBM dominated, businesses preferred personal and mini-computers. IBM's stock paid the price during that period.

- If you are a low-risk taker, 40 percent of your investments should be in fixed income investments and 60 percent in stocks.

If You're 30 to 50

You have to be a little less aggressive now, even if your risk profile is high. If you are comfortable with aggressive investing, you should have 30 percent in fixed income investments and 70 percent in stocks. If you're not an aggressive investor, you should have 50 percent in fixed income investments and 50 percent in stocks.

If You're Over 50

You need to be realistic the older you get. Your ability to replace lost capital is impaired by the limited time you have, not by your work skills. However, this does not mean your money should go under the mattress to be counted every night. Nor does it require you to buy treasury bills every three months.

> **WARNING**
> If you're older, you need to have balance in your portfolio with a larger fixed-income and fewer small-cap stocks. Remember, even if inflation is dormant, it will come back. Use stocks to fight the certainty of inflation.

- If you want to be more aggressive, invest 50 percent of your funds in fixed income and 50 percent in stocks.

- For moderate-risk takers, put 60 percent in fixed income and the remainder in stocks.

- If you want the least risk, put 70 percent in fixed income and 30 percent in stocks.

The Internet offers several sites that can assist you in developing diversification strategies. Check out brokerage firm Legg Mason's Web site (www.leggmason.com) that uses an online questionnaire to help point you in the right direction (see figure 2-7). Fidelity Investments (www.Fidelity.com) also offers an asset diversification planner.

>> News

Acquisition News
>Legg Mason closed on its acquisition of Royce & Associates, which is widely known for its top-performing, value-oriented family of small-cap and micro-cap mutual funds, The Royce Funds... *more* ▶
>Press Release on Private Capital Management, L.P., a leading high net worth money manager headquartered in Naples, FL... *more* ▶

Cal Ripken, Jr. Tribute
In celebration of Cal Ripken, Jr.'s career, Legg Mason will display his number "8" on all four sides of the Baltimore Headquarters at 100 Light Street. The tribute will begin Monday, October 1st continuing through Saturday, October 6th, during the hours of 5:30pm to 6:00am. *more* ▶

Market Commentary
The latest weekly market commentary from Richard E. Cripps, Chief Market Strategist.
"As investors sort through the political and economic impact of a changed world, they will soon look beyond the market bottoming process and begin assessing the outlook for equity returns over a longer period of time..." more ▶

Legg Mason IRA Center
Learn about various types of IRAs along with their features and benefits. Even open an account! *more* ▶

New Individual Investor Tools
We've recently updated our Private Client Site to better meet the needs of individual investors. When you access your account online, take advantage of our exciting news features including: market commentary, quotes, charts, financial news, online seminars, company and industry profile reports and MUCH more. *Why not visit us today and enjoy greater online convenience at the touch of a button! more* ▶

Start Saving for College
If you've looked at the projected cost of a college education, you're probably searching for the best possible way to save for that goal. As college costs rise faster than the rate of inflation, you'll need a powerful savings program to keep up. Learn more about college planning with our online seminar.

New 2001 Tax Laws Offer Investor Opportunity
The Impact of Tax Reform on Your Financial Future.

FIGURE 2-7   Legg Mason Menu

Step #7: Develop a Minimum Loss Strategy

The general market is represented by leading market indices like the S&P 500, Dow Jones Industrial, and Nasdaq composite. You need to carefully evaluate these indices so that when they top or turn down, you will know when to buy or sell. Seventy-five percent of stocks follow the market trend, regardless of how good you think they are. Growth stocks and lower quality companies usually get clobbered in a market down turn. They'll often drop two or three times the market averages. Some will never rebound or take years to rebound.

In the stock market game, the best offense is a great defense. You absolutely can't win unless you have a strong predetermined defense to protect yourself against large losses. If you invest in stocks, you are going to make mistakes in your selection and timing of purchases. Poor decisions will lead to losses, some of which can become significant. No matter how smart you may think you are or how good you believe your information or analysis is, you simply are not going to be right all of the time.

As a general rule, cut your loss when a stock in your portfolio drops 7 to 10 percent below the price you paid. If your stock moves up into a good profit position beyond what you paid for it, raise your stop-loss position so that if it suddenly falls, you can still get out of the stock and make a profit.

Figure 2-8 shows you how easy it is to enter a stop-loss order. In the screen's scenario, I have instructed the online brokerage firm (Ameritrade) to sell 100 shares of IBM if its market price dips to $92. Notice that I have also checked "Day" on the menu to indicate that this order is good for the business day I entered it. If it is not executed, it will automatically get cancelled when the markets close on that day. I could have selected "Until Cancelled" to keep the order open until I entered a cancellation order sometime in the future.

There is no rule that says you have to wait until every single loss reaches 7 percent to 10 percent before you sell a stock. If you sense that the market or your stock isn't acting right, sell it. Don't think about it or wait a few more days to see what might happen. It now becomes an automatic decision with no more vacillating. The fact that you are

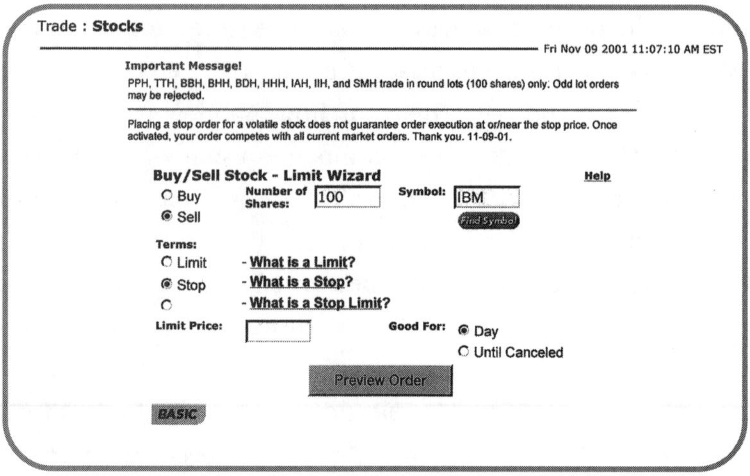

FIGURE 2-8   Stop Loss Screen

down below your cost is the reason you are selling. You don't need any other reason and nothing else should have a bearing on the situation.

All investment decisions you make need to take into consideration your attitudes about risk. The amount of risk you can tolerate often depends on your knowledge of investments, experience, age, and personality. Knowing your risk tolerance level can help you select investments that are right for your portfolio. The Internet provides two sites that will help you determine your risk level:

- Bank of America's Web site (www.bankamerica.com) offers a survey of 12 questions. Enter your answers and the online calculator suggests an investment strategy that suits your current needs and situation.

- Frank Russell Company (www. russell.com) features a "Comfort Quiz" to help you allocate your investments in a mix that's right for you.

Select investments that meet your financial goals and risk tolerance level. How much time do you have to invest? Do you want to be an

---

CONTROLLING LOSSES WITH SPECIAL ORDERS

Limit Orders

Choosing the terms of limit indicates that you wish to seek the purchase or sale of a stock at a specific price or better. To place a limit order, you must specify a price at which you wish the order to be filled.

Stop Orders

Choosing the terms of stop indicates that you want your order to become a market order once a specific "stop" price has been reached. Once the order becomes a market order, it will then seek an immediate execution, with buy orders usually executing near the current ask price and sell orders executing near the current bid price. The stop order is designed to protect against potential loss by liquidating a position if the market price changes in a direction that negatively affects the position's valuation.

Stop Limit Orders

Choosing the terms of stop limit indicates that you want this order to seek an execution at a specific price once that stop limit price has been traded at or through. The order becomes a limit order at the same price once the stop limit price has been reached.

---

active or passive online trader? Analyze your investment alternatives before you make any buy or sell decisions. Determine at what price you will either sell a stock to make a profit or cut losses so you'll never have to use a "should-have-done" excuse again.

Step #8: Set-up a Good Recordkeeping System

The essence of good planning is keeping track of where you've been so you will know where you're going. Investing requires recordkeeping discipline. Brokers, transfer agents, and mutual funds make it easy for investors to keep track of their investments by sending regular statements that show your trading history and current investment holdings. If you throw those statements into the garbage, you might find yourself in a world of pain down the road, especially when you prepare your tax return.

When you sell stock, you have to account for the sale on your income taxes. To determine if you have a gain or a loss on the sale, you need to know what you paid for the stock. When you buy shares, your brokerage statement will show you exactly what you paid. This is important, since it represents the "cost basis" you will use when you sell shares.

The cost basis may change over time, depending on whether the stock splits or the company spins off certain assets. Let's say you buy 100 shares of Microsoft for $50 per share. Your cost basis is $50. Now, let's say Microsoft splits its stock 2 for 1. After the split, you need to adjust for the cost of the additional shares. The stock split lowers your cost basis to $25 per share. The essence of good record keeping is keeping track of the cost basis of your investments. When you sell shares of stock, you can use either the specific-share method or the first-in, first-out method.

The specific-share method lets you use the specific cost at which you purchased shares of stock as the cost basis. Let's say that you've made three purchases of Microsoft's stock: a 100-share trade for $50 per share, a 100-share trade for $40 per share, and a 100-share trade for $60 per share. Under the specific-share method, if you sell 100 shares of stock, you can choose any of the 100-share purchase prices for your cost basis. In most cases, you'll choose the highest-cost shares, since this would lower your potential capital-gains tax. On the other hand, you could choose the first-in, first-out method, which means that you would use the shares you bought first to determine your acquisition cost.

Step #9: Install a "Protect Your Principal" Sign

Psychologists tell us that good sex is 10 percent in your body and 90 percent in your mind. Good trading evolves from the same ratios. It's about 10 percent methodology and 90 percent mental discipline. You can study charts and indicators until your eyes cross, but unless you develop a specific mindset that guides your trades, you'll be walking a tightrope without a safety net. To start with, let's establish a rule that you need to etch into your mind for the rest of your trading life: Always protect your principal.

That sounds easy enough to do, right? Unfortunately, it's not. Protecting your principal is much easier promised than accomplished. Virtually everything you learn in this book points back to protecting your principal. As a successful investor, your tools consist of market knowledge, mental discipline, and your trading account. Protect the money in your trading account at all times. Don't abuse it or treat it carelessly, or others will take it from you. Money is your most cherished tool, and you must guard it with your life. If you keep it uppermost in your mind and insert the concepts into your investment plan, you'll be a successful investor.

Have you ever watched a television program or read an article that tells the story about a day trader who lost all their money? I bet we've both heard the same statistics that between 80 and 90 percent of all day traders lose money. As you read this, traders somewhere in the world are "chasing" a stock, ignoring their stops, holding losers, overtrading, taking home dangerous or oversized positions, and buying against a down-trend. Translation? They are treating their precious trading capital recklessly.

Even if you avoid all unnecessary risks, a percentage of your trades will lose money. Don't add to these by making careless trades or you'll wake up one morning to a rapidly declining account balance. True trading professionals who rake in profits protect their principal like a mother tiger protects her cubs. They trade cautiously and look at occasional good-trades-gone-sour as routine business expense. And they don't compound them with losses due to carelessness.

Okay, how do you protect your principal? When you're making a trade, repeat to yourself, "At all times, I protect my principal." Say it out loud and shout it with enthusiasm. Before you click the "buy" button, ask yourself: Why am I entering this trade? Does my trade coincide with the present market trend? Do primary market indicators support my decision? Is my entry point technically perfect? Do I have a rational, well thought-out game plan? What's my stop-loss price if this trade goes sour? Where's my proper exit point if it performs well?

With practice, you'll soon be able to answer these questions in five seconds or less. If your answers are quick, concise, and positive, then the trade should be as close to a "sure thing" as possible. If you fumble or try to justify one of the answers, cancel the trade. Please take a personal oath right now to protect your principal. Paste the commandment on your monitor. Tape another copy on your bathroom mirror and refrigerator door. Write it on the back of your hand or do whatever it takes to make sure it happens.

Step #10: Learn to Make Trades Not Dollars

We all want to make money trading online, so step #10 appears to contradict what we all want. Traders who routinely rake in big bucks don't mentally count the dollars while they're trading. They don't think, "Wow, I'm up two points in AOL. Let's see, a thousand shares, times two dollars a share, equals two thousand dollars." Nothing blows your concentration and clouds your judgment more than keeping a mental calculator running in your head, tallying up the actual dollars you've made and lost each minute. It's all phony money until you actually sell, so why think about it?

In fact, stating a set goal in dollars you must make every day, especially if you're a beginner, assures that it probably won't happen. The need to make a certain amount of money colors your perception of the markets. It pressures you to enter trades that are bad bets because you

> **GOOD TRADING IS AN ART FORM**
>
> Throwing a flawless, 30-yard pass to a moving receiver, performing open-heart surgery, and landing a fighter on an aircraft carrier at sea all require "touch" skills and sheer determination. So does executing a perfect trade. Money represents the by-product of the art of good trading and if you make good trades, you'll have plenty of time to count the money at the end of the day.

promised yourself, or worse someone else that you would bring home the dollars.

You'll be prone to make trades when the indicators warn you'd be best to stay on the sidelines. But your pledge to make money echoes in your mind, so you force trades and lose money. Now you're embarrassed and annoyed with yourself. That punishes your self-esteem, which leads to more losses. The cure for this malady: From now on, your goal is not to make money. Your goal is to trade well and the dollar making part of the formula will fall into place. Banish money from your mind and think of stock prices as numbers, not dollar amounts.

Your profits will add up a zillion times faster than they do when making money was your primary goal. Why? Online traders who trade well cut their losses and let their winners run. They cherish and protect their principal. They leave unnecessary risks to others. They recognize whippy, choppy market conditions and stand aside, content to keep their money safe. They control their emotions and make no promises to anyone, including themselves about making money.

Good online traders "let the market come to them." They insist on entering the trade at the perfect entry point and exiting at the perfect exit point. If those points don't arrive, they discard the trade. They know another opportunity is just around the corner. They keep their list of trading guidelines in their investment plan at all times, and

---

EVEN BABE RUTH STRUCK OUT

If you're willing to wait forever, all of your stocks will go up if the companies they represents stay in business. The only certainty about the stock
market is that there is none. Every successful investor constantly makes mistakes so don't be afraid of failure. While Babe Ruth had 714 homers, he
also had 1,330 strikeouts that the media never talks about.

---

always trade within those guidelines. To sum it up, traders who trade
to trade well are perfectionists about their craft and become wealthy.

PUTTING IT ALL TOGETHER

If you don't know where you've been, you won't know where you're
going. Even the greatest of all stock market investors make mistakes.
They know where they've been and as Peter Lynch once said, "I never
make the same mistake twice." Suffice to say, you will make mistakes if
you invest in the market, but take it in your stride, and move forward.
Make prudent decisions along the way and don't let your emotions
override your better judgment. If you make a practice of quickly dump-
ing your losers and replacing them with winning stocks, you will win.

We've taken you through the ten essential steps you need to complete to create a viable financial plan. Keep in mind that whatever plan
you create, it must be dynamic. Change it instantly when you discover
new and better investment strategies that will accelerate you toward
reaching your financial goals. As your portfolio grows, so will your
interest in the game. You'll soon find yourself trading stocks, hunting
for bargains, scouting for qualified hot tips, joining investment clubs,
comparing your performance with your friends, and crafting your own
strategies to land that next big winner.

Don't worry about your inexperience. Even America's most successful investment managers were inexperienced novices at one point in
their lives. But they took the first step, bought their first stock, and

began to learn how the game was played. Investing is no different than any other pursuit. You can follow sports for years, but until you lace up the Nikes and get in the game, you cannot possibly understand how it's played. Similarly, you can follow investing from the sidelines, read some books, attend some seminars, and watch the financial news, but the only way to learn the real lessons of the market, the emotion, the discipline, and the execution is by putting your own money on the line. As the old adage goes, you can't win gambling with your hands in your pockets.

CHAPTER-RELATED WEB SITES

📁 Frank Russell Company (www.russell.com) features a "Comfort Quiz" to help you allocate your investments.

📁 Investor Home (www.investorhome.com) provides information about the investment process and how to bulletproof your portfolio.

📁 Bank of America's Web site (www.bankamerica.com) offers a survey of 12 questions. Enter your answers and the online calculator suggests an investment strategy that suits your current needs and situation.

📁 Morningstar (www.morningstar.com) provides a portfolio set-up menu that is easy to use.

📁 Stock Point (www.stockpoint.com) offers a free personal portfolio-tracking program.

📁 Financial Portfolio (www.finportfolio.com) tells you how to construct your portfolio to meet your financial goals and evaluates your investments to determine how much you should buy to keep your portfolio in balance.

📁 Hovers (www.stockscreen.com) provides a special module for retirement planning.

CHAPTER-RELATED WEB SITES, continued

 Money Central (www.moneycentral.com) walks you through the process of setting up a retirement plan, including calculating your living expenses and determining your income requirements.

 Schwab Investor Profile (www.schwab.com) offers an investor's profile questionnaire that matches you to one of six retirement-oriented portfolios.

Seek and You Shall Find an Online Broker

"A broker's guess is liable to be as good as anyone else's."

—WILL ROGERS

ALTHOUGH TRADING ONLINE IS A RELATIVELY RECENT PHENOMENON, its impact on the brokerage industry has been revolutionary. December 1997 was a watershed for the brokerage industry when Charles Schwab & Company reported that 50 percent of their commission trading for the month was done online and Internet brokerage sales accounted for 41 percent of their total sales. Today, investor interest in online trading has caused a rapid growth in the number of brokerage firms going online. In 1997, there were 15. Today, there are over 200 brokerage firms that are taking advantage of the explosive growth in online trading.

When companies race to a new market, consumers usually benefit by lower prices. Online trading commissions have fallen from an average trade price of $35 in 1997 to less than $8 today. And, the services that online brokerage firms are offering today are far superior to what they were just a few years ago.

WHY ONLINE TRADING IS POPULAR

What is it about online trading that has attracted so many investors? Obviously, the low commission is a major attraction, but price does not explain all of the allure. There's a high degree of independence and freedom that comes with the ability to turn on your computer and make a trade. No broker calls or passes judgment over your decisions and you have the freedom to buy and sell any security you wish. In an age when more and more investors feel comfortable calling their own investment shots, online trading provides the power to trade instantaneously on your terms.

You simply log onto an online brokerage site where you enter buy or sell orders, track your portfolio, transfer funds, or conduct investment research all with the click of a mouse button. And, you avoid one of the major problems of trying to conduct trade transactions through a live broker. Most brokers simply don't have time for you, which is not their fault.

A successful stockbroker has at least a hundred clients. If that broker were to call each client during the trading day, they could only spend four minutes per client answering questions and taking trade orders. If the market is in a sudden down-turn or up-turn, your chances of getting through to your broker are next to impossible. How much time do you think a broker can spend on your account? Not much! Unless you're a major player in the market generating lots of commission dollars, you'll get about four minutes a day.

ONLINE TRADING IS COST EFFECTIVE

Online trading is cost effective because it eliminates the stockbroker. The average cost of an online trade in 2001 was $11 versus $75 for a "live" broker trade. That's a whopping 85 percent savings if you trade online. Investment industry experts talk about the advantages of online trading, which include 24-hour access to trade information, convenience, and significant savings in trading fees. They also warn that investors can get carried away with the ease of online trading by not conducting adequate research on a stock before making a trade.

However, a recent Fidelity Investment survey found that four out of five online traders researched and closely followed all of their investments. "Our online clients are buy-and-hold investors, and they're self-directed," said Robert Blunt, vice president and manager of Fidelity's Scottsdale branch. According to Blunt, "Eighty percent of Fidelity's customers use the Internet. It's more than just trading. You can check your accounts, transfer funds and conduct research. And, you have access to your account 24 hours a day, seven days a week."

Some investors like to read through the brokerage company's research reports they routinely receive. These reports offer you an opportunity to see how the broker's analysts view the market and where they think specific stocks are going. Unfortunately, they seldom send you negative reports so you're never sure if you're getting the full story. After spending a great deal of time reading these reports, I have discovered a couple of things. By the time you get them, the information is obsolete and the analyst's is likely to be just about as good as anybody else's.

> **WARNING** !
>
> Woody Allen once said, "A stockbroker is someone who invests your money until it is all gone." Always remember that nobody cares more about your money than you do. Therefore, protect it at all times.

THROW THE DART

In his classic book, *A Random Walk Down Wall Street*, Burton Malkiel debunks virtually every popular theory of stock selection employed by the gurus of Wall Street. Malkiel and his dart-throwing chimp theory caused much controversy. He contends that a blindfolded chimpanzee throwing darts at *The Wall Street Journal* could select a portfolio that would do as well as one carefully selected by the experts in the late 90s.

Unfortunately, most stockbrokers parrot the information that's published by their firm's research department. You are usually better off conducting your own research and buying stock through an online broker. Why pay high trade commissions just to get an obsolete monthly research report that's probably biased anyway? You'll save a bundle on commission fees and probably end up with a better "self-directed" portfolio by trading online.

ONLINE BROKER DEPENDENCY TEST

Before you select an online broker, there are questions you should consider to help you determine the level of services you'll need. For example, do you actively solicit stock tips from friends? Are you the kind of lone wolf who'd rather chew off a paw than ask for advice? The following quiz will point you toward the type of online broker you should consider. After you've completed it, add up the points to the right of each question to arrive at your final score.

1. When you invest in the stock market, you're:
   - ❑ Generally pessimistic. I expect the worst and usually get it. (3)
   - ❑ Somewhat optimistic. I don't know what to expect but hope for the best. (2)
   - ❑ Generally optimistic. I expect the best. (1)

2. Are you willing to share your investment strategies with others?
   - ❑ Very willing. In fact, every chance I get. (3)
   - ❑ Not very willing. Only if I'm backed into a corner. (2)
   - ❑ Not at all. I like to keep most of my investment strategies to myself. (1)

3. How emotional are you with regard to the investments you make?
   - ❑ Overly emotional. (3)
   - ❑ Somewhat emotional. (2)
   - ❑ Not very emotional. (1)

4. How would your friends describe you when you're about to make a tough investment decision?
   - ❑ Friendly and relaxed. (3)
   - ❑ Cool and calm. (2)
   - ❑ Mean and irritable. (1)

5. If you're lost in a city, do you:
   - ❑ Immediately stop for directions. (3)
   - ❑ Consult a map, then try to find your own way. (2)
   - ❑ Drive around until you run out of gas. (1)

6. How communicative are you?
   - ❑ I don't make decisions without consulting someone. (3)
   - ❑ I may consult with someone but make most decisions myself. (2)
   - ❑ I can make most decisions on my own. (1)

7. Do you consider yourself:
   - ❑ An artsy person? (3)
   - ❑ A renaissance person? (2)
   - ❑ A quantitative person? (1)

8. Which leadership profile best describes you?
   - ❑ Lineman: Just tell me who to go out there and hit. (3)

❑ Quarterback: I want to have some control over the outcome of the game. (2)

❑ Coach: I want to call every play. (1)

9. Which of these statements sounds most like you?

❑ Tell me what to do. (3)

❑ I have an idea I'd like to discuss. (2)

❑ I know what I want so get out of my way. (1)

How Did You Score?

If Your Score Was 22-27. You tend to be dependent on others for advice. You would probably be better off with an online firm that offers full brokerage services.

If Your Score Was 14-21. You are not overly confident about investing. Use an online broker that offers good training tools and a customer service department that is proficient in answering investment questions.

If Your Score Was 1-13. You are self-reliant and ready to go. Station yourself in front of a computer and let the trading begin with an online brokerage service that offers low trading fees and a minimum amount of support services.

WHAT DO FULL-SERVICE BROKERS OFFER?

A full-service broker researches many companies and securities, helps you organize your goals, and gives you advice on specific securities that match these goals. As a general rule, full-service brokers provide recommendations and inform you of initial public offerings (IPOs), insider trading, and tax-related questions. For example, if you own stock in a firm that is a takeover target, a full-service broker may provide you with relevant information regarding offers to buy your stock.

When you want to buy or sell securities, a broker can help you decide what type of order to place (i.e., market or limit order) and oversee its implementation. All brokers (full-service and online) physically handle your equity orders and maintain a history of your transactions. But, most do not provide you with the performance reports.

Full-service brokerage commissions can take a large bite out of your profits. For example, assume that you invest $2,000 and pay a $200 commission to a full-service broker. Your securities must increase to $2,200 for you to break even. One way to avoid high commissions is to use a discount broker or a deep-discount broker.

In the past, discount brokers offered no advice and conducted no research. Today, many discount brokers, such as Quick and Reilly, Fidelity, and Schwab, offer investment advice, IPO information, and research tools to customers who desire expanded levels of service. Consumers have the option of seeking advice for special transactions or placing orders directly. Discount brokers subsequently have tiered fee structures that vary depending upon the level of service you desire.

WHAT DO ONLINE BROKERS OFFER?

Trading on the Internet with an online broker has revolutionized the stock market. If you wanted to buy stock in the "old" days, you drove downtown and entered a stately office building. Soon, a dignified stockbroker wearing a dark suit and a condescending manner ushered you into a mahogany-paneled office and opened an account for you. When you bought or sold stock, the commission cost you $100 or more.

How things have changed. Nowadays, online brokerage houses offer an array of inexpensive services and eagerly await your business. You'll probably never see their office or personally meet their staff. Instead, you contact an online brokerage firm (see directory in the Appendix II) and request an application form through e-mail. After your account is open, you can research stocks online and make buy or sell decisions with the click of a mouse. You can also place orders by telephone. But once you get used to trading via the Internet, placing telephone orders will seem slow and cumbersome. Here's what to look for when you search for an online broker:

- A Web site that's accessible and easy to navigate with graphics that don't take forever to appear on your screen. You want a site that allows you to move quickly from screen to screen.

- A well-organized trading screen with edits built in to guard against data entry errors.

- Access to real-time quotes. Real-time quotes mean stock prices are current when displayed. Some companies give quotes that are delayed as much as 15 minutes.

- A quick confirmation system with current portfolio account balance updates.

- Alternative ways of reaching your broker (i.e., telephone) if their site or your Internet provider site goes down.

- Low trading rates. You'll be surprised at how much rates differ. Can you open an account with a reasonable minimum dollar amount?

- Extensive research services. Many online brokers have a plethora of stock research tools. The better the tools, the more you're likely to pay in trade fees.

BUZZWORD

Deep discount brokerage firms charge even lower commissions than discount brokers do. **Deep discounters** exist only for the purpose of carrying out stock trades. Investors get little or no research assistance or advice. Deep discounters are ideal for investors who conduct their own research and merely need an online broker to place their trades.

- A wide range of investments that you can buy online. Some online brokers don't allow you to buy certain types of investments like mutual funds online.

Word of mouth counts for a lot when it comes to selecting an online broker. Ask people you know who are trading online which brokers are reliable and efficient. Then call the most highly recommended ones and ask them to mail you information. We've listed the Web sites of the primary online brokers in Appendix II. Take your time and do as much research as possible. If you sign up with the wrong broker, it can make your trading life miserable.

> **INSIGHT**
> Online investors want a lot from online brokers, such as fast downloads, instant trade executions, and great customer service, all at a cheap trading price. Look beyond a broker's commission if you want more services.

CHOOSING AN ONLINE BROKER

What's Their Reputation?

The Securities Investor Protection Corporation (SIPQ) insures brokerage accounts in a way that's similar to how the Federal Deposit Insurance Corporation (FDIC) insures bank accounts. Each customer's account is insured for up to $500,000 and some brokerages have additional insurance. If your brokerage firm goes belly-up, you're covered for that amount.

Look into the background of a brokerage firm before you begin investing with them. The Central Registration Depository (CRD), a registration and licensing database used by regulators throughout the securities industry to collect data about securities firms and their brokers, is available at your state securities agency or the National Association of Securities Dealers (www.nasdaq.com). Additionally, each month the New York Stock Exchange releases a disciplinary action list from their Web site (www.nyse.com).

How's Their Customer Support?

Send a few e-mails to brokers that interest you to see how quickly their customer service department responds. When you call them, do you get a message saying "Please hold for the next available representative"? How long do you have to hold or do you instantly get a real person on the line? If you do get a person, is he or she knowledgeable and can answer questions to your satisfaction? If that person refers you to someone else, do you get a prompt and knowledgeable answer? Are there hidden fees? Some online brokers charge you a start-up fee or a monthly "connect" fee that you pay even if you don't make a trade.

What Special Features Do They Offer?

Commission structures change radically from firm to firm. One reason for this is that some Internet brokers offer a wide variety of special features. When deciding which broker is best for you, factor in the features you consider important. Here are several features you may want to consider:

- Low monthly fees with minimum equity balance
- No additional charges for postage and handling
- A summary of cash balances and a summary of order status at the end of each month
- An online summary of your portfolio's value that's updated daily
- Confirmation of trades via e-mail, phone, or U.S. mail
- An online historical review of your trading activities
- No charges for retirement account maintenance
- Consolidation of your money market, investments, checking, and savings accounts
- Unlimited check-writing privileges
- Dividend collection and reinvestment
- Debit cards for ATM access

- Interest earned on cash balances
- Wire transfers accepted
- No IRA inactivity fees

You should ascertain which of the following types of investments the broker enables you to trade:

- Stocks (foreign or domestic)
- Options
- Corporate and government bonds
- Treasury securities
- Zero coupon bonds
- Certificates of deposit
- Precious metals
- Mutual funds
- Investment trusts

> **WARNING**
> Make sure your broker doesn't charge you for services that are free elsewhere. For example, some online brokers charge a flat fee of lets say $15 per trade, but then add on a postage and handling fee of $4 so the real trading fee is $19.

Finally, you need to determine whether the brokerage offers the following analytical and research features:

- Real-time online quotes
- Reports on insider trading
- Economic forecasts
- Company profiles and breaking news
- Earnings forecasts

HOW DO YOU FIND GOOD ONLINE BROKERS?

Fortunately, there are several Web sites that compare prices and services of online brokers to help you select one that's right for you. A good place to start is at www.internetinvesting.com. Paul Shread launched the site a few years ago and divides his listing of online brokers into two categories:

brokers suitable for garden variety online investors and brokers suitable for day traders. The site summarizes commission expenses, account minimums, and different features offered by online brokers. Paul also provides links to helpful Internet investing books and other Web sites.

Money magazine routinely rates online brokers on such criteria as commissions, availability of real-time quotes, research links, account information, technology support, fees, and

> **POINTER**
>
> No two brokerages are alike and they're constantly changing their services and fees to keep pace with their competitors.

product availability. You're first asked to respond to six questions that

FIGURE 3-1   Online Brokers Screen Page

help their system select brokers that meet your requirements (see figure 3-1). The questionnaire helps you determine what kind of broker you're looking for based on the feature they offer.

Based upon your input, *Money's* Web site displays a list of online brokers that best fit your selection criteria. They're rated on a five-star scoring system where five stars are best (see figure 3-2). What a great service and best of all, it's free courtesy of *Money* magazine.

FIGURE 3-2 *Money* Magazine's Best Online Brokers

THE MOONLIGHTER'S SHORT-TERM TRADING BIBLE

APPLYING FOR AN ONLINE ACCOUNT

Brokerage firms are basically cash-and-carry enterprises. They all require investors to open an account before trading, a process that takes from two to three weeks. Account minimums vary from $0 to $10,000. When you place an order, your broker withdraws money from your cash account to cover the trade. If you sell stock or receive a dividend, the broker adds money to your cash account. If you develop a good history, your broker may allow you to place trades without funds in your cash account if you settle the deficit within three days.

You're required to complete an application form when you apply for an online account and depending on the online broker, submit a minimum amount to open the account. Brokerage firms are required by law to have your signature on file. Figure 3-3 shows a typical online brokerage application courtesy of Ameritrade (www.ameritrade.com).

> **INSIGHT**
> Think about it. If you know what stock you want to buy, shouldn't you just enter the stock symbol and number of shares you want, hit the buy button, and be done? It doesn't make sense to ask a full-service broker to enter the same one-minute transaction and then pay a big brokerage fee.

To speed up the application process, you can complete application forms online or fax them to the online brokers. You must follow up by sending the signed forms within 15 days or your application will be canceled. The broker then verifies all the information on the form and opens your account. You'll receive a personal identification number (PIN) by mail. Once you receive your PIN, you're ready to begin trading.

> **POINTER**
> See Appendix II in the back of the book for a complete directory of online brokerage firms.

Open An Account

Choose one of our three convenient ways to open your account.

1. **Express Application**
   The fastest account opening method available. Complete, submit, and fund your application online.

2. **Online Application**
   Complete your application online, print it, then submit it via U.S. mail or fax.

3. **Request Account Information**
   Receive an account packet for any of the account types we offer via download, fax or U.S. mail. Complete the application, then submit it via U.S. mail or fax.

Express Application — complete, submit, and fund your application online

Choose from the following account types:

- Individual Account
- Joint Account
- Individual Retirement Account (IRA)

Please review the following guidelines for Express Account Opening:

- You will be opening a **cash only** account — you can request an upgrade for margin/options approval.
- You must be a **citizen of the United States or a Permanent Resident** and must **not be affiliated with the NASD**.
- You will not be able to open Tenants by the Entireties accounts, Rollover IRAs, Simplified Employee Pension IRAs, or Savings Incentive Match Plan for Employees IRAs.
- You will not be able to open an IRA if your primary beneficiary is a trust or if you are married and your primary beneficiary is not your spouse.

FIGURE 3-3   Ameritrade Account Application Form

PITFALLS OF ONLINE TRADING

Unfortunately, the benefits that make online trading a blessing can become a curse as well. Instantaneous trading provides incredible power and freedom for investors to literally move at the speed of light to execute whatever trade they want. But power and freedom are double-edged swords if not used properly. It's easy to fall into a trading mentality of buying and selling stocks at every blip in the market. A short-term trading mentality is not the only potential problem with online trading. Remember that online trading is only as good as the technology behind the trading system.

If your Internet service provider is encountering problems, you may not be able to get onto the Internet, let alone connect to your broker. And, if you believe your online trades will always be conducted in nanoseconds, think again because they can be delayed for several minutes, depending on

> **WARNING**
>
> Online trading systems are vulnerable to security problems. Although Internet security has improved significantly in recent years, security breaches are still possible. For that reason, security provisions should be important when considering online brokers.

the brokerage firm you're using. A prudent approach is to open a couple of accounts with brokers who also take telephone orders. That way, you give yourself more options should system problems develop.

Finally, if you're not careful when you execute an online trade, it can cost you dearly. Make sure you review confirmation screens (see example in figure 3-4) before you execute an order to avoid any surprises due to a key entry error. My editor tells me that the following sentence is poor grammar but I will use it anyway: Always, always, always review your confirmation screen before you push the order button. The confirmation screen appear's as soon as you enter buy or sell order information and is the last chance you have to cancel your order if you've made a mistake.

Please review the following before placing this order:
You have requested an order to:
BUY 100 shares of IBM, INTL BUSINESS MACHINES
at **MARKET**, on Account **165938697**

Current Quote

Symbol	Bid	Ask	Last	Change	B/A Size	Last Trade	Exchange
IBM	96.84	96.96	96.90	-0.41	100x100	10-05-2001 14:08:04	NYSE

Place Order   Do NOT Place Order

Unplaced orders will cancel in 90 seconds.

It is your responsibility to verify that the order information is correct and that your account has the required funds or position specified before selecting "Place Order."

Once you have placed your order you must go to the Review Orders page to edit or cancel the order.

**Important Disclaimer

FIGURE 3-4   Confirmation Screen

PROFILE OF ONLINE TRADERS

Age: 30 percent of online traders are under 35, with 57 percent under 45.

Education: 59 percent of online traders have college degrees.

Gender: 67 percent of online traders are men while 51 percent are women.

THE FUTURE OF ONLINE BROKERING

There's no denying that online trading has been a boon in providing low-cost easy access to the financial markets for millions of investors. Cheap online trades have the potential to turn individual investors into trading machines who buy and sell stocks many times a week. This is good news for online trading companies.

Until recently, you haven't seen firms like Merrill Lynch on the online trading list. Is that because Merrill Lynch has not figured out how to use online technology? Of course not. It's because they have a huge network of brokers earning top commissions. However, Merrill Lynch has started to push their online trading program and as a result, have simultaneously attracted more accounts to their full-service-brokers.

Schwab's online experience has been particularly telling. They still take telephone orders for a fee, but they encourage online trading by telling their customers it's cheaper. In the future, all brokers will offer online trading if they want to stay in business. And, online commissions are projected to go even lower. In fact, there is talk of rebates where brokers pay customers for doing trades. How can brokers charge $8 a trade, zero dollars a trade, or even pay for a trade?

Brokerage firms make money by lending stock held in their accounts to make trades, from the interest on margin loan, and from the cash balances held in accounts. Another source of revenue is what's called "payment for order flow." This payment is, in effect, a kickback to brokers for steering trades to certain market makers. The upshot is that for large accounts, the time may come when investors are paid to make a trade.

PUTTING IT ALL TOGETHER

Becoming a stock broker is not a profession you want your children to go into. The advent of online trading with its low commissions is dramatically affecting the brokerage industry, especially full-service brokers. However, online trading is not the only factor making the brokerage business a tougher place to make a buck these days. There are several ways for investors to access the market without any broker or financial intermediary. No-load mutual funds where investors go directly to the fund's Web site to to buy funds have been stealing brokerage commissions for years. Even if you're utilizing the services of a full-service broker, you owe it to yourself to have at least one online account so that you can enjoy the benefits that both options afford you.

CHAPTER-RELATED WEB SITES

Here is a partial list of online brokers:

📁 Accutrade (www.accutrade.com) 800-494-8939

📁 American Express (www.americanexpress.com) 800-658-4677

📁 Ameritrade (www.ameritrade.com) 800-454-9272

📁 Brown & Co. (www.brownco.com) 800-822-2021

📁 CSFBdirect (www.CSFBdirect.com) 877-355-5557

📁 Datek (www.datek.com) 888-463-2835

📁 Discover Brokerage (www.discoverbrokerage.com) 800-688-3462

📁 ETrade (www.etrade.com) 800-387-2331

📁 Fidelity (www.fidelity.com) 800-544-8666

📁 Muriel Siebert (www.msiebert.com) 800-872-0444

📁 National Discount Brokers (www.ndb.com) 800-888-3999

📁 Net Investor (www.netinvestor.com) 800-638-4250

📁 Quick & Reilly (www.quickwaynet.com) 800-837-7220

📁 Schwab (www.schwab.com) 800-435-4000

📁 Suretrade (www.suretrade.com) 800-394-1452

📁 Wall Street Access (www.wsaccess.com) 800-925-5782

📁 Waterhouse (www.tdwaterhouse.com) 800-934-4448

Covet Great Stocks

"I want to buy stocks that nobody knows about and sell them after everyone discovers them."

—John Markese

THROUGH MAGAZINES AND NEWSPAPERS, AND RADIO AND TELEVISION talk shows, we're all bombarded regularly with stock recommendations from experts of all kinds. Even your barber, taxi driver, or good friends have hot stock tips they're eager to share with you because it makes them feel important. They probably got their "hot tip" from another buddy and you can rest assured they haven't done any research on the stock they think you should buy. Ask them what their hot stock's earnings per share (EPS) are. When they give you a blank stare and say "just trust me," you'll have your answer. They don't know what they're talking about, which is eloquently illustrated in Western Investments ad in figure 4-1.

A friend of a friend of mine told me about this hot stock.
You ought to buy some. Trust me, you can't lose.

FIGURE 4-1   Western Investments Ad

If you're not prepared to perform your own analysis on a stock you're considering buying, then quite frankly, you are a fool. You won't know what you're really buying, which will substantially increase your investment risk. Analysis is the process you go through to help you understand the volatile and financial characteristics of a stock so that you can make an informed investment decision. It doesn't take all that much time to qualify a stock. In this chapter, we'll show you how to conduct "time efficient" analyses of stocks that interest

BUZZWORD

Stocks are almost always priced fairly based on current market information. That's what is known as the **fair market value** because stock prices fully reflect all known information at any given moment in time.

you, how to determine what a stock's strengths and weaknesses are, and how to quickly determine when it's time to buy or sell.

INSIGHT

If I had a buck for every piece of bad investment advice I've gotten from my buddies, I would be a millionaire today.

HOW EXPERTS RATE STOCKS

Some investors rely on market pundits or analysts who tout stocks on TV and in business publications for stock tips and advice. But, be careful. These pundits want to sell you their stock. Do you really think they are going to say anything negative about something they're trying to sell? Be wary of what the so-called experts recommend in the newspapers, radio, or television. You usually don't know anything about their expertise or motivations.

Companies like Vector Quest track stocks and include analysts' evaluations in their stock reports (see figure 4-2). America Online and Prodigy's investor section include analysts' evaluations in their respective

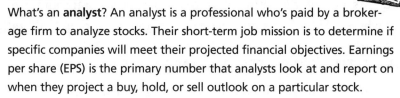

BUZZWORD

What's an **analyst**? An analyst is a professional who's paid by a brokerage firm to analyze stocks. Their short-term job mission is to determine if specific companies will meet their projected financial objectives. Earnings per share (EPS) is the primary number that analysts look at and report on when they project a buy, hold, or sell outlook on a particular stock.

Current Ratings		
Strong Buy	(1)	7
Moderate Buy	(2)	11
Hold	(3)	8
Moderate Sell	(4)	0
Strong Sell	(5)	0
Mean Rating (1 to 5 scale) =		2.0

This report is based on mathematical calculations and, as such, no investment decision should be based solely on its conclusions. Data serving as the basis for such calculations is provided by, among others, S&P Comstock, Market Guide, Vickers Stock Research, Zacks, and J&J Financial.

FIGURE 4-2   ZACKS Analysts Report

Web sites. They show how analysts rate a stock in accordance to five buy-sell categories: strong buy, buy, hold, sell, or strong sell.

Buy-sell ratings are less objective than you might expect because analysts are discouraged from giving a stock a "sell" rating. CEOs naturally hate sell ratings, and often complain bitterly to brokerage companies who list their company's stock as a "sell." They also tend to become less cooperative with the analyst who publishes negative reports, making it more difficult for the analyst to research the company. For that reason, analysts rarely give "sell" ratings. The worst rating most analysts are likely to give a stock is "hold." As a result, the entire rating system has been compromised to the point where a "hold" has now become the equivalent of a "sell" rating.

> **POINTER**
> Be wary of merger or other "it's going to happen" rumors. Most of them never materialize and even if they do, the stock could fall if the big traders decide to sell on the news.

NEWSLETTER, NEWSPAPER, AND MAGAZINE LEADS

It's debatable whether financial magazines and newspapers are any less timely than the myriad of expensive investment newsletters that supposedly specialize in timeliness. About 80 percent of newsletters, financial newspapers, and investment magazines don't beat the market over long periods of time.

For years, Mark Hulbert has published a monthly newsletter called the Hulbert Financial Digest that rates the performance of leading investment newsletters. Hulbert's research suggests that their guess is liable to be as good as anybody else's. If you're shopping for a good newsletter, *Hulbert Financial Digest* will steer you to the newsletters that have rated the highest over the past few years.

> **POINTER**
>
> For a one-year subscription, send $59 to Hulbert's Financial Digest, 316 Commerce St., Alexandria, VA 22314.

Hulbert has several suggestions for investors interested in finding quality investment media. He recommends that you read different newsletters, newspapers, and magazines to get a feel for the type of advice they offer. Look for the following key factors:

- *Risk level.* How risky are the media's recommendations? You may find a newsletter or magazine that has done very well over the past several years but its portfolio has been fully margined. You may decide that's not for you.

- *Tone.* If the media does a lot of apologizing, that's a give-away that they're more interested in protecting their ego than in making you money.

- *Follow-up.* Does the media source tell you not only what to buy but when to sell?

- *Approach.* Are you comfortable when you read their articles and recommendations? If you find their approach irritating, egotistical, obnoxious, or worthless, throw it away.

Ultimately, you should choose media sources that seem to have the most relevance to your investment situation. It will help you learn to invest with your eyes and not your ears. When you use your ears, you are passively listening to opinions, which usually aren't worth much as we have discussed. Facts that you can see with your eyes have value. There is no substitute for using your own hard work and judgment to gather the facts on a stock from a reliable media source before you invest. Use the facts to learn more about a company's products and prospects. Study the stock's historical performance on the charts and analyze fundamental data. In particular, review the key elements that separate the winners from the losers.

WHAT'S THE SECRET TO FINDING GREAT STOCKS?

The secret to finding great stocks is that there really is no secret. The search techniques for finding winners are tried and true. It's how you assemble and apply them that makes a difference. Although the techniques don't work all the time, they work most of the time and if you use them, you'll substantially improve your odds of making a lot of money.

Collecting the right information on a company is the key to your investment success. Knowing how to interpret the information you've collected will be critical because information is even more important than timing. When you find a company that looks promising, you don't have to buy the stock today or even this week. If it's a good stock, it will stay good while you watch its performance and investigate it further before you buy. You can get all of the information you need to size up a company's prospects on the Internet or through the media.

You'll use a combination of fundamental and technical analysis techniques to find winning stocks. Fundamental analysis looks at a company's earnings growth, sales, profit margin, and return on equity among other things. Technical analysis involves interpreting a stock's price and volume chart so that you can time your buy and sell decisions right.

Before we show you how to do that, put your feet up on the desk, lean back in your chair, and think about some of the greatest stocks of the '90s like Dell, Cisco, AOL, Wall-Mart, and Circuit City. What did they all have in common? They had super fundamentals like sales and earnings that were consistently growing year after year. They had good margins and high returns on equity, and were also the leaders in

> **INSIGHT**
> Hitch your portfolio up to quality stocks popping out of solid bases and you're in for a great ride.

fast growing industries. Those are the kinds of companies you want to find.

START WITH THE FUNDAMENTALS

Great stocks have great fundamentals so start with the fundamentals first. Search for companies with superior earnings and growth. They should also have top-notch profit margins and a good return on equity. Is the company a leader in a fast-growing industry? The firms that are gobbling up market share are likely to keep delivering the best results year after year.

Look for companies whose earnings have grown at least 20 to 25 percent every quarter over at least the past two years. Demand the same for sales growth. Although you can use a slew of ratios to gauge a company's performance, the basics don't go away. A company must make a healthy profit, which is virtually impossible without strong sales. A company's sales figures show you whether there is a demand for their products or services and, more importantly, whether that demand is increasing.

Look for quarterly sales that have increased at least 25 percent over the last three to six quarters. An ideal company will have accelerating sales growth where each quarterly increase in sale is larger than the previous quarter. Pay special attention to companies with significant earnings increases over the last six to twelve quarters. Sales growth is one of the best ways to judge a company that's truly on the move. Here's a summary of other important points to consider when you analyze a stock:

- *Industry.* Is the company in a growing industry with strong long-term potential?

- *Position within the industry.* Does the company have a strong niche position within its industry? Is it in the top ten percentile of the companies that make up the industry?

- *Product or service line.* Is the company expanding its product or service line? Is it spending a good share of its revenue on research and development? Do its key products have solid long-term potential?

- *Profit margin.* The higher a stock's profit margin relative to the industry profit margin, the more attractive the stock. A high-growth profit margin is an indication that a company might still be in the early stage of its growth curve.

- *Relative strength.* Look at the strength of the stock's price performance relative to its market and industry. Is it one of the leaders?

- *Management ownership.* Look for companies in which the management owns a significant share of the stock, which is a strong indication that management believes in their company.

Is there an easy way to get at the fundamental data of a stock that interests you? You bet, through Investment Business Daily (IBD), a premier newspaper that publishes five key functional indicators on every stock in the major exchanges daily (see figure 4-3).

Each day, IBD features stocks that are on the move in the New York and Nasdaq stock exchanges. It's a great way to quickly find stocks that may be of interest to you through one source without wasting your time chasing 20 other sources. The illustration in figure 4-3 is

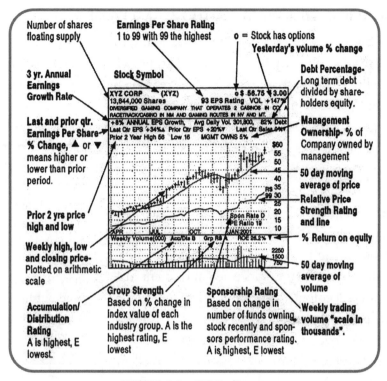

FIGURE 4-3   IBD Indicators

self-explanatory. It provides you with a wealth of key financial indicators for XYZ Corp, including earnings per share, price earnings ratio, and return on equity. Notice that the stock's mini-graph is plotted next to its 50-day moving average to give you an indication of consistency or inconsistency of the stock's price movement. The accumulative distribution and sponsorship ratings tell you if the institutions are attracted to the stock. An "A" rating is high and a "D" rating is low. This valuable information is also available to IBD subscribers online (www.invest.com).

WARNING

Buying a market-leading stock is great on the way up. Holding it on the way down is another story.

A PICTURE IS STILL WORTH A THOUSAND WORDS

If the fundamentals of a company look good, then it's time to conduct a technical analysis. Check out their graph. How has the stock performed over the past six months, one year, or five years? Some stocks may be extended and could easily pull back, while others may be lagging in the market. But the big winners are already outperforming most of the other stocks. The time to buy is just as a strong stock resumes its up-trend after it has gone through a consolidation period. If all of this sounds complicated, it isn't. It's easy to interpret a stock's chart so that you can properly time your buying and selling opportunities.

A stock's chart shows its price movement history in vivid color. A mere couple of inches on a chart provide a motion picture of a stock's movement over whatever period of time you select. Fortunately, there are several excellent charting services available on the Internet at little or no cost. *Money* magazines' Web site (www.money.com) offers free charting services (see figure 4-4). Most stock charts are updated every 15 minutes during market hours.

> **INSIGHT**
>
> If you start with the fundamentals and finish with the technical analysis, you'll weed out the losers and find the winners every time.

Both CompuServe and its parent company, AOL, offer stock charting services to their customers. You don't need any expertise in charting techniques to spot whether a stock is in a down-trend or whether its price action has overcome negative momentum and it's on an up-trend. Only rarely will it be true to say, "I'm not sure. It seems to be right at the point of reversing." If that's true, look at it again in a week to see where it's headed.

A typical stock chart consists of vertical bars that plot the stock's price range for a day or a week, depending on the type of chart you use, and a short horizontal bar that marks the closing price. The daily

FIGURE 4-4   Money.com Stock Chart

chart in figure 4-5 shows each subsequent day when another price bar is added, forming the stock's trend over time. Notice the corresponding vertical lines underneath the price bars. These are volume lines, representing the number of shares traded each day. Trading volume indicates supply and demand, how strong or weak a trend is, and how likely it is to continue.

Dell Computer Corporation offers us a classic example of a stock that has gone through some great and not-so-great times as illustrated in figure 4-5. As Dell entered the new millennium in 2000, its stock slid from $55 to $35 a share in just two months; this represents a 22 percent loss in value. Notice that it climbed back up in March when a bullish run of the tech stocks drove Dell to a high of $60 a share. However, investors in general feared that most of the tech stocks were overvalued as we approached the end of March and Dell lost $20 a share over the next two months.

The company successfully recovered most of its loss in June and July, but when personal computer sales began to soften toward the end of the summer, Dell stock plummeted all the way down to the low $20 range. If you had not been following Dell's stock chart, you could have easily lost over 50 percent of your investment in the company over this 12-month period of time.

Focus entirely on the factual reality of a stock's chart. Do not back into a nondecision through the insidious process that expert investors

---

A STOCK'S CHART IS LIKE A CRYSTAL BALL

One objective of chart reading is to spot which way a stock is headed. Once a trend is established, whether it's moving up or down, a stock is more likely to stay in that trend than to reverse. Think of the trend as your friend. When changes in a stock's trend occur, an analysis of the chart will help you recognize and quickly capitalize on these situations.

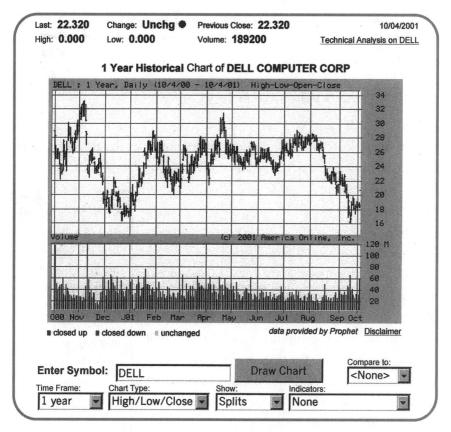

FIGURE 4-5   Dell Computer Stock Chart

call "analysis-paralysis." The market keeps moving with or without investors. So do not wait for just a little more news or technical confirmation. There is never going to be a final answer or a point of total closure. You should exercise discipline, evaluate a stock's chart, and make a buy or sell decision accordingly.

The most helpful charts span 6 to 12 months of trading activity. You can miss the bigger picture if you use charts of shorter length. Falling prices accompanied by abnormally heavy volume are usually a bad sign, because they generally indicate the selling of large blocks of shares by big institutional investors. However, falling prices aren't necessarily bad news if volume is less than normal. It may mean selling is not significant and is drying up.

QUARTERLY AND ANNUAL REPORTS

Entire books have been written on how to read a company's annual report. Some investors like to study every detail of the financial statement, combing through the balance sheet, cash flow figures, and footnotes in search of undiscovered nuggets of information that could help them decide whether the company is destined for stellar performance.

You can get a good indication of a company's success within the first two or three pages of the report. If a company is doing well, you can rest assured the numbers and graphs will be in the front of the report in vivid color showing sales revenue, net income, and earnings per share growth. The lack of such figures probably means the results have been disappointing and instead the company will show meaningless statistics such as the growth in number of employees or assets.

POINTER You can dig for data all over the Internet but the tried-and-true annual and quarterly reports are still one of the best places to investigate a company's financial health.

Finally, there are earnings estimates that Wall Street expects companies to report in the coming quarter or year. Look for estimates that represent positive indications of growth. Remember, these are only estimates, and are no substitute for a solid track record of past performance. A good quarterly earnings report or an optimistic brokerage recommendation will generate optimism in the heart of any investor. Here's a summary of what you need to know and look for when reading an earnings report:

- *Price-to-earnings ratio.* Stock price divided by last four quarters of earnings. The lower the ratio, the better.

- *Return on equity.* Net income divided by shareholders equity. The lower the better.

- *Net profit margin.* Net income divided by sales. The higher the better.

- *Cash.* On the asset side of the balance sheet, look for liquid assets like marketable securities and short-term investment. The higher the number, the better.

- *Debt.* On the liabilities side of the balance sheet, look for long-term debt due one or more years out. The lower the number, the better.

Many companies maintain their annual reports on their Web sites. If you want a published copy, call their corporate office and request one. Good public libraries keep annual reports of major corporations at their research desk. Hovers is a company that specializes in tracking and publishing (i.e., *Hovers Directory*) important information on most publicly traded companies. They also offer this same information on their Web site (www.hovers.com).

FOLLOW THE LEADERS

Institutional investors are the mutual funds, pension funds, banks, and other financial institutions that do the bulk of stock trading on any given day. They account for about 80 percent of all trading activity. So when institutions target a stock for purchase, it's more likely to go up in price thanks to the increased demand they create. This is called institutional sponsorship.

Institutions employ analysts, researchers, and other specialists to gather comprehensive information about companies. They meet with company executives, evaluate industry conditions, and study the outlook for every company they plan to invest in. That's why their stock selections are widely watched. Wouldn't it be great if you knew exactly what stocks institutions are buying and when?

Although institutions don't disclose their buy and sell activities, you can track their moves by watching for clues in a stock's trading activity. One of the most useful ways to spot current institutional trading is to study volume percent change figures or how much trading increased or decreased in a day compared to the average daily trading volume over the past 50 trading days.

Because this data comes out daily in financial papers like *The Wall Street Journal*, it's the quickest way to detect the level institutions are trading in a stock. When volume spikes up 50 percent or more at the same time the stock goes up in price, that's generally a clear sign that major investors are moving into the stock. This usually precedes a significant rise in the stock price. If a stock's price drops on heavy volume, it's a sign large investors may be moving out of a stock. If a stock's trading volume advances but the price goes nowhere, it could mean the stock is reaching a peak.

You can't afford to ignore the influence professional money managers exert on stock prices. The stocks with the highest increase in trading volume are listed online and in magazines. Information about volume changes appears in the stock tables of *Investment Business Daily*, *The Wall Street Journal*, and *Baron's*. *Mutual Funds Magazine* features the top stocks held by the hottest funds along with other relevant information (see figure 4-6).

WHAT'S A STOCK WORTH?

If anyone doubts the schizophrenic nature of how stocks are valued, go back to New Years Day of 2000 when American Online (AOL) announced that it would buy Time Warner (TWX). Early in January, the price of both stocks soared. Most investors were excited about the

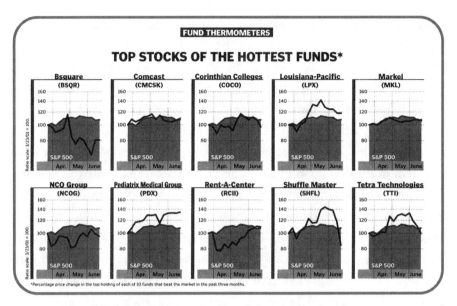

FIGURE 4-6 Top Stocks of the Hottest Funds

fact that a phenomenal upstart was acquiring a proven provider of information and entertainment. And, slow moving Time Warner was getting hitched to one of the fastest growing tech companies on the market. It had to be a marriage made in heaven.

But the market suddenly began taking back much of its applause along with the gains it had awarded the two stocks. When analysts took a second look, AOL was saddling itself with a slow-growing media behemoth and Time Warner's healthy cash flow was about to be drained to prop up AOL's slim profit margins. Investors threw up their hands, unsure how to value either stock.

When the merger was finally approved in January 2001, the stock values of the two companies began to return to their normal levels. In today's wild roller coaster market, how can you determine what a stock is really worth? In order to evaluate a company's stock value, investors long ago developed a measure called the price-to-earnings, or

PE ratio. It's derived by dividing a company's price per share by its earnings per share. If a company has a PE of 20:1 for instance, that means investors are paying $20 for every $1 of earnings. If the PE is 18:1, they're only willing to pay $18 for that same $1 profit. Most people only use the top number when referring to a company's PE.

PE ratios fluctuate with investor perceptions of companies. That's why two companies with the exact same earnings per share (EPS) may have different multiples. If Company A and Company B each earn $1 a share, but Company A is trading for $20 and Company B is trading for just $18, the market is making a judgment on their future earnings prospects. Investors think Company A's earnings are poised to grow more quickly based on any number of factors such as their financial health, competitive positions, management style, and industry leadership. Consequently, they're willing to pay $2 more for Company A's stock over Company B's stock. A company's PE ratios are published in the financial newspapers and appear online when you request a stock price quote from a quality service like Investors Advantage (see figure 4-7).

Most established companies trade up and down in a range depending on how investors are weighing their earnings prospects. Sometimes disappointing news such as a lackluster quarter or a poor earnings report can depress a stock's price. Conversely, good news can spark a flood of investor interest. This ebb and flow is reflected in the PE ratio,

Anchor Gaming (Nasdaq-NM: SLOT)					
Last Trade	58.010	Change	⬇0.04	Shares Outstanding	14.573M
Bid	58.000	Volume	29,200	P/E Ratio	22.92
Ask	58.110	Last Trade Size	100	EPS	$2.53
Open	58.650	52 Week High	64	Dividend Per Share	N/A
Today's High	58.680	52 Week Low	17 3/16	Exchange	Nasdaq-NM
Today's Low	57.300	Previous Close	58 1/32	Industry	

FIGURE 4-7   Investors Advantage PE for Anchor Gaming

which can be compared both to a company's historical stock price range and to that of other companies in its industry.

If you take the time to conduct research to determine the value of any stock you're considering, you will be richly rewarded. Fortunately, there is more information available to you than you can use. Peter Lynch wrote in his book, *One Up on Wall Street*, "I can't imagine anything that's useful to know that the amateur investor can't find out. All the pertinent facts are just waiting to be picked up." And yet, there are people who say they can't invest because they don't know where to get information. Here are two excellent Web sites to check out:

> **POINTER**
>
> In the stock market, an investor with money in hand is like a kid in a candy store. There are well over 10,000 stocks and about 8,000 mutual funds to choose from. To put it lightly, you can afford to be picky.

- *Thompson Investor Net (www.thompsoninvest.net)*. This site provides more than 7,000 in-depth company reports that are updated twice a month. In addition to general information, you get a comparison of the firm's financial ratios to its industry. Thompson charges a fee for this service, but its reasonable.

- *Yahoo Market Guide Report (www.Yahoo.marketguide.com)*. The site provides free information on hot stocks along with a sector listing, an industry listing, and educational information. Yahoo also features a "company of the day" article to highlight an outstanding company. For a small fee, you can subscribe to additional services that include company facts, company profiles, detailed company reports, earnings estimates, and stock screening tools.

NEVER BUY THE CHEAP STUFF

All investors like to buy cheap stocks. There's nothing wrong with that as long as there is value in the cheap stock. Unfortunately, many buy cheap stocks simply because they can buy more shares. However, the number of shares you have has nothing to do with the cash value of your portfolio. The growth of each stock's share price is what's significant. That's where the real value is. Astute investors have an entirely different view of what constitutes a cheap stock versus a value stock. In terms of value, a $100 stock may actually be cheaper than a $10 stock. Value investors look for low price-earnings ratios, exceptional annual earnings growth, and other critical financial information.

INSIGHT One of the great mistakes investors make is paying too much attention to stock prices instead of stock values.

What looks like a bargain in the stock market is often no bargain at all, but big trouble in the making. Say you follow a stock for a period of time to get a feeling for its normal trading range. Then one day you notice the price begins to drop. You keep watching and the price continues to fall. You check its financials and see that its most recent earnings report was positive. Yet the price continues to drop to the point where you can no longer resist it. You buy shares at what you think is a bargain price and after you buy, the stock falls even further. Only when its next earnings report comes out do you realize why the stock had dropped so dramatically. As the new report undoubtedly reveals, the company has hit some serious financial turbulence.

Be wary of stocks that unexpectedly begin to fall, particularly during a period when the overall market is moving up. The company's most recent earnings report may be of no value to you in assessing the strength of the stock because the problems are probably more recent. Dig deeper and call the company. Talk to their investment relations manager and ask what's going on.

POINTER When the bear is chasing everybody down Wall Street and there's blood in the street, buy everything you can.

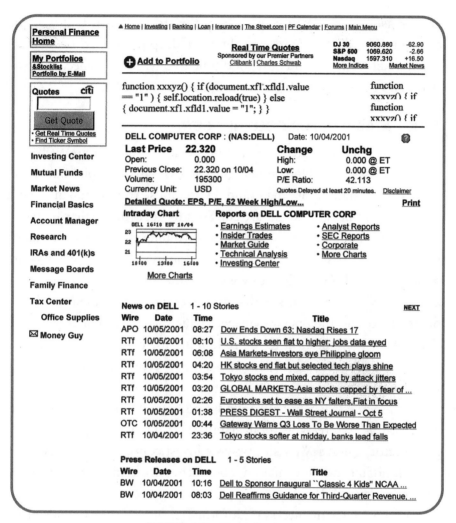

FIGURE 4-8   News Features

Don't be shy because their job is to talk with investors like you.

Search for recent news on the company to see if they are encountering any financial trouble. Most Web sites that feature stock quotes include new features on specific stocks similar to the ones shown in figure 4-8. Chances are there are good reasons for the price drop and good reasons for you to stay clear of the stock. If you find that the company is still doing well, and the price drop is just part of the normal market flow, it could be a good time to buy. Always check the current news on any stock before you initiate a buy order.

MINE DATABASES FOR GOLD NUGGETS

Your most reliable sources for specific stock information are Web sites with databases that help you find great stocks based on solid functional and technical data rather than random opinions. You can tap into these databases to find stocks that are consistently reporting stellar financial performance, one of the hallmarks of a winning stock. Two outstanding Web sites to start with are *Smart Money* magazine's www.smart money.com and Vector Quest's www.eduvest.com. *Smart Money* offers a screening room at their site that allows you to search their databases of stocks to find the one(s) that meet your specific search criteria (see figure 4-9). For example, if you're looking for bargain growth stocks or value stocks in a particular industry, the screening room tools will find them for you.

Let's assume that you have found a potentially great stock by using *Smart Money's* screening room database. Your next step is to check into Vector Quest's Web site (www.eduvest.com). It will ask you to enter fundamental information about the stock in a format that's shown in figure 4-10.

Once you enter the necessary information into Vector Quest's questionnaire, it goes to work for you and produces a multi-page technical analysis on the stock you're interested in buying. Figure 4-11 shows you the first page of a five-page report for IBM. The complete report includes valuable information such as a company's long-term debt, current dividends, and projected earnings, along with other important financial data. Vector Quest also tells you what it believes the stock is worth.

Stock Screener

Easy to Understand

Extensive help text and
annotation makes this screener
a tool anybody can profit from.

Total results: 213

CHKP

Make report

1-yr price chart

Stock Ticker	Company Name	V	Price/Sales
GMST	Gemstar-TV Guide Inte...		20.2
QCOM	QUALCOMM Inc.		18.1
AMGN	Amgen Inc.		17.8
CHKP	Check Point Software ...		17.9
TMIC	Trend Micro Inc.		15.6

The new SmartMoney Stock Screener is a premium tool available only on
SmartMoney Select.

Why should you subscribe? Because you'll gain access to the best stock screener
on the Web (or anywhere else, for that matter). We've combined a powerful
database and elegant design to make the SmartMoney Stock Screener a tool
anybody can use profitably, from beginner to pro. If you're serious about using your
computer to find good investments, you've found the right software.

Check out these features:

· Tap a database of more than 7,000 NYSE, Nasdaq and AMEX stocks.
· Choose from 100 different screening criteria, from forward P/E to free cash flow.
· View your results in three different, innovative ways
· Drill down to SmartMoney Investor Snapshots for advanced charting and research
· View extensive help text on how to screen and how to interpret each criterion
· Save your favorite screens for repeated use.
· Try a hard-wired SmartMoney screen, from Bargain Growth to Momentum
· Create a spreadsheet and download an extensive report on all your companies
  using our vast database of financial and performance data.

Still not convinced? Then try SmartMoney Select for yourself RISK FREE. Sign up
now for a two-week FREE trial and get one FREE Multex.com research report ($10
value) as our gift.

FIGURE 4-9 *Smart Money's* Screening Room

Value Point Analysis Model

All Input Factors are Hyperlinked to their Definitions

INPUTS:

Value Point Analysis/VectorVest Base Case Stock Analysis:
Look for and note the input entries for the **(GRT) Earnings Growth Rate** and
the (projected) leading 12 month **(EPS) Earns Per Share** for use in a Base Case Value
Point Analysis:

Enter a Stock Symbol: [   ]   Analyze

Enter Stock Symbol for **WSRN** Data Source: [   ]   Search   Clear
Look at both *Quick*Source files in **KeyLinks:** and for
Projected Earning Estimates in **Earnings Estimates:**

1 - Enter Stk Name, Sym, and Exchange (30 chars or less) [   ]
2 - Enter the Number of Shares in Millions, Gtr than 0 [   ]
3 - Enter the Long Term Debt in Millions of Dollars [   ]
4 - Enter Current Dividend in dollars/sh(xx.xx), annual [   ]
5 - Enter Book Value or Net Worth in dollars/sh [   ]
6 - Enter Projected Earnings in dollars/sh, annual [   ]
7 - Enter Projected Average Growth in Earnings (%) [   ]
8 - Enter Projected Average Growth in Sales (%) [   ]
9 - Enter Current Yield of AAA Bonds(%), Gtr than 0 [7.04]
This optional entry represents the latest week
Index of 10 high grade corporate bonds.
Source: Market Laboratory*Bonds Section, Barron's(10/01).

10- Enter Projected Change of AAA Bonds(%) [0]
Optional base case entry.

11- Enter Current Earnings in dollars/sh, annual amount [   ]
12- Enter Current Price in dollars/sh, Gtr than 0 [   ]
13- Enter Number of Years the Earnings Growth Rate is [1]
     Expected to be Sustained. e.g. 1, 1.5, 2 etc.
This optional entry represents a one year base case.

FIGURE 4-10   Vector Quest's Analysis Model

VectorVest Stock Analysis of Intl BusMach

Thank you for requesting an analysis of Intl BusMach from VectorVest. The ticker symbol for Intl BusMach is IBM. IBM is traded on the New York Stock Exchange and options are available on this stock.

PRICE: IBM closed on 11/08/2001 at $113.81 per share.

VALUE: IBM has a Value of $77.04 per share. Value is the foundation of the VectorVest system. It is a measure of what a stock is currently worth. Value is based upon earnings, earnings growth rate, dividend payments, dividend growth rate, and financial performance. Current interest and inflation rates also play an important role in the computation of Value. When interest and/or inflation rates decrease, Value goes up. When interest rates and inflation increase, Value goes down. Sooner or later a stock's Price and Value always converge.

RV (Relative Value): IBM has an RV of 0.79. On a scale of 0.00 to 2.00, an RV of 0.79 is poor. RV reflects the long-term price appreciation potential of the stock compared to an alternative investment in AAA Corporate Bonds. Stocks with RV ratings above 1.00 have attractive upside potential. A stock will have an RV greater than 1.00 when its Value is greater than Price, and its Relative Safety (see below) and forecasted earnings growth rate are above average. In some cases, however, a stock's RV will be above 1.00 even though its Value is well below Price. This happens when a stock has an exemplary record of financial performance and an above average earnings growth rate. In this case, the stock is currently selling at a premium, and the investor is banking on future earnings growth to drive the stock's price higher. This information is very useful not only in knowing whether or not a stock has favorable price appreciation potential, but it also solves the riddle of whether to buy high growth, high P/E, or low growth, low P/E stocks. We believe that RV ratings above 1.00 are required to consistently achieve above average capital gains in the stock market.

RS (Relative Safety): IBM has an RS rating of 0.93. On a scale of 0.00 to 2.00, an RS of 0.93 is fair. VectorVest looks at safety from the viewpoint of an equity investor (one who is buying stock of a company) rather than that of a purchaser of debt (one who is lending money to the company). From this perspective, consistency of financial and operating performance, stock price appreciation history, and price volatility are the key factors used in the evaluation of Relative Safety (RS). Debt to equity ratio, capitalization, sales volume, business longevity and other factors are also considered, but to a lesser degree.

VectorVest favors steady, predictable performers. All stocks are rated on a scale of 0.00 to 2.00. A stock with an RS greater than 1.00 is safer and more predictable than the average of all stocks. A stock with an RS less than 1.00 is less predictable and riskier than the average stock.

FIGURE 4-11   Vector Quest Technical Report

Never buy a stock if the price makes you uneasy. Instead, find an alternative investment with more attractive values. There are screening programs at various Web sites that let you specify valuation criteria. After you enter your criteria, such as PE ratios and EPS, the program will search databases for stocks that meet your parameters. Hoover's Online offers a free screener program (hbn.hoovers.com/search/forms/stockscreener) that has over 8,000 stocks in its database. Additional screening sites are listed in the Appendix II under the heading "Search and Screening Tools."

> **POINTER**
>
> See the different Web sites that are listed under "stock quotes" in Appendix II to obtain the information you need to complete Vector Quest's questionnaire.

DOES IT FEEL RIGHT?

Sometimes you have to look beyond a company's bottom line to determine whether you want to own its stock. If you don't like the company, don't buy it, no matter how healthy its earnings. Many investors decline to own the most profitable stocks on the New York Stock Exchange. Philip Morris has led the market in total shareholder return for the past 60 years. But because it's the world's leading cigarette producer, some investors refuse to own the stock. Teetotalers sometimes avoid the stock of brewers such as Anheuser-Busch. On the other hand, a lot of Bud drinkers own the stock because they love the beer. Environmentalists often refuse to buy stocks of companies that are notorious for polluting the environment. Pacifists typically decline to invest in defense contractor stocks.

Of course, you really don't need a reason to decline buying a stock. You might decide against investing in a retailer because you don't like its stores, or a restaurant because you don't like its food. You might not invest in a manufacturer because you don't like its products. My friend refuses to buy Microsoft stock because she owns an Apple computer and has always considered Microsoft a competitor. Personal preference should be a part of your stock selection process. It's your money. Invest in the stocks you like after you have thoroughly checked them out.

WATCH FOR OPPORTUNITIES

Smart investors watch for buy opportunities when the market pushes the price of a stock down because of a temporary problem that may have no bearing on the company's long-term prospects. That's when they swoop in and buy the stock to hold until the company rebounds. What could be easier? Yet as elementary and logical as it may sound, buying low and selling high is not that easy.

What makes the concept so difficult is that it clashes with every fiber of human impulse and emotion. When stocks are blazing through a strong bull rally, and every news show reports a new market high, it's hard to resist the impulse to jump in while the market is hot. Then, when stocks begin to go south and the economic outlook dims, emotion prods us to pull the plug and sell out before things get even worse. The result for the uninitiated is that they buy when stocks are pushing new highs, and sell when stocks sink to their lowest levels.

The truth of the matter is, it takes nerves of steel to buy low, to put your money on the line when the market is floundering, and to sell out when everyone else is buying in. But that's what separates winners from losers. Only after you understand the psychology of the market and know its history does it become easier to get in and out of the market at the right time. There will be fluctuations in stock prices, with high points and low points every year. Try to use these fluctuations to maximize your returns, bolstering your holdings when stocks are down, and lightening up your position when euphoria has driven prices up beyond reason.

Even good companies can go through a tough year or quarter. And when they do, Wall Street punishes them mercilessly. A disappointing earnings report can cause the price of a stock to tumble far beyond what it should. Bad news about a company can also cause the stock price to drop. In 1994, when Intel reported that its Pentium chip was causing some mistakes in large calculations, its stock price dropped from $65 to $56 a share. But once the company resolved the problem, the stock not only moved back up to its original high, but continued to climb to $156 a share in just seven months.

In 1996, America Online instituted an unlimited use policy for customers willing to pay $19.95 per month for their services. The response was so over-whelming the company couldn't meet demand. This seems like exactly the kind of problem most businesses would love to have, but Wall Street hammered the stock, knocking it from a high of $71 to a low of $25 in just two months. A year later, the stock had bounced back into the 70s, and investors smart enough to buy the stock in its time of trouble earned a return of more than 180 percent in just one year.

> **INSIGHT**
>
> Wall Street generally rewards companies that demonstrate they can do more with fewer employees. In part, that is because people represent one of the most expensive parts of running a business. The more productive a company's employees are, the less people they need.

John Rogers of the Ariel Funds likes to buy stocks when no one else wants them. "We like to buy small and mid-size companies when they're cheap and out of favor. We look at the private market value of the companies. We look at what comparable companies are being sold for. When talking about market value, we are really trying to get a sense of what an informed buyer would pay for the company. When we come up with a value for a company that interests us, we divide that number by the number of total shares outstanding to get a true value for the stock."

Look for undervalued stocks that the market has punished or forgotten. Try to use the emotion of the market as an opportunity to buy good companies at low prices. I've seen times when a single negative earnings report would cut the price of a stock by 50 percent. Those are the stocks that should grab your interest. Obviously, you don't want to invest in every stock that takes a hit, but take a close look to see if there's an excellent chance it will rebound, and if there is, buy it. Look for a company that has done something to correct its problems. Don't invest in that stock unless you believe their management team has figured out how the company is going to bounce back. Maybe the answer is new management, or maybe it's a new subsidiary, a new product, or some cost cutting measures.

Always remember that Wall Street will ultimately value every stock correctly relative to every other stock. Watch for windows of opportunity when prices are out of whack with the rest of the market. Over the short term, emotions can cause a good company's stock to drop further than it should. Disappointing earnings, a failed product launch, or other bad news can cause the market to overreact. That's when you want to make your move. It's a lot like turkey hunting. You have to be patient, sit back quietly, and let the bird walk in front of you before you shoot. Pull the trigger when the price is right.

PUTTING IT ALL TOGETHER

Great stocks come in many different sizes, colors, and styles. Don't always look for the trendiest stocks because some of the dullest companies make great stocks. For example, RPM Corporation manufactures paints and coatings. Although it's not glamorous stuff, the company has posted 49 consecutive years of record earnings, while its stock price has moved up 15 percent on average per year. Dull can be very profitable.

Focus on stocks that are in consistent industries. Don't buy a little bit of everything to make sure you have all industries covered. Work on the industries that have the most predictable earnings streams. Look for companies in household goods like the ones you see in your grocery store (e.g., Procter & Gamble). Consider concentrating on small to mid-sized companies like Clorox, First Brand, McCormack Spice Company, Herman Miller, General Binding, and American Media. These companies generate positive cash flow, have high returns on assets and equity, and have a strong brand name in their specific industry niche. When it comes to bleach, you think of Clorox. When it comes to tabloid journalism, you think of the *National Enquirer*.

If you are not prepared to conduct a functional and technical analysis of a stock you're thinking of buying, then don't buy it. Always be on the lookout for winning stocks that can historically demonstrate great fundamentals like solid earnings growth and stellar sales performance. Read the company's annual report and search for the key information you need to make a buy decision. Look at what the stock analysts are saying, and check out their advice before you buy into their recommendations.

Examining a stock's chart can often tell you where that stock has been over a period of time, information that may not show up when you do a fundamental analysis of that stock. Don't allow yourself to get sucked into exciting short-term up-trends. The true measure of a great stock is how well it has done when the market was riding its own up and down trends.

CHAPTER-RELATED WEB SITES

Zacks Investment Research (www.zacks.com) reports on what analysts are saying about most of the stocks on the U.S. exchanges.

Merrill Lynch (www.ml.com) allows you to download research reports by such well-known experts as Merrill's chief economist Bruce Steinberg. Click on the research tab on the right side of their main menu to find the reports.

Paine Webber (www.painewebber.com) provides specific analytical reports by company even if you're not a customer. The firm's top-ranked strategists produce the reports.

J&E Research (www.jeresearch.com) is a site that specializes in financial modeling, research, and analysis. Their stock analysis program uses an Excel spreadsheet that you can use to complete the fundamental analysis of any stock.

Company Sleuth (www.companysleuth.com) will email you daily news updates on companies you're following.

The Neat Sheet lists hot stocks to watch and caters to people who do not have a lot of time to research and monitor stocks. Subscribers also receive a straight-shooting annual report. For subscription information, call 800-339-5671 or visit their Web site at www.neatmoney.com.

Individual Investor Online (www.iionline.com) offers delayed quotes, stock prospecting tools and screens, portfolio management tools, and financial news.

Honor the Market's Trends

"If you start with the fundamentals and finish with the graphs, you'll find gold most of the time."

—GINO RICARDO

PICKING GREAT STOCKS WILL EVENTUALLY MAKE YOU A LOT OF money. But even leading issues need a healthy market to help them make their greatest moves. In a bear market, three out of four stocks will fall, regardless of how great they are. Always keep a sharp eye out for market trends. The most important market yardsticks are the major stock averages and daily trading volumes of the New York and Nasdaq stock exchanges. These gauges help you spot rallies or market declines.

One of the best known averages is the Dow, the blue chip index that contains 30 of America's most prestigious companies. The Dow is price weighted, so higher-priced stocks sway the index more than lower-priced ones. Some critics distrust the Dow because of its small sample. Professional money managers like the S&P 500, which represents 500 premier companies and is therefore one of the most common benchmarks. But the Dow has worked well as a market gauge over the years. Since 1982, it has gained 1,189 percent compared to an almost identical number for the S&P 500 (1,085 percent). With so few stocks, a market watcher can quickly see what's going on inside the Dow.

MARKET CORRECTIONS

Not many people like winter rain and snow. But those showers bring in the spring flowers in much the same way the market needs to go through periodic corrections. They're no fun, but smart investors know corrections refresh the market for the next rally. They allow strong stocks to form healthy bases and allow new leaders to emerge; these leaders are usually the first out of the gate when the market turns up.

Mutual funds, pensions funds, and other major institutions control market corrections since they comprise as much as 80 percent of the market's daily trading volume. So, the cause of market declines becomes a "no brainer." When institutions decide to pull their money out of the market, the market declines. When institutions decide to buy back in, the market changes course and rallies. How can you tell if the market is about to rally? The most effective way is to watch for a follow-through day. Its occurrence will tell you the institutional money is flowing back into the market. Without a follow-through, your best bet is to stay on the sidelines and sit on your cash.

How do you spot a follow-through day? Lets assume that after a long slide, the market closes up on one or more of the three major indexes (i.e., Dow, Nasdaq, or S&P 500). Stocks seem to be coming alive for a few sessions, but that's not enough evidence that institutions are coming back into the market. At the beginning of the third day after the reversal, start looking for follow-through days. The first signal will occur when one of the major indexes gains 1 percent or more on increased trading volume. The strongest rallies tend to stage follow-throughs four to seven sessions out.

MARKET TIMING

The underlying principle of market timing is that you purchase stocks when prices are low and sell when prices are high. This seemingly simple strategy is based on reams of historical data used to discover patterns and relationships that affect investment returns. Market timing software uses this data to anticipate changes in market patterns. Market timers note that the market can under-perform for long periods of time. This low performance can reduce returns for buy-and-hold investors who decide to pull out of the market before the next upswing.

A recent study at the University of Michigan showed that the S&P 500 annualized return from 1982 to 1987 was 26 percent. If an investor was out of the market for ten of the biggest gain days, their returns would have been reduced to 18 percent. If they were out of the market for 40 of the biggest gain days, returns dropped to 4 percent. These percentages point out the biggest problem with market timing: the need to predict when to get into the market and when to get out of the market. A buy-and-hold strategy makes certain that the investor is in the market for the days when the biggest gains occur. For more information about market timing, check out these sites:

- *First Capital Corporation (www.firstcap.com)*. This site provides two free newsletters. *Market Timing* presents a short-term technical approach for the stock and bond markets. *Global Viewpoint* provides a weekly technical analysis of world markets that includes interest rates, foreign exchange, spot stock indices, and commodities. You can also search for back issues online. Both newsletters include recommendations, tips, illustrations, and charts.

- *Roger Hagan's Market Timing for Mutual Funds (www.halcy on.com/rhagan/).* This site includes ordering information for a mutual fund timing spreadsheet, last week's signal graph, graphs of favorite funds, links to other sites, and who's hot and who's not.

- *Timely (www.timely.com).* This site posts free charts and quotes on all U.S. and Canadian stocks and indexes. It features include customized charting, company-specific links, indexes that indicate today's market action, and cross-indexed information for locating key market activity.

INDUSTRY TRENDS

Have you ever wondered why there are so many industry groups in the United States? Our economy is fragmented and industries tend to spawn related businesses that become industries in there own right. For example, the computer sector is not just PC makers. There are also Computer-Graphics, Computer-Integrated Systems, Computer-Local Networks, Computer-Memory Devices, Computer-Peripheral Equipment, Computer-Services, Computer-Optical Recognition, and Computer-Software within the computer industry. Industry classifications make it easier to pinpoint specific areas that may be leading or falling behind within a broad industry group.

In America's economy, many segments or subgroups make up an industry. And, new subgroups are forming all the time as new products, technologies, and ways of doing business make possible things that were inconceivable only a few years ago. Stocks, like people, move in groups where each market cycle is led by specific industries. In the 1991 bull market, it was the computer and electronic issues that set the pace.

Although there are exceptions, leading industries in one bull market don't usually come back and lead in the next bull market. In the 1995 bull market, technology stocks were the rage as corporations poured money into new computers to boost productivity and profits. It wasn't just computer manufacturers that participated. In fact, manufacturers of personal computers lagged behind other computer subgroups even though they out-performed the broad market.

Sometimes, a major development happens in one industry and related industries reap follow-on benefits later. For example, in the late 1950s, the airline industry underwent a renaissance with the introduction of jet passenger planes. The increase in air travel a few years later spilled over to the hotel industry, which was more than happy to expand to accommodate the rising number of travelers. More recently, we've witnessed the ascent of the Internet industry. The Web, in turn, has helped the securities industry attract thousands of online investors. Retailing, media, and other industries are enjoying the coattail effects of the Internet as well.

However, some industries and stocks don't ride the leaders' coattails. Don't assume that just because it's the rainy season, umbrella manufacturers will suddenly surge. Look for quality companies capable of producing healthy earnings and sales as a result of exceptional products and services.

It's important to track the performance of an industry before you invest in it. As a rule, watch for the best stocks among the top 40 of the 197 industry groups. Here's a case where herd mentality works to your advantage. Studies show 37 percent of a stock's move is directly tied to the performance of their industry. Another 12 percent is due to strength in a stock's overall sector. Roughly half of a stock's move up or down is based on the strength of its respective industry.

The phenomenon is quite natural and is usually due to positive events that are taking place within an industry. For example, among the best-performing groups in the consumer-led boom of the '80s were apparel manufacturers and retailers. The subgroups that did best were those involved with women's apparel, thanks largely to the influx of women into the work force. Manufacturers such as Liz Claiborne and retail chains like The Limited enjoyed years of booming sales and earnings as women shopped for career clothes and had money to pay for them.

A sector is a broader grouping of companies than an industry group. For example, industry groups within the leisure entertainment sector include media, which is further broken down as follows:

- Media-Books
- Media-Cable TV
- Media-Newspapers
- Media-Periodicals

If you don't check on a stock's industry before you buy, you could find yourself owning a loser. Look what happened to Sun Microsystems in the fourth quarter of 2000 when the company had met all of its earnings and sales projections. Because the personal computer market had gone soft when companies like Compaq and Dell announced disappointing earnings, Sun Microsystems got sucked down by its own industry even though its earnings were up (see figure 5-1).

Take a look at the computer systems industry graph in figure 5-2. This graph represents a composite of the average price of stocks in the computer systems industry. It's the industry that Sun Microsystems participates in and as you can see, it started down trending in November 2000 at the same time Sun started down trending. In fact, the industry graph and Sun's graph follow almost identical down-trend patterns. The lesson to learn is that even great industry leaders like Sun Microsystems can't overcome their own industry when it falls.

You don't have to scan every stock to find out which industries are leading the market. *Investor's Business Daily*, a well-recognized investment newspaper, ranks 197 different industry groups by the price performance of all stocks in each group over the latest six months (see figure 5-3). This is a realistic period in which to observe market trends.

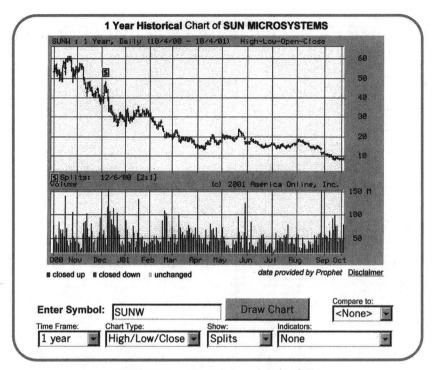

FIGURE 5-1   Sun Microsystem's Chart

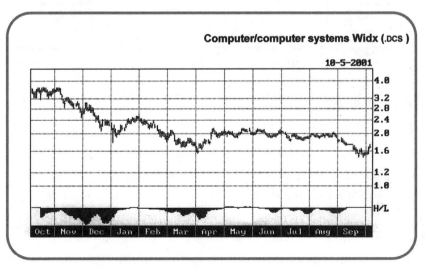

FIGURE 5-2   Computer Systems Industry Graph

Investor's Business Daily Industry Prices

197 Industry Groups are ranked 1 through 197 on price performance of all stocks in the industry in the latest 12 months (1 = best performance). Top ten industries in performance are boldface. Worst 10 are underlined.

Rank This Wk	Last Wk	3 Mo. Ago	Industry Name	No. of Stocks in Grp	% Chg. Since Jan. 1	Daily % Chg.
1	1	16	Medical-Biomed/Genetics	142	+52.4	+1.7
2	2	0	Elec-Semiconductor Mfg	83	+87.7	+3.3
3	3	6	Computer-Memory Devices	37	+67.6	+3.4
4	4	2	Elec-Laser Sys/Component	30	111.7	+0.7
5	6	1	Elec-Semiconductor Equip	46	+98.8	+2.6
6	7	11	Medical-Products	135	+58.0	+1.2
7	8	20	Medical-Ethical Drugs	78	+40.7	+1.2
8	5	46	Computer-Local Networks	51	+45.2	+3.5
9	9	10	Elec-Misc Components	66	+56.1	+2.4
10	10	33	Retail-Convenience Strs	9	+54.1	+1.0
11	11	9	Elec Products-Misc	55	+40.6	+1.8
12	33	59	Insurance-Prop/Cas/Titl	119	+25.8	+0.6
13	12	29	Medical-Instruments	92	+51.8	+1.6
14	13	14	Computer-Software	206	+49.1	+2.0
15	14	7	Computer-Peripheral Eq	99	+38.5	+0.5
16	18	28	Elec-Parts Distributors	22	+53.4	+1.4
17	19	32	Computer-Services	71	+47.4	+1.1
18	26	53	Finance-Sbic&Commrcl	11	+40.6	+1.1
19	17	12	Telecommunications-Equip	140	+41.4	+2.4
20	23	21	Finance-Mrtg&Rel Svc	31	+55.5	+0.9
21	15	5	Transportation-Airline	29	+86.5	+3.5
22	25	8	Elec-Measrng Instruments	34	+57.2	+2.0
23	16	24	Media-Radio/Tv	48	+48.8	+0.5
24	20	17	Retail/Whlsle Computers	31	+33.9	+1.5
25	29	39	Medical/Dental-Supplies	85	+32.1	+0.8
26	24	30	Financial Services-Misc	36	+57.7	+1.4
27	27	40	Computer-Mini/Micro	31	+42.2	+4.7
28	28	18	Finance-Consumer Loans	24	+68.6	+0.7
29	42	51	Banks-Money Center	7	+51.3	+0.9
30	30	63	Comml Services-Misc	134	+27.4	+0.9
31	22	19	Elec-Military Systems	44	+46.7	+0.8
32	32	27	Metal Prod-Fasteners	8	+57.1	+0.8
33	36	26	Computer-Integrated Syst	43	+50.6	+1.9
34	34	35	Machinery-Gen Industrial	52	+25.7	+0.6
35	39	22	Finance-Investment Bkrs	37	+56.7	+1.1
36	31	31	Oil & Gas-Drilling	19	+45.2	-0.1
37	41	68	Retail/Whlse Office Supl	8	+44.5	+4.4
38	40	36	Comml Svcs-Schools	19	+46.9	+0.3
39	47	45	Computer-Graphics	22	+41.6	+3.1
40	37	50	Banks-West	70	+35.5	+0.1
41	52	41	Funeral Svcs & Rel	6	+46.3	+1.3
42	21	4	Mining-Gems	17	+75.3	-0.5
43	38	67	Telecommunications-Svcs	68	+33.3	+0.7
44	55	52	Aerospace/Defense Eqp	45	+27.9	+0.6
45	43	37	Computer-Optical Recogtn	19	+29.0	+1.1
46	44	34	Comml Svcs-Security/Sfty	53	+23.5	+0.5
47	35	65	Machine-Tools & Rel Prod	23	+29.1	+0.8
48	50	13	Elec-Scientific Instrumn	40	+50.3	+1.3
49	51	38	Pollution Control-Svcs	108	+15.7	+1.0
50	53	99	Retail-Misc/Diversified	80	+10.6	+0.2
51	67	105	Banks-Southwest	17	+35.8	+0.3
52	46	15	Machinery-Mtl Hdlg/Autmn	21	+49.3	+0.7
53	59	48	Finance-Savings & Loan	295	+36.6	+0.4
54	54	23	Leisure-Gaming	81	+17.2	+0.3
55	69	79	Agricultural Operations	29	+29.4	-0.1
56	61	64	Food-Dairy Products	12	+32.9	+0.2
57	60	148	Leisure-Hotels & Motels	26	+20.3	+1.0
58	56	107	Medical-Outpnt/Hm Care	87	+16.6	+1.3
59	45	166	Retail/Wholesale-Jewelry	21	+8.4	-0.1
60	49	44	Retail-Restaurants	130	+19.0	+0.9
61	48	54	Bldg-Resident/Commrcl	40	+22.8	+1.1
62	62	55	Banks-Northeast	180	+30.8	+0.3
63	57	118	Leisure-Movies & Related	55	+8.1	+1.8
64	64	76	Banks-Southeast	120	+28.7	+0.9
65	63	25	Electrical-Control Instr	24	+28.3	+1.1
66	79	161	Shoes & Rel Apparel	34	+16.6	+1.2
67	65	109	Textile-Apparel Mfg	72	+8.3	+0.5
68	58	89	Insurance-Life	52	+25.0	+0.6
69	72	69	Diversified Operations	82	+29.1	+0.7
70	90	100	Pollution Control-Equip	52	+23.5	+1.5
71	71	153	Retail-Home Furnishings	25	+16.0	+0.7
72	68	49	Leisure-Toys/Games/Hobby	41	+19.3	+1.0
73	97	94	Insurance-Diversified	8	+47.3	+2.6
74	92	84	Tobacco	9	+32.2	+0.8
75	82	98	Machinery-Const/Mining	11	+36.6	+1.5
76	75	130	Cosmetics/Personal Care	57	+14.8	+0.6
77	85	178	Bldg-Mobile/Mfg & Rv	33	+20.4	+0.8
78	78	86	Office Supplies Mfg	26	+27.2	+0.1
79	70	74	Finance-Investment Mgmt	24	+24.6	+0.2
80	83	124	Comml Svcs-Printing	16	+26.0	+0.9
81	77	104	Retail-Mail Order&Direct	32	+11.5	+1.3
82	80	71	Transportation-Svcs	15	+45.0	+1.5
83	86	62	Banks-Super Regional	22	+40.5	+0.3
84	76	91	Oil&Gas-Intl Specialty	14	-29.2	+1.3
85	66	182	Telecommunctns-Cellulr	28	+5.2	+0.2
86	87	114	Comml-Leasing Cos	39	+21.5	+0.7
87	84	97	Retail/Wholesale-Food	20	+14.6	0.0
88	122	87	Leisure-Photo Equip/Rel	11	+18.5	+0.6
89	107	66	Chemicals-Fertilizers	12	+37.3	-0.2
90	100	111	Banks-Midwest	120	+21.8	+0.4
91	81	80	Metal Proc & Fabrication	45	+14.4	+0.5
92	101	3	Machinery-Printing Trade	10	+63.7	-0.1
93	108	72	Metal-Steel Pipe & Tube	11	+29.8	+0.2
94	96	70	Insurance-Acc & Health	22	+31.6	+0.5
95	121	181	Leisure-Products	63	-1.1	+0.4
96	98	149	Media-Newspapers	19	+24.0	0.0
97	95	58	Aerospace/Defense	8	+38.4	+0.9
98	106	123	Consumer Products-Misc	40	+12.3	-0.9
99	104	126	Metal Ores-Misc	16	-16.6	-0.8
100	91	160	Household-Appliances	15	+26.0	0.0
101	136	175	Auto/Truck-Replace Prts	25	+6.7	-0.4
102	74	106	Metal Ores-Gold/Silver	44	+13.3	-0.3
103	119	176	Comml Svc-Engineering/Rd	25	+10.0	+1.3
104	115	134	Retail-Drug Stores	11	+25.2	+1.4
105	93	82	Bldg-Constr Prods/Misc	52	+21.9	+0.6
106	135	96	Comml Svcs-Advertising	19	+18.2	+1.4
107	88	121	Retail-Discount&Variety	36	-0.4	+1.5
108	102	65	Chemicals-Specialty	60	+21.7	+0.7
109	99	92	Retail-Apparel/Shoe	59	+8.4	+1.2
110	109	141	Containers-Paper/Plastic	28	+12.2	+0.8
111	103	159	Transportation-Ship	9	+10.8	+0.4
112	113	133	Medical-Hospitals	19	+23.9	+0.6
113	73	56	Oil&Gas-Machinery/Equip	16	+24.8	+1.5
114	129	135	Office-Equip & Automatn	17	+29.2	+2.0
115	105	144	Auto Mfrs-Foreign	9	+10.3	+0.8
116	89	103	Steel-Specialty Alloys	12	+21.6	+0.4
117	132	95	Food-Misc Preparation	49	+21.4	0.0
118	130	115	Insurance-Multi Line	10	+28.2	+0.6
119	140	168	Food-Confectionery	6	+20.0	+0.6
120	123	77	Finance-Mortgage Reit	51	+12.9	+0.1
121	153	117	Medical-Drug/Diversified	8	+30.2	-0.7
122	127	147	Energy-Alternate Sources	22	+5.3	+1.4
123	117	173	Metal Ores-Non Ferrous	8	+14.2	+1.5
124	150	184	Comml Svcs-Linen Supply	7	+11.2	+1.0
125	120	127	Auto/Truck-Original Eqp	52	+7.5	+0.5
126	124	102	Real Estate Development	23	+17.8	+0.7
127	118	93	Oil&Gas-U S Explo&Prod	142	+9.2	+0.5
128	114	187	Retail-Consumer Elect	19	-7.5	+0.4
129	112	42	Paper & Paper Products	39	+23.6	+1.0
130	143	138	Beverages-Alcoholic	13	+23.2	+1.3
131	125	110	Leisure-Services	36	+16.4	+0.2
132	149	155	Utility-Telephone	23	+16.7	+0.3
133	110	60	Media-Cable Tv	33	+28.0	+2.0
134	126	189	Household-Audio/Video	23	+5.1	+1.7
135	138	119	Electrical-Connectors	11	+13.1	+1.2
136	128	169	Metal Prod-Distributor	7	+13.5	-0.3
137	116	145	Transportation-Rail	18	+31.5	-0.1
138	148	112	Beverages-Soft Drinks	13	+32.5	-0.8
139	131	139	Chemicals-Basic	15	+21.1	+0.4
140	111	78	Machinery-Farm	10	+31.6	+0.1
141	141	47	Medical-Generic Drugs	17	+30.9	+0.5
142	165	150	Food-Canned	9	+21.5	+0.3
143	134	143	Medical-Hlth Maint Org	29	+5.0	+1.5
144	142	137	Banks-Foreign	36	+11.4	+0.8
145	94	120	Bldg-Heavy Const	19	+21.9	+0.9
146	146	129	Retail-Supermarkets	35	+13.6	+0.8
147	145	190	Medical-Nursing Homes	27	+4.6	+0.5
148	163	116	Electrical-Equipment	22	-14.0	+0.2
149	147	90	Bldg Prod-Wood	18	+20.6	+0.4
150	137	73	Oil&Gas-Field Services	38	+18.6	+0.8
151	164	170	Medical-Whsle Drg/Sund	23	+11.0	+0.9
152	133	164	Auto Mfrs-Domestic	4	+13.8	+0.8
153	152	83	Bldg-A/C & Heating Prds	14	+17.6	+0.8
154	151	101	Media-Books	17	+22.6	+0.3
155	157	179	Transport-Air Freight	7	+31.6	-0.5
156	144	180	Household-Textiles Furns	15	+6.1	-1.0
157	139	88	Real Estate Operations	34	+14.1	-1.3
158	154	136	Oil&Gas-Refining/Mktg	30	+9.8	+0.2
159	166	156	Utility-Electric Power	110	+13.3	+0.9
160	156	108	Media-Periodicals	15	+9.2	-0.3
161	159	128	Oil&Gas-Prod/Pipeline	29	+14.9	0.0
162	158	122	Chemicals-Plastics	29	+12.5	+0.6
163	172	186	Hsehold/Office Furniture	27	+2.3	+0.5
164	162	81	Retail-Major Disc Chains	5	+22.7	+0.4
165	181	152	Bldg-Hand Tools	9	+19.2	-0.1
166	160	61	Computer-Mainframes	7	+20.6	+0.1
167	174	163	Finance-Equity Reit	187	+5.0	0.0
168	169	57	Oil&Gas-Cdn Exp&Prod	123	+5.9	+0.2
169	171	171	Retail-Department Stores	17	+10.4	+0.4
170	179	167	Bldg-Maintenance & Svc	17	+12.5	-0.2
171	175	177	Retail/Whlsle-Bldg Prods	31	-0.9	+1.1
172	168	154	Bldg-Cement/Concrt/Ag	17	+10.8	+0.7
173	178	151	Oil&Gas-Cdn Integrated	8	+15.7	+0.2
174	177	174	Utility-Gas Distribution	52	+8.7	+0.2
175	181	146	Finance-Public Td Inv Fd	401	+13.3	+0.2
176	176	172	Finance-Publ Inv Fd-Frn	125	-1.3	+0.3
177	188	195	Food-Sugar & Refining	3	-0.8	+0.8
178	191	162	Soap & Clng Preparatns	11	+7.3	+0.7
179	170	43	Machinery-Thermal Proc	5	+21.9	-0.4
180	155	191	Steel-Producers	23	-11.2	-0.6
181	187	183	Utility-Water Supply	16	+5.0	+0.9
182	173	140	Food-Flour & Grain	8	+20.9	-0.4
183	167	132	Trucks & Parts-Hvy Duty	11	+3.4	-0.5
184	182	157	Oil&Gas-Intl Integrated	5	+12.4	+1.1
185	184	142	Insurance-Brokers	10	+7.9	-0.2
186	185	131	Bldg-Paint & Allied Prds	14	+10.3	+0.6
187	189	188	Household-Housewares	12	+2.0	-0.2
188	183	165	Retail/Whlsle-Auto Parts	24	+1.1	-0.3
189	186	197	Energy-Coal	5	-16.0	+0.1
190	180	75	Food-Meat Products	18	+22.1	+2.0
191	192	196	Transportation-Truck	48	-13.8	+0.3
192	196	192	Textile-Mill Products	17	-4.9	+0.2
193	190	113	Container-Metal/Glass	10	-2.9	-0.5
194	194	194	Transportation-Equip Mfg	10	-8.9	+0.8
195	195	193	Oil & Gas-U S Royalty Tr	20	-3.7	-0.9
196	193	158	Oil&Gas-U S Integrated	14	+6.0	+0.7
197	197	185	Auto/Truck-Tires & Misc	10	-0.9	-0.2
64	64	64	S & P Industrial Index		-25.9	+0.8
64	64	64	S&P 500 Index		+27.6	+0.8

FIGURE 5-3 IBD Industry Prices

STOCK TRENDS

When you look at a stock's price and volume chart, think of it as the stock telling you what it's doing. If the price is moving up, it's telling you it's under accumulation, that there's more buying than selling. The steeper the uptrend, the stronger the buying is in relation to the selling. If the volume is heavier than normal, the stock is telling you the buyers are institutional investors who deal in large quantities. Their purchases of thousands of shares at a time have much greater impact on a stock's price than the few hundred that most individual investors buy. A stock rising on heavy volume is significantly bullish. But when the volume begins to taper off, the stock may be telling you that serious buying is nearing an end, and along with it the stock's up-trend.

If the stock's price is moving sideways, it's telling you that buyers and sellers are about evenly matched. If the volume's heavy, it's also telling you that a battle of titans is under way. Until the stock moves higher or lower out of its directionless pattern, you don't know which side will prevail. If the price is moving lower, the stock is telling you it's under distribution. The heavier the sell volume, the more ominous the pattern. A stock falling on lighter than normal volume is less worrisome. And, a weak stock that's stabilizing on very light volume is telling you that the selling may be drying up.

Technical analysts believe there are certain price and volume patterns that presage bullish moves, or at least improve the chances of a stock working for you rather than against you. These patterns are referred to as bases or consolidation areas where buyers and sellers are evenly matched. When a stock moves up and out of its base on increased volume, it's telling you buyers are regaining the upper hand and that the path of least resistance in the stock is up rather than down.

Well-drawn trend lines help you decide when to buy or sell a stock. Trend lines tell you if a stock is rising too fast or running out of gas. When they're used to confirm sell signals, they can help you lock in on gains by selling before a stock fizzles. One of the market trends to watch out for is the closing wedge.

The advent of a closing wedge during an up-trend often pre-stages a major reversal. Many traders will sell when they spot one. Here's how you determine if one of your stocks is trending into a closing wedge. Draw two trend lines along your stock's recent high and low prices. In a closing wedge, the lines will intersect like they did with Sun Microsystems in figure 5-4. It's a clear signal that the buy volume for

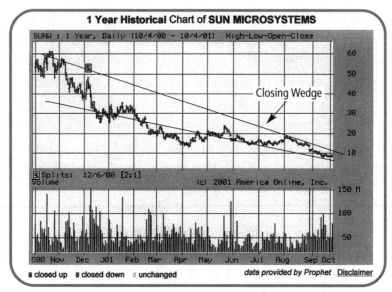

FIGURE 5-4   Sun Microsystems' Closing Wedge

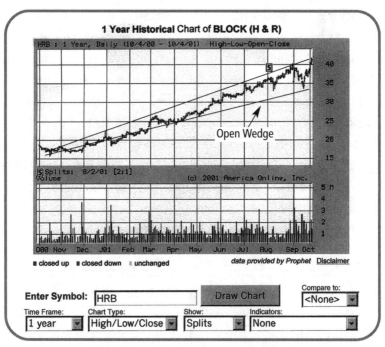

FIGURE 5-5   H&R Block's Opening Wedge

your stock is being undercut by the sell volume. In short, there are more sellers than buyers and it's time to get out of the stock.

Conversely, an open trend line can signal a buy or hold opportunity for a stock. The open wedge trend line is basically the reverse of a closed trend line. Draw two trend lines along your stock's recent high and low prices just as you did in the previous example. In an open wedge, the lines will diverge as shown in figure 5-5. It's a clear signal that the buy volume for a stock is exceeding the selling volume. In short, there are more buyers than sellers and it's time to buy the stock or hold onto it if it's already in your portfolio.

50-DAY MOVING AVERAGE TREND

If it were a perfect world, all stocks would move in straight, predictable lines instead of like roller coasters. Fortunately, there's a tool called the 50-day moving average that straightens out the seesaw path. It's a simple calculation that plots the arithmetic mean of a stock's last 50-day closing prices. The resulting trend line smoothes price fluctuations and depicts the general route of a stock. Use the 50-day moving average to spot trends. As each trading day passes, the average is recalculated by replacing the oldest closing price with the newest closing price. The process is repeated every day to form the moving average (see figure 5-6).

Most stocks have a way of telling you whether they're going up or down, depending on their 30-day moving average. When a stock is trading above its moving average, most of its recent investors have bought their shares at a lower price, so they tend to be positive about their investment. If a stock is trading below its moving average, you have a different story. Recent buyers got in at a higher price and are now looking for a way out to recover their investment or minimize their loss.

Some investors use the 50-day moving average to guide their buy and sell decisions. They'll buy just when a stock's price swings up and touches the moving average with the hope that it will continue to rise

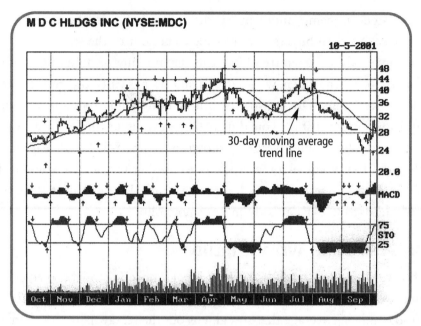

FIGURE 5-6   MDC's 50-Day Move Average

well beyond the moving average line. Conversely, they'll sell when a stock's price swings down and touches the moving average if they are convinced that there are more sellers than buyers for the stock.

THE ANIMALS OF WALL STREET

In the late 1800s, New York City gradually swallowed Manhattan's farmland, but the animals managed to migrate over to Wall Street. Today, four animals dominate the market: bulls, bears, hogs, and sheep. An old street saying goes: "Bulls make money, and bears make money, but hogs and sheep get slaughtered." A bull fights by striking up with his horns. If you're a bull, you believe the stock market is going to rise in value. You're a buyer. Bears fight by striking down with their paws. As a bear, you speculate that stock prices will fall and make your profits from a declining market because you're a seller and a bargain hunter.

Where do the hogs and sheep fit in? Hogs bet all of their money on big, risky positions and then get slaughtered when the market turns against them. The market always knows when hogs overeat and it skewers them every time. Instead of relying on their own knowledge and experience, sheep follow stock tips and believe what anyone tells them. But when the market suddenly turns volatile, the pitiful sheep get sheared in a hurry.

Each market day is a giant tug-of-war between the bulls and the bears. As a trader, you'll have to decide who's in power if you want to make money in either market. In a strong, rising market, bulls rule and you'll profit from the soaring prices. Unless you're a contrarian or a market participant who takes the opposite side of the current trend (not a good idea for new trades), you'll strap on your horns and buy. When the market turns weak and prices fall, bears rule by profiting as prices trend lower. In a bear market, you either stand aside or learn the art of selling short.

When volatility indicators show that the bulls and bears are engaging in a no-win battle, wise traders observe from the sidelines. Knowing when to trade and when not to trade is the hallmark of a seasoned trader. Believe it or not, it takes immense discipline to watch the market whirl around you, and not jump in. Forcing trades when market conditions are whippy and unpredictable is not a wise move.

> **WARNING**
>
> Some investors think they need to keep trading during a market slump. It's difficult for even the most nimble investor to make money in a bear market. Most stocks follow the market down trend so if you invest in a given stock, you're fighting the tide.

The market almost always bids up any company that delivers higher earnings growth rate. And, the market can become even ecstatic when a company accelerates its profit growth over the previous year. But, beware when earnings growth decline, which usually happens before a company formally reports its financial position. Institutions employ armies of analysts to watch their holdings like a hawk. If they sniff out downside company earnings, they'll dump thousands of shares in a minute leaving you holding the bag.

What can you do to protect yourself? If you followed our earlier advice and religiously put in stop-loss orders on every stock that's in your portfolio, you have already protected yourself from serious downside losses. However, cut your losses even shorter the moment you get news that one of the stocks won't meet its earnings expectations. Chances are that if you sell immediately, you will avoid a much bigger loss once the official earnings are announced.

LET BEARS RUN THEIR COURSE

When a grizzly comes into a campsite, smart campers curl themselves into a ball and lie completely still until the animal loses interest and goes away. Wise investors take a similar approach in the face of a bear market. It might be tempting to rush in when others are fleeing. But the fact is, three out of four stocks will follow the bear market's negative trend. It's best to let the bear run its course before you step back into the market.

A bear market occurs when at least one major stock average declines 20 percent or more from its latest high. Conversely, smaller corrections let stocks take a break before they resume their advance. But a bear-style drop is the market's way of burning off excessive gains in stocks. Trying to predict the bottom of a bear market can pose serious risk to your portfolio. You could buy a stock thinking it's cheap, only to get mauled as it drops further. A better and safer approach is to sit still and wait for the inevitable recovery.

No two bear markets are exactly alike. Since the early 1970s, bear markets have been as short as a few months to as long as two years. Their duration depends in large part on the state of the U.S. and global economies. In times of severe recession and galloping inflation, the Dow Jones has fallen 30 to 50 percent. When things aren't so bad, the decline has ranged from 20 to 30 percent.

The good news is that historically, each bear market is followed by an even stronger bull market. Knowing when the market is about to shift from a bear to a bull is essential to successful investing. If you sense that the bear is over, don't start buying. Wait to see if the market can prove itself with a follow-through, which usually takes place four to seven sessions after a new rally starts. In the follow-through session, at least one major index will rise more than 1 percent on higher volume than the previous day.

Follow-through is a path a stock follows on its chart as its price climbs to just above its 50-day moving average. It may hover there for several days before it starts to inch up again on heavy trading as institutions follow through by acquiring the stock. A deep market follow-through is a signal that big institutional buyers are coming out of their closets and driving the rally with their sheer buying power. Without their support, no market rally can sustain its advance. The ultimate test of a rally is to see new groups of stocks jumping out of sound price bases and leading the market higher. They may jump out, but if they quickly fall back, you will have your answer. The big institutions aren't buying into the rally.

Don't let small losses turn into major casualties. If you think you can weather a market down turn by sitting tight on your sinking portfolio,

> **WARNING**
>
> It took the S&P 500 six years to recover the 50 percent it lost in the 1973-74 bear market. In March of 2000, over a thousand stocks on the Nasdaq exchange alone dropped 50 percent or more. Cutting your losses quickly is the single most important rule of investing. Don't let small losses turn into something that may take months to recover.

think again. History has taught us that significant market down turns can drag on and on as we learned in the bear market of 2000 and 2001. Step back into history and consider the bear markets from 1958 through 1998. They lasted anywhere from 3 to 20 months. Even after the bear officially goes back into the woods, it can take even longer for the market to dig its way out of the bottom.

Since the S&P index was first computed in 1928, there have been 11 bear markets when it lost 20 percent or more of its value after climbing to new historic highs. After the S&P index recovered from bear markets and achieved new historic highs, there have always been at least three minor corrections of from 3 to 11 percent. Each correction was followed by a recovery to yet another historic high before the market entered a more pronounced bear market of greater severity.

The most impressive aspect of the bull market of the '90s was its subdued character prior to the record setting peak gain of 29 percent in 1995. The bubble that peaked in February 1994 established a new peak trading day duration record of 116 days. In December 1995 this record was broken with a series of 77 new historic highs for the S&P composite spread over a 210-day trading period without a correction of three percent or more. The 29 percent peak-to-peak gain associated with this bubble was more than ten percentage points higher than the previous record of 19 percent, which was established during the bull market of 1985–87.

It's not easy to predict the demise of a bull market. The data suggest that bull markets are more likely to end after a relatively small peak-to-peak gain following a spectacular series of new historic highs that have been achieved without an intervening decline of at least 3 percent. There have only been two cases (the bull markets of 1967–68 and 1980) where the last peak-to-peak gain in stock prices was the largest bubble in that bull market.

TROLL FOR NEW LEADERS

Picture a thousand salmon struggling upstream during spawning season. Some get caught by the bears, but others fight their way against the current and complete their incredible trek. Stocks go through the same motions in a bear market. Three out of four stocks follow the market's general down trend, so most stocks are on the mend when the bear is roaring. Yet as market and public sentiment sour, some stocks quietly wade through all the selling and creep up to higher prices, avoiding the bears.

When the market finally bottoms and begins a new rally that's being pushed by bulls, certain stocks will shoot out to new highs on heavy volume. Savvy investors fish for such stocks, which have the highest potential for outstanding gain. Be on the lookout for new leaders during a bear market. Coal and oil stocks accelerated to higher ground after the punishing 1973–74 bear market. Homebuilders and toys took off after the 1981–82 bear market thanks to pent-up demand and the second baby boom. In the bear market of 1998, financial and Internet stocks took off. In 2000–2001, financial services were almost immune to the bear because of low interest rates and the subsequent strong housing market.

The Dow has weathered every market drop in the past century by constantly switching the members of the average to reflect new leading firms. When the Dow was launched in 1928, it was made up of a slew of steel makers and other metal-related firms. None of them are found in the Dow today. In 1972, the 30 firms that made up the Dow included no financial service firms. Today, American Express, Citibank, and J.P. Morgan are members reflecting the strong growth in the financial industry.

Individual sectors in the Dow often see changes in leadership at the start of the bull market. Woolworth was one of the original 30 Dow stocks in 1928. In the late 1990s, Woolworth could not compete against big discount stores and was dropped from the Dow and replaced with Wal-Mart. The moral of the story is, if you hold a slumping blue chip thinking it will come back, you could find yourself waiting a long time and miss prime opportunities elsewhere in the market. Sears and Coca-Cola peaked in 1998 just before the Dow slid 21 percent. The Dow has since recovered 43 percent from where it was in the bear market of 1998 but both Sears and Coca-Cola were still fighting down trends three years later.

CONTROL YOUR EMOTIONS IN TOUGH MARKETS

Everyone feels great when stock prices are being chased uphill by the bulls. But when they abruptly turn around and start running the other way, it's a whole different story. A down market can turn confident investors into nervous wrecks. Uncontrolled emotions can cause you to make unwise decisions and result in even bigger losses. Choose only high quality companies among sectors that are outperforming the market. That will give you a solid system to preserve your capital and keep the following emotions at bay:

- *Complacency.* When a bull market is near its end and market averages are soaring, hordes of stocks appear to be moving full-steam ahead. Investors are buying any stock that's in a hot sector throughout the advance. Suppose the stock you bought suddenly takes a nosedive as the bull begins to leave the market and falls below your stop-loss point. You decide not to sell because you're sure it will rebound. It never does and you ride it all the way down into major loss territory because of your complacency. Don't get complacent.

- *Denial.* Suppose the market tops and then leading stocks start to fall from their peaks. Stocks in your portfolio take the heat as you watch gains you enjoyed during the bull market evaporate. When your stocks drop below your stop-loss point, you stray away from your defense system and hold on, denying that the market decline is real. You keep telling yourself it's just a temporary pullback as your portfolio sinks lower and lower. By the time the market whacks 25 percent or more off your portfolio, your investment decisions no longer ride on logical thinking but rather on pure emotion. That's when denial sets in. You're now hoping that your stocks will at least return to your buy price so you can sell and won't have to admit how stupid you were not to have sold earlier.

- *Despair*. A bear is roaring and all of the major indexes are down well over 20 percent. Leading stocks have sunk 40 to 70 percent from their 52-week highs. Your losses have snowballed to the point where you sell out in despair. Instead of analyzing your mistakes, you put a blanket over your head and forget about stocks indefinitely. You're giving up at the worst possible time because the market always comes back after it has been roasted. New sectors of stocks will sprout up and build solid bases as new leaders burst ahead on exploding trade volume. You'll miss the really big gains if you give up.

In summary, you should never let emotions cloud your trading judgment. To exploit market psychology, you must act in a contrarian fashion, taking the contrary course when the crowd falls prey to its emotion. Extreme optimism often coincides when the market tops. People think the sky is the limit and send stock prices flying. Savvier investors sell into this frenzy and horde their cash. When the market begins to tank, extreme pessimism can be bullish. Toward the end of the decline, the last bulls throw in the towel and sell everything with a vengeance. Cooler heads dive into the market buying bargain-priced equities that are about to launch into the next rally.

> **WARNING**
> A word to the wise. Sentiment gauges shouldn't be used in isolation. Your primary indicators are still the major indexes.

FINDING MARKET TREND INFORMATION

The Dow theory was developed by Charles Dow, the first publisher of *The Wall Street Journal* in the early 1900s. In a nutshell, the theory states that the averages that make up the Dow Jones Industrial Average reflect at any given time all that is known or can be foreseen concerning financial matters. Based on that premise, the Dow theory states that any market trend must be confirmed by the Dow averages.

The fact that the Dow theory has stood the test of time gives credence to its ability to forecast market turns. Historically, if the turn is down, eight out of ten stocks will follow its path. Understanding market trends will help you determine when to buy or sell stocks to maximize your returns. Here are excellent online sources that provide market trend information:

- *Financials.com (www.financials.com)*. This site provides stock ratings and market data, as well as links to Data Broadcasting Corp., U.S. Industry Market Summaries, company stock prices by industry, Griffin Financial Services "Weekly Market Outlook," and Market Vision's "World Markets at a Glance" data about foreign exchange, futures equity, indexes, and U.S. Treasuries.

- *Thomas Register (www.thomasregister.com)*. This site includes buying information for the products and services of more than 155,000 companies, divided into 55,000 categories. The register includes 3,100 online supplier catalogs. After you register and select a password, use of the catalogs is free. This site is an excellent source for discovering a company's chief competitor.

PUTTING IT ALL TOGETHER

Market trends are driven by many simple and not so simple forces that drive the prices of stocks up and down every day. Some of the forces are quantitative and some are based on pure emotion. If interest rates suddenly spike up, financial institutions will likely take a hit. On the other hand, if consumers are feeling good about everything and decide to buy more goods and services, retail stocks will do well. If the market trend is up and buyers significantly outnumber sellers, we are in what analysts like to refer to as a bull market. Conversely, if there are more sellers than buyers, we are in a bear market.

Watch market trends carefully because not everything is as black and white as the pundits would like you to believe. The fact that we may be in a "confirmed" bear market does not mean that every stock shares that bear market conviction. Certain industries or sectors within those industries may not even be affected by the bear or the bull. Your subsequent challenge as an investor is to seek out and find value-based stock in either market and make the most of whatever the market gives you at the time.

CHAPTER-RELATED WEB SITES

📖 The Bureau of Economic Analysis (www.bea.doc.gov) calculates economic indicators such as the gross domestic product and other regional, national, and international data, all of which are displayed on their Web site.

📖 American Society of Association Executives (www.asaenet.org) provides high-quality industry overviews, including briefings of industry trends.

📖 *Fortune* magazine (www.fortune.com) includes special market reports as well as stock and fund quotes.

📖 ABC News (www.abcnews.com) features business and industry news and market commentary.

📖 CBS Market Watch (www.marketwatch.com) offers feature articles on the market and breaking news targeted at investors.

CHAPTER-RELATED WEB SITES, continued

 The Wall Street Journal is the Big Kahuna among investment newspapers, although its authority isn't as unquestioned as it used to be. For subscription information, call 800- 778-0840 or visit their Web site at www.wsj.com.

Follow the Heavenly Economic Cycles

"If all the economists in the world were laid end to end, they would not be able to reach a conclusion.

—George Bernard Shaw

Since stocks were first invented, economists have attempted to derive economic formulas that would tell them when a bull or bear was in the neighborhood. They've studied charts of the market's ups and downs for decades, looking for telltale signs of wiggles in the patterns. Back in 1920, economist Leonard Ayre noticed a telling connection between changes in interest rates and stock prices. He discovered that when interest rates went up, stock prices generally fell, and when interest rates fell, stock prices increased. Over the next several decades, countless other economic events that affected the stock market were identified and analyzed by economists in finite detail. What they confirm is that it's vitally important to have a basic understanding of how certain economic events affect the stock market so that you can immediately take evasive action if economic indicators indicate the market is going down, or invasive action if indicators indicate the market is going up.

OUR "NEW" ECONOMY

While complacency is never wise, a growing number of economists believe that so much has changed in the U.S. economy since the 1980s and 1990s that the old rules don't apply anymore. Increased competition in a global marketplace has forced U.S. companies to become more efficient. Technical and communications advances have given them the tools to generate fatter corporate revenue so that they can absorb higher wages and other costs without raising prices. With inflation in check, many companies have succeeded in muting demands for wage hikes by establishing incentive pay and profit sharing plans that are tied to productivity. And, as prices of computers and communications equipment have rapidly declined, businesses have had more incentive to substitute cheap machines to increase their productivity.

There's no denying the fact that a more efficient economy has changed the inflation model. However, some skeptics still worry that the strong economy will ultimately create imbalances. They believe a shrinking pool of available workers is bound to lead to wage inflation, regardless of impressive productivity gains. The wealth effect created by a booming stock market, that's feeding off a benign inflation environment, can create spending pressures on the economy. For that reason, the Federal Reserve Board (Fed) strives to preempt potential inflation rather than react to pricing pressures by tweaking interest rates. All of this of course was happening before we entered into the new mellinium.

HOW THE ECONOMY CAN DESTROY STOCKS

Did you or one of your friends get mauled by the bear that ripped through the 2000 and 2001 stock markets? As we entered the new millennium, the economic messages may have been unpleasant, but at least they were easy to read: The U.S. economy is slowing down. Not reversing, not stopping, still growing, just not so fast. Investors can face it now or face it later, but as in all cases, facing it now is better. Then, the terrorist attack on the World Trade Centers in September 2001 almost brought the economy to a screeching halt and stock price fell through the floor.

According to Warren Buffet, how big those problems are depends on what you own. If Wall Street adversely responds to earnings warnings from major corporations as it has over the past couple of years, and more recently, the threat of more terrorist attacks, investors are in for some bad times. Let's take a brief look at what happened from an historical viewpoint so you're better prepared to deal with the future.

Dark omens started accumulating when many companies cautioned that they wouldn't hit profit estimates in the second half of 2000. As the third quarter ended, company after company realized there was no way they could make their earnings estimate. And Wall Street was merciless in its response. Many firms admitted that their profits wouldn't meet expectations in the coming quarters and many of their stocks plummeted 50 percent or more overnight. Look what happened to "bellwether" Motorola (see figure 6-1).

Motorola was having problems in the second half of 2000 and fell from $36 to $18 a share in less than 12 months. The market snapped again in September of 2000 when "mighty" Intel announced third-quarter earnings problems. Their stock dropped 22 percent in a day and drifted lower for days after. When Kodak announced similar news, it too got hammered and went down 25 percent in a day, to a five-year low. By the end of 2000, 60 U.S. companies issued advisories that profits would be better

FIGURE 6-1   Motorola Graph

than expected and 332 announced profits would be worse, which raises the question: Why did so many companies get into trouble and what could you have done to avoid getting mauled by the bear?

Why were Wall Street gurus so surprised by the shortfall epidemic of 2000? They should not have been. At the time, oil prices were the highest in decades, and even in an information-based economy, that can mean trouble especially with winter approaching. It's a serious problem for any company that's dependent on petroleum-based chemicals or a heavy user of transportation.

The euro was so weak at the time that some thought it was doomed. The effect on U.S. companies was the familiar double whammy. Prices of our products became relatively expensive when euros were exchanged for fewer dollars, and this effectively reduced export demand for our products. In addition, we started seeing evidence that the tight labor market was leading to higher employment costs. Put these economic events together and it's not surprising that a lot of companies got into earnings trouble. Analysts also got blindsided when Wal-Mart issued a third-quarter 2000 warning because of a broad weakness in retail sales.

The story was the same at Priceline, whose stock plunged 42 percent the day it warned of third-quarter trouble. A slow September 2000 blew Priceline's estimates despite a great July and August. Enlarge that picture and you get an image of an economy that's still growing, but no longer at extraordinary rates. The slowest the U.S. economy has grown in the '90s was at a zippy 5 percent (1998) annual pace, and the fastest was an almost incredible 8 percent in 1999. When that kind of growth slows to 3 percent or 4 percent a year as it did in 2000 and 2001, most economists will claim we're healthy as a horse, just not roaring along like a Formula One race car.

THE BULL GOT GORED

The end to super growth of the 1990s helps explain why investors were so wrathful at being disappointed. They couldn't understand why stocks with towering PE ratios got pummeled when their earnings quivered. This is what happened to Intel. It was trading at a multiple of 55, which is nosebleed territory for a huge, capital-intensive manufacturer. Its disappointing third-quarter 2000 earnings report knocked its stock down 36 percent in one day.

Other household-name stocks also got clobbered. Many were already trading at pitiful discount prices and got kicked some more. Alcoa tumbled from a PE of 19 to 14 and DuPont went from 16 to 13. Rockwell International was trading at a measly 12 and still got squashed down to eight. Why such severe punishment? Investors believe that missed quarterly earnings wasn't the end of the story. High raw material prices, a weak euro, and increased wage pressure added to the prospect of a general economic slowdown.

The general opinion was that we were looking at many quarters of earnings below the estimates on which prewarning prices were built.

What's more, investors were jittery. They knew the S&P 500 multiple had doubled in the past five years to historically unheard of levels, and wondered how long it could last. They were expecting an economic slowdown and saw evidence that it was finally arriving. With most equities in the hands of institutions, no fund manager wanted to be holding a "slowdown" stock, so there was a stampede to abandon any company showing weakness.

These stunning shifts in the stock market reflected the radical transformations that are still taking place in the U.S. economy. If you're going to invest in the stock market, you need to have a basic understanding of how key economic indicators affect it and you must know how to interpret these indicators so that you can buy stock at the right time and sell before it's too late.

HOW SUPPLY AND DEMAND AFFECT THE MARKET

The economic laws of supply and demand affect the heart of the stock market, driving it up or down, depending on the economic cycle we're in. Unfortunately, economic gurus do everything they can to make their theories as complicated as possible. However, if you peel away all the charts and graphs, the principles of economics are quite simple to understand. If someone wants to sell something and others want to buy it, the agreement they reach is called the equilibrium point, or sell price. If demand rises faster than supply, buyers bid up the scarce resource and prices rise. If there's too much supply, prices fall. It's that simple.

Those in the petroleum industry know how to play the economic game very well. They understand that if demand for gasoline remains constant and they can produce gasoline at the same cost, the price will stay where it is. A price balance between buyers and sellers has been reached (i.e., the equilibrium point). But suppose there's a sudden boom in the popularity of gas-guzzling sport utility vehicles (SUVs), which happened in 2000.

SUV owners start demanding more gas for their guzzlers. As they bid for the same amount of supply (i.e., gasoline), the price of the gasoline continues to rise. If the petroleum industry can't or won't increase production to meet the new demand, the price of gasoline rises dramatically, as it did in 2001. Now, imagine what happens if oil prices spike overnight because of tensions in the Middle East or OPEC decides to reduce its production of crude oil. The price of gasoline goes up again. The economic supply and demand principles work the same way in the stock market. If you have more buyers for a stock, its price generally goes up or conversely, if you have more sellers, its price drops.

INFLATION AND THE MARKET

What a dollar will buy fluctuates daily. If the price of a new home rises 20 percent, the value of your money relative to housing drops 20 percent. If it costs 15 percent more to buy a gallon of gas, a dollar relative to gas purchases is worth 15 percent less. This is what we call inflation or the erosion of money's purchasing power brought on by a period of steadily rising prices. While changes in the pattern of supply and demand often result in higher prices for individual goods, they don't necessarily trigger inflation across the broad economy. Inflation doesn't occur unless many prices increase simultaneously, eroding the general purchasing power of each dollar bill you hold.

For example, if prices rose 3 percent and you just got a 3 percent raise, inflation wouldn't matter much, would it? That's basically what's been happening for the past decade. Inflation has been chugging along at about 3 percent, but the economy has adjusted for the difference. There is tacit agreement between employers and employees that annual raises will grow in line with inflation. If take-home income and prices both go up 3 percent, what difference does it make?

Unfortunately, inflation can't be counted on to remain so predictable. Once spurred into action, it can erode the purchasing power of your money much more quickly than the economy can adjust. A 10 percent inflation rate is fine if you get a 10 percent raise. But what if you don't? And what about those bonds you have in your retirement account, the ones returning a mere 6 percent? With inflation running at 10 percent, your real rate of return would be minus 4 percent.

Inflation is ghostly and hard to pin down. Even the best economists are never quite sure where it's coming from. What's insidious is that it travels like a disease through the economy. University of Washington economics professor Paul Heyne says in his book *The Economic Way of Thinking*, "Economic systems transmit viruses. A setback or unexpected bit of good fortune in one sector of the economy generates setbacks or good fortune for other sectors. Pretty soon, a relatively minor event is having a broad aggregate effect."

The threat is an inflationary spiral that begets strong consumer spending and puts upward pressure on prices. That spurs employees to demand cost-of-living increases, which their employers pay for by raising prices. The cycle builds until it breaks. Prices can go up only so far before they start to destroy prosperity and people's ability to invest in stocks and mutual funds. As a result, the subsequent lower demand for stocks in general forces stock prices to decline.

INTEREST RATES AND ECONOMIC CYCLES

Inflation also leads to higher interest rates, which are enormously disruptive for businesses. Not only do they boost borrowing costs, they also slow the economy by limiting demand for goods and services, which is bad for stock prices. As prices increase, it becomes more expensive for companies to do business. The added costs put downward pressure on their earnings, which reduces what investors are willing to pay for their stock.

Money greases the cogs of the economy. Restricting its flow can slow the economy down, and increasing its flow speeds things up. If we're in an inflationary period, and the Feds raise interest rates to reduce the supply of money, consumers have less to spend on goods and services, effectively reducing prices. The most important thing to know about interest rates is that when the Fed raises them, it tends to limit the money supply and slows the economy. When it lowers them, the money flow increases and the economy tends to speed up. Consequently, if the Fed fears inflation, it will raise interest rates. If it fears recession, it lowers them.

In hindsight, it's easy to see how things can go woefully wrong with the economy. During wars, aggregate prices usually rise as governments increase spending on war materials. During the Vietnam War, increased military expenditures pushed the economy to its capacity when President Lyndon Johnson refused to pay for the expenditures with tax increases. Instead, he borrowed money, which increased the money supply and was largely responsible for the inflationary period we encountered in the early seventies.

At the same time, several external economic events further fueled the inflation engine. The Organization of Petroleum Exporting Countries (OPEC) aggravated the situation by drastically slashing oil production in response to the Arab-Israeli conflict. Supply shortages sent oil prices soaring and triggered severe shortages in 1974–75 and 1979–80. Adding salt to the wound, there was a surge in food prices caused by weather-related crop damages and an explosion in raw materials prices due to growing worldwide demand. Between 1972 and 1974, U.S. inflation leapt from 3 percent to 11 percent and in 1980 it rose to 14 percent.

Prices were so high in the mid-1970s that personal consumption began to decline, eroding aggregate demand. Businesses cut back on production, laying off workers, and driving up the rate of unemployment. Normally, such conditions would bring inflation to a halt as recession took hold. At the time, the Nixon Administration was more worried about the political implications of a recession than the inflation crisis. More money was injected into the system in an attempt to jump-start the stagnating economy. That merely drove prices higher and made the pain worse. The term for this unusual and unpleasant combination of low growth and high inflation is stagflation.

The spiral wasn't broken until the Carter Administration's Federal Reserve Chairman Paul Volcker spent 1979 and 1980 engineering a recession by driving interest rates from 6 to a 20 percent range. Fortunately, OPEC increased oil production at the same time. Rising interest rates tempered borrowing, wages dropped back to sustainable levels, and prices fell. It seems as if all the Fed has to do is utter the word "imbalance" and stocks topple over like dominoes. Sure, the market usually corrects itself a couple of days later after dragging billions of dollars in market value down. But, when the Feds start raising interest rates, there will be turmoil and uncertainty in the market.

ECONOMIC VITAL SIGNS

In economics, outcomes are often hard to predict. If the market is working correctly, stock prices reflect investors' future expectations for the economy. In fact, stock prices often drop six months or so in advance of economic slowdowns and soar about six months before a recovery. So even if you're supremely confident about the economy, be wary of using that knowledge to make big bets on specific stocks.

Will the slowing economy fall into recession or will the Federal Reserve succeed in breathing new life into the economy and the stock market by cutting interest rates? Will the booming economy continue to boom? It would be great if there were a simple way to get answers to such questions. But short of having economists and physicists join forces to develop economic fortune cookies, it won't happen. The only real option investors have for trying to gain a sense of what might happen in the future is to track a select group of economic indicators.

No set of economic indicators is going to provide you with a connect-the-dots path to the future. As anyone who's watched CNBC or surfed the Web knows, you can quickly find yourself drowning in a flood of confusing economic minutiae. Our goal is to help you home in on a few easily accessible statistics that provide insights into several areas of the economy and don't require a Ph.D. in economics to understand. There are three key economic gauges that can have a major impact on the market.

> **POINTER**
>
> STAT-USA (www.stat-usa.gov) is a Web site sponsored by the U.S. Department of Commerce that provides financial information about economic indicators, statistics, and economic news.

Employment Report

The employment report is released at the beginning of the month by the Bureau of Labor Statistics (BLS) and provides a quick update on the job market. Growing employment leads to increases in consumer spending, which accounts for two-thirds of the U.S. economy. Most economists consider the report an advance peek at future economic growth. The financial press usually zeroes in on the unemployment rate.

Basically, job growth is a harbinger of economic growth. When investors are more concerned about the economy overheating than fizzling, strong job gains can actually send the stock market down by raising the specter of rising inflation. For example, in 1997 and 1998 we added jobs at a frenetic pace of more than 250,000 a month. In 1999 the monthly rate slowed to fewer than 230,000, and it slipped below 160,000 in 2000, a drop of 70 percent from 1999 (see figure 6-2).

Although that kind of decline doesn't guarantee a recession, it certainly suggests much slower growth for the economy and corporate profits in the months ahead. If job creation numbers actually go negative for several months, that can definitely be a red flag, since sustained

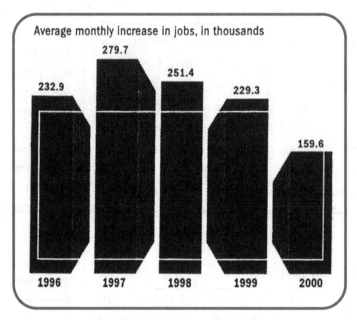

FIGURE 6-2 Employment Report

job losses typically occur only during recessions. You can find the employment figures on the BLS Web site at www.bls.gov/ceshome.htm.

Consumer Confidence Index

Employment and unemployment data can tell you about consumers' ability to spend. Economists turn to a variety of surveys that gauge the fickle phenomenon known as consumer sentiment. One of the most widely followed is the Conference Board's monthly consumer confidence index. The idea behind the index is simply to measure changes in consumer attitudes about the economic situation. If there's a dramatic shift from spending to saving, it can apply the brakes to economic growth.

The board polls 5,000 different households each month, asking people how they feel about current and future business conditions, the job market, and their own income prospects over the next six months. The

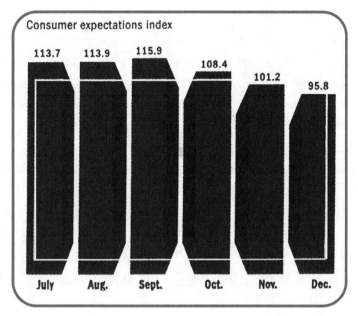

FIGURE 6-3 Consumer Expectation Index

board's number crunchers massage responses into an index that measures confidence in the economy. A rising trend in the index suggests that consumers are becoming upbeat and more likely to propel the economy forward. A downward trend indicates that consumers are more likely to pare back on spending.

Although the consumer confidence index grabs a lot of attention, you get a better reading on what lies ahead from the board's expectations index. The index is derived from the overall confidence index and measures how well we think the economy and our personal finances will be doing six months down the road (see the example in figure 6-3).

You can get the current readings on the consumer confidence and expectation indexes by going to the Conference Board's Consumer Research Center Web site at www.conference-board.org/products/c-consumer.cfm.

Purchasing Manager's Index

The industrial sector of the economy is the place to turn to for clues about the economy's future direction. For a timely assessment of our industrial might, most economists track what's called the purchasing managers' index (PMI). Each month, the National Association of Purchasing Management (NAPM) surveys roughly 400 manufacturing executives who buy raw materials and oversee inventories, querying them about production and new orders at their firms. NAPM computes an index from the responses for that month.

Most pundits focus on whether the index falls above or below 50, the break-even point for the manufacturing sector. For gauging the direction of the overall economy, the key index level isn't 50, but 43. If the index comes in above that number, the economy continues to grow; anything below 43 means the economy is contracting (see the example in figure 6-4).

FIGURE 6-4   PMI Index

Leading Economic Indicators

If you don't have the time or inclination to track a variety of gauges, consider tracking several benchmarks rolled into one, the index of Leading Economic Indicators (LEI), published monthly by the Conference Board. Initially developed during the Great Depression to help predict changes in economic growth, the index reflects ten separate components, including the length of the workweek, building permits, interest rates, the money supply, and stock prices. Basically, when the LEI is rising, the economy will continue to chug along in the near future. An example of how the LEI is presented is shown in figure 6-5. You can find the latest leading indicator figures in the "Business Cycle Indicators" section of the Conference Board Web site at www.tcb-indi cators.org.

The economic indicators that we've covered in this section have done a good job over the years of anticipating slowdowns. However, their record of predicting recessions is more mixed, leading some

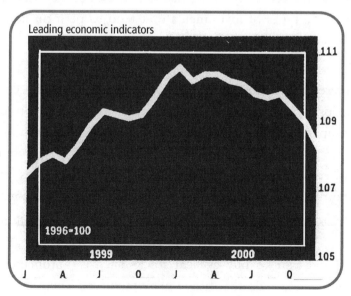

FIGURE 6-5   LEI Index

economists to dub the index "the misleading economic indicators." For example, the oft-invoked rule of thumb that three consecutive monthly declines in the indicators means we're headed for recession has generated at least one false signal during six of the past eight expansions. Of course, in the fast-changing world of markets and the economy, all outlooks are subject to revision. So unless that forecasting "Magic Eight Ball" actually becomes a reality, I suggest you keep an eye on the economic indicators.

WHAT ARE THE ECONOMIC CYCLES?

If you understand economic cycles and how the economic indicators work, and know the effects they have on stocks, you will significantly improve your odds of making money in the market. Certain types of investments tend to do better during specific stages of the economy. You wouldn't want to make all your buying decisions based on economic cycles, but you'll improve your performance by shifting your portfolio as the economy shifts. The five phases of a typical economic cycle and the types of investments that tend to perform best in each cycle are summarized as follows:

- *Economic slowdown.* The economy begins to decline. Short-term interest rates move up sharply, peaking as consumer confidence drops. The slowdown is exacerbated by inventory corrections as companies, fearing recession, try to reduce their inventory levels. Manufacturers cut back on production while wages continue to rise, resulting in increased inflation. Most stock prices fall significantly, which makes it a good time to stay out of the market.

- *Recession.* Characterized by falling production, peaking inflation, and weakened consumer confidence, recessions are usually a good time to buy cyclical stocks such as automakers, paper companies, and other heavy manufacturers. Their earnings may look anemic and their stock prices may be floundering, but they are among the first stocks to take off when the economy turns around. Long-term bonds are also a good place to park your money because the Feds tends to lower interest rates to help spur the economy. As interest rates go down, bond prices go up.

- *Recovery.* Marked by stimulatory economic policies, falling inflation, and increasing consumer confidence, the recovery period is a good time to buy stocks. Smaller emerging growth stocks often do especially well during a recovery and cyclical stocks should still have some growth left. Real estate is also a good investment during recovery periods.

- *Early upswing.* The recovery period is past, confidence is up, and the economy is gaining momentum. This is the healthiest period of the cycle in a sense, because economic growth can continue without any signs of overheating or sharply higher inflation. Consumers are prepared to borrow and spend more, and businesses that need to increase capacity begin investing in capital equipment and hire more people. Higher operating levels allow many businesses to cut unit costs and increase profit margins. The early upswing stage could last for several years and the stock market should remain strong during this period. Unload any cyclical stocks that you own whose growth is probably over.

- *Late upswing.* The economic boom is in full swing. Manufacturing capacity nears a peak, prompting an investment rally as unemployment continues to fall. Real estate prices move up, prompting a construction boom and increasing investors in the stock market that are tied to the real estate market. Inflation picks up as wages increase in the wake of labor shortages. With interest rates rising, bonds and bank stocks become less attractive.

It is important to become confident in your decisions based on your own experience and knowledge of the economic indicators. Don't chase hot trends and don't panic every time a market expert predicts a fall in prices. Develop your own strategies and a system for playing the market and the economy. In the end, there is one fact with which all the experts agree: over time, the market always moves up.

HOW TO NEUTRALIZE ECONOMIC CYCLES

Dollar cost averaging is an investment strategy that evens out the fluctuations in stock throughout the different economic cycles. Here's an example of how dollar cost averaging works. Let's say you choose to buy 100 shares of XYZ Corp. on the 15th day of every month for four consecutive months. Assume the share prices are as follows:

Date	Price Per Share	Shares	Cost
Jan 15	$30	100	$3000
Feb 15	$50	100	$5000
Mar 15	$100	100	$10,000
Apr 15	$40	100	$4000
	Total	400	$22,000
	Average Price/Share		$55

By dividing the total amount you paid ($22,000) by the number of shares you purchased (400) you find that the average price is $55 per share. Now let's examine what happens when you invest a set amount of dollars each month. If you invest the same amount of money as the previous example over four months, you would invest $5500 on the 15th of each month. You get the following:

Date	Price Per Share	Shares	Cost
Jan 15	$30	183	$5500
Feb 15	$50	110	$5500
Mar 15	$100	55	$5500
Apr 15	$40	138	$5500
	Total	486	$22,000
	Average Price/Share		$45.27

You purchased 486 shares with a total investment of $22,000. By dividing $22,000 by 486, you arrive at an average price of $45.27 per share. This is a savings of $9.72 per share from the $55 per share in the previous example. You purchased more shares for the same investment. You can see that when prices are low, you can buy more shares. Conversely, when prices are high you buy fewer shares. Thus, when it comes time to receive dividends, you will have more shares on which you can earn dividends.

LEARN TO RUN WITH THE BEARS

There's nothing like a little market carnage to unleash a flood of what's called "bear-market advice" stories. For example, "It took 302 months for investors to break even after the crash of 1929." If you don't have a bear market survival plan, you had better develop one. When you tune into CNBC or CNN during a bear market, you can easily get the impression that Armageddon has arrived and it's just a matter of time before marauding bands of disgruntled investors start pillaging the stock exchanges.

But bear markets, typically defined as a decline of 20 percent or more in one of the exchanges, are facts of investing life. The S&P's 500 has had 14 of them since 1929. Bears can be severe and can maul one exchange and leave the others alone. We saw this occur in 2000 when the tech-heavy Nasdaq was thrown into a bear market while the DJIA remained relatively stable. The Nasdaq sank by over 50 percent in 2000 and hit a two year low in 2001. Smart investors didn't panic because they knew that each bear market always gives way to another bull market.

Over the years, you probably remember hearing advice about diversifying your holdings among stocks and bonds. If you're like many investors, you ignored that advice because putting even more money in stocks like Qualcomm and Oracle used to be "where the action was."

BEARS ARE ECONOMIC ANIMALS

Make sure you know what constitutes a bear market and how to recognize the beginning symptoms before the bear takes over. That will give you a chance to get out of the market before it turns ugly. As a general rule, even if you're invested in great stocks, a bear market will drag them down. Your best move is to get out of the market, sit on the sidelines, and wait until it bottoms out. Then be patient when you buy back in and it begins to move up into bull market territory. You'll find plenty of bargains along the way.

If you've gotten a taste of what it's like to lose money in a bear market, it's a good time to rethink how to diversify your portfolio.

As you reallocate your portfolio, don't sell your high-quality stocks that have momentarily fallen. Instead, sell off all your losers that seemed like a good buy at the time. You know, mistakes like the IPO you bought for $200 on its first trading day that's now selling for $20. While you're at it, reexamine your sector weightings. A 60 percent tech stake seemed to have all upside and no downside in the '90s. Now that you've seen how far and how fast tech shares can dive, scale back your tech weighting to a more conservative number.

The hardest part of a bear market plan is to continue to follow the market. When stock prices melt away, all our instincts tell us to unload our stocks and avoid buying new ones. We're afraid they'll go even lower. But this attitude makes little sense if you're investing for the long term. If history is any guide, you'll be better off if you continue to buy, which is appropriately illustrated in the headlines of the Associated Press article in figure 6-6.

Researchers at T. Rowe Price recently looked at the six bear markets in the S&P 500 over the past 30 years to see how three different types of investors would have fared if each invested $10,000 on the eve of a bear market. The "stock investor" kept all his money in S&P 500 stocks and

Incomes, spending rise

The Commerce Department said Monday that Americans' incomes, which include wages, interest and government benefits, rose 0.5 of a percent. Meanwhile, consumer spending rose by a moderate 0.3 of a percent last month, slightly faster than expected.

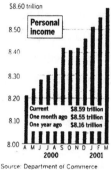

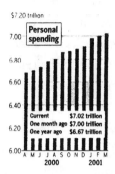

Source: Department of Commerce

Associated Press

Consumers cut spending on big items

Associated Press

WASHINGTON — Consumers were selective when it came to opening their wallets and pocketbooks in March. They spent briskly on services but were more thrifty on big-ticket items like cars. All told, the Commerce Department said Monday that consumer spending rose by a moderate 0.3 of a percent last month, slightly faster than expected.

At the same time, Americans' incomes, which include wages, interest and government benefits, rose 0.5 of a percent, matching many analysts' expectations.

Economist Ken Mayland of ClearView Economics said people cut back on purchases of costly manufactured goods last month because they decided they could make due with, for instance, the old car or refrigerator, given the un-

certain economic times.

But consumers maintained spending on services — such as medical care and home utilities — because they are necessities, he said.

Consumer spending accounts for two-thirds of all economic activity and has been a main force propping up the economy, which grew at an annual rate of 2 percent in the first quarter.

On Wall Street, blue-chip stocks declined, giving back earlier gains in the session. The Dow Jones industrial average lost 75 points to close at 10,735. Even with the Dow's decline, U.S. stocks finished their best month in almost a decade. The Wilshire 5000 Total Market Index, the broadest gauge of U.S. shares, advanced 8.1 percent in April, its biggest monthly climb since December 1991.

FIGURE 6-6   Associated Press Article

added an additional $100 every month. The "cash investor" bailed out once the index declined 10 percent, and put all his money and subsequent additions of $100 a month into T-bills. The "switch investor" did exactly what the cash investor did except he put all his money plus $100 a month back into stocks once the S&P 500 regained its prebear peak.

So how did they do? In the relatively brief bear markets of the 1980s and 1990s, stock investors quickly caught up with the cash-and-switch investors. For example, within two years of the 1987 crash, stock investors had the most money. In the generally longer and tougher bears of the 1960s and 1970s, it took more time for stock investors to come out ahead, but they always did.

Of course, you could come up with thousands of scenarios with different outcomes, depending on how much money you start with, how much you add, and what kinds of stocks you buy. But the strategy of putting most of your money in stocks makes as much sense today as it ever did. Assuming that you are a long-term investor who makes rational, informed decisions and knows that volatility is a natural part of stock investing, you'll do just fine. If you're not that kind of investor, consider the market's plunge as your wake-up call to put your money into a money market account.

Tom Peters put the right spin on the word "mistake" when he said, "The essence of innovation is the pursuit of failure, one's ability to try different things and not be concerned about making mistakes, as long as you don't repeat the same mistake. The assumption all great investors share is that they all need to experiment, innovate, and be daring in their thinking. You can't be innovative with your investment plans and not make mistakes."

WATCH FOR FALLING STOCKS

Stocks fall faster than they rise during bad economic times. While it's often good to buy stocks when they're down, it can be a mistake to jump on board too soon. When a stock takes a hit after a disappointing earnings report or a down-trending bear market, bargain hunters are often quick to buy into the stock before the market pushes the price back up. However, in most cases there is no need to hurry. Stocks tend to fall much faster than they rise. If the market has had a major correction, or a stock you follow has had a sudden free fall, be patient. Wait for the stock and the market to begin showing some upward momentum. You may not get in right at the bottom, but you can avoid buying a falling star midway through the fall.

When the market dropped 25 percent in 1987, it ultimately began to move back up. But it took more than a year to regain all the ground it had lost. There was plenty of time to analyze the situation, find upward trends, and buy into the market while prices were still depressed. As an investor, my biggest weakness probably has been my impulse to buy a stock shortly after a steep drop. I once owned several hundred shares of telecom equipment maker Viasat (VSAT) when it was trading in the $50s. When the company issued a disappointing earnings report, the stock suddenly plunged to $15 a share. I watched for a couple of days, saw that it was hovering around $25, and decided to double up my holdings before it moved back up. It never did. The stock had dropped another 40 percent to about $15 a share (see figure 6-7). Time did not heal the downtrend that Viasat was traveling on!

There are certainly times when a fallen stock can rebound quickly. But, just in case things go the wrong way, there's one precaution you can take to ensure that you won't get mauled too badly by the bear. Put in a stop-loss order to sell any stock the moment after you buy it. For instance, let's say you buy XYZ at $15 a share after a steep drop. You put in a stop-loss order at $13.50 so that if it drops another $1.50 or 10 percent, you automatically sell-out at a small loss rather than ride it down 50 or 60 percent like I did with Viasat. If the company turns

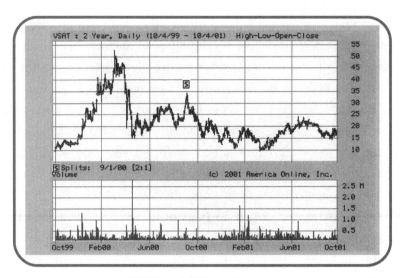

FIGURE 6-7   Viasat's Graph

around, you can always buy back into the stock later. Just don't rush it. Stocks, after all, fall faster than they rise.

WHY GREAT STOCKS THRIVE IN GOOD ECONOMIC TIMES

The explosive growth of a stock doesn't happen in a vacuum. Usually, new products, services, or management propel a stock to new highs. That's why it's important to keep up with developments that could launch the next great stock. These changes are what can propel stocks into leadership roles. Stocks don't double, triple, or move even higher in a vacuum without a news story that's behind the major price advance. Where would Microsoft be today without its Windows operating system? If you look through the list of greatest stocks, there were plenty of breakthrough products that fueled their advances:

POINTER

Only buy financially strong stocks with strong upward trend lines and avoid weak stocks. They're weak for a reason that you may not know about.

- Syntex rocketed 450 percent in six months in 1963 when it began selling the first oral contraceptive pill.

- McDonald's surged 1,100 percent from 1967 to 1971 as its low-cost, fast food franchising business model swept the nation.

- From 1978 to 1980, Wang Labs' shares grew 1,350 percent with the development of word-processing office equipment.

- International Game Technology surged 1,600 percent from 1991 to 1993 thanks to the development of game technology based on microprocessors.

- Accustaff rose 1,486 percent from January 1995 to May 1996 as outsourcing grabbed hold of Corporate America, sending this temporary-staffing firm to big profits.

- America Online surged 593 percent from 1994 to 1996 as the company rose to become the leading Internet service provider to a nation eager to log on to the Web.

- Qualcomm rose 376 percent from February 1999 to December 1999 on the rising popularity of the company's Code Division Multiple Access technology for wireless telephones.

> **WARNING** !
>
> Don't try to catch a falling knife with your bare hands or you'll cut yourself. Stocks get slammed for various reasons. If you want to jump in on a free-falling stock market, make sure your reasons for doing so are well founded. Sometimes "dead cats" don't bounce but they can sure claw you on the way down.

A great company's success isn't something that happens by accident. They never stop innovating and evaluating the future of the marketplace. As soon as one product is out the door, they're working on the next generation and new ways to sustain their leadership. If you don't have great or at least potentially great companies in your portfolio, get rid of them.

ACCELERATION IS CRITICAL

Most stocks that make major advances have another trait. Their earnings accelerate over the previous three or four quarters. Acceleration represents an increase in the earnings growth rate quarter after quarter. Improving bottom-line growth nearly always precedes a burst in stock price. What's important to realize about this is that it's not just rising earnings that make a good stock. The key is to focus on companies whose earnings may be drawing institutional investors' attention, the phase when a stock prepares to spring higher.

A recent study by Western Publications evaluated the greatest stocks dating back to 1953 and found that 95 percent of these winners had breakthrough products, new management, or new ways of doing business that boosted these stocks to staggering heights. These and other success stories didn't achieve greatness without proven products.

Watch out for the company that promises the cure for cancer or some other breakthrough technology. It's wiser to wait for products to prove themselves in the marketplace before investing in something untested. If a product really hits it big, the stock will be in demand for a long time.

PUTTING IT ALL TOGETHER

As we discussed in the beginning of the chapter, economists have spent decades evaluating different economic events to determine their impact on the stock market. And, they have gotten pretty good at it. We have covered several of the major events like changes in interest rates and consumer confidence levels, that you should take into consideration whenever you buy or sell stocks.

All economic events affect the laws of supply and demand. You now know the different economic cycles, some of which are impacted by low and high demand and/or supply. Each cycle is unique and offers its

---

own set of advantages and disadvantages when investing in different types of stocks. In the end, always be on the lookout for great stocks. They thrive in good economic times.

CHAPTER-RELATED WEB SITES

📑 Census Bureau (www.census.gov) provides information about industry statistics and general business conditions.

📑 STAT-USA (www.stat-usa.gov) is sponsored by the U.S. Department of Commerce and provides financial information about economic indicators, statistics, and economic news.

📑 The Bureau of Economic Analysis (www.bea.doc.gov) calculates economic indicators such as the gross domestic product and other regional, national, and international data, all of which are displayed on their Web site.

📑 Merrill Lynch (www.ml.com) allows you to download research reports by such well-known experts as Merrill's chief economist Bruce Steinberg. Click on the research tab on the right side of their main menu to find the reports.

📑 Bloomberg Personal Finance (www.bloomberg.com) is loaded with timely business news, data, and an analysis of the market.

📑 S&P's publishes the *Outlook* weekly. It is one of the most widely read investment newsletters. For further information, call 800-852-1641.

📑 *USA Today* (www.usatoday.com) features a money section that includes investment articles and news, economic information, and information on industry groups.

Thou Shall Know When to Sell

*"Selling your winners and holding loser
is like cutting your flowers and watering
the weeds."*

—Bill O'Neal

ONE OF THE MOST DIFFICULT ISSUES INVESTORS FACE IS KNOWING when to sell a stock. They're constantly looking for the right moment. Ideally, the perfect time to sell a good stock is never. If a company continues to maintain strong financial performance, increasing its earnings and revenue year in and year out, why sell? This is exactly the kind of stock you want to own. There are a number of great blue chip stocks that have continued to perform well, such as Philip Morris, Kellogg, and Merck. One of the biggest advantages of stock ownership is that you pay no taxes on your gains until you sell. If you hold a stock, it can grow five or ten-fold, or more, and you still pay no taxes on the gains until you sell. So much for the winners.

Why do investors tend to hold onto their stocks long after they become losers? There's a general agreement among psychologists that humans are constantly looking for ways to decrease their amount of pain and raise their amount of pleasure. Pain avoidance and pleasure are familiar concepts that certainly dominate marketing, advertising, and investing. While numerous other forces are undeniably at work as investors face decisions about selling and comfort seeking, pain avoidance is extremely powerful.

At its most obvious level, making a profit represents pleasure to all of us, while suffering a loss equates to feeling pain. Here we will focus on how our subconscious pain-avoidance and comfort-seeking tendencies cause us to drop our guard after we buy a promising stock, then suffer later.

WHY SELLING FEELS UNCOMFORTABLE

The act of selling requires a significant change in our thinking. When you bought that "great" stock, its prospects were outstanding because it represented value and opportunity. Now, choosing to sell represents adopting an opposite view whether the stock has done well or faltered. Liquidating means that what we once thought was correct is no longer so in our minds. This company is no longer underpriced or its prospects are not what we expected.

Maybe we've already been on the wrong side of the market and are now admitting a change is warranted. Either way, selling is like saying our earlier beliefs are no longer valid. Many of us find it difficult to admit that we were wrong. If you place a strong value on self-esteem, selling at a loss is likely to be an especially difficult battle zone for your ego.

We live in a time of high expectations, driven in part by computers, which makes precision possible and often expected. Time is telescoped and we've become impatient with delays. We expect perfection in an environment that demands zero defects and demands immediate paybacks. Our favorite professional sports team is labeled a failure if doesn't win the Super Bowl.

Perfectionism makes us recoil from the decisions involved in selling our stocks. We avoid such choices, and therefore hold by default, which is the least uncomfortable course of action. You know that when you sell you won't receive the top price unless you're extremely lucky. Thus, you feel doomed to being wrong sooner or later. By selling, we expose ourselves to yet another instance in which we can be proved less than perfect. We therefore tend to avoid selling.

So we hold rather than sell because, at the very least, holding postpones coming to closure. It seems to be a way to avoid further financial loss. However, investors pay dearly to avoid the emotional pain of selling, since losses only get worse. Selling is a powerful deterrent to sustained losses, but it requires courage to implement.

Surprisingly, holding rather than selling makes us feel better. To sell a loser is like admitting defeat, which none of us want to do. If we sell a loser, it cannot be recovered and we fear we might actually compound our first mistake should the stock's price increase after we sell. So we preserve hope of ultimately being a winner and feeling better by holding. An objective assessment of a stock's prospects may provide little optimism. But, we continue to hope for a major miracle and wait to see what comes next.

POINTER

Write down your thoughts and impressions of the market on a daily basis. Make note of seasonal tendencies, patterns, and market-moving news. If you put on any trades jot down the reason why. The wonderful byproduct of keeping a diary is that you'll begin to internalize the rhythm of the market and you can review your performance. Learn from your mistakes and duplicate your successes.

When you're thinking of selling, tear down any protective shields around your ego and accept the consequences of your decision. One of the worst aspects of losing in the stock market is that it reflects on our thinking. A loss not only leaves us poorer but also makes us feel foolish, stupid, or perhaps inadequate.

COMMISSION PHOBIA

Some investors balk at paying brokerage fees; this is called commission phobia. It's a smokescreen that can prevent you from realizing potential profits or minimizing losses from a stock sale. Like taxes, commissions are neither a surprise nor a rule change in the stock market game. Therefore, paying them cannot be a valid objection at the time of sale. There's no way to sell stock without paying commissions.

Commissions are more visible in stocks, commodities, and options than in most other products or services because securities prices are publicly quoted in the media. Investors pay commissions to trade stocks as a way of rewarding the time or expertise of the people who actually do the trading. When other products are purchased, commissions are built into the purchase price. In fact, built-in commissions for goods such as cars, shoes, or washing machines are much higher than stock commissions.

Investors often display commission phobia when their investment goes down or has gone up so little that commissions wipe out its gain. Few people complain about commissions when their stock creates a sudden gain. If you're an online trader, relatively cheap commissions should make "commission phobia" a non issue.

TAX PHOBIA

No matter how investors viewed the economic results of eliminating favorable tax treatment of long-term capital gains, the Tax Reform Act of 1986 had at least one positive result: it removed an artificial excuse for not selling stocks. The Act legally erased the distinction between long- and short-term capital gains. Until then, many investors used the tax incentive to hold stocks for the long term as a justification for not selling. Unless an extremely large gain was involved and the time remaining to qualify for long-term status was short, tax reasons for not selling were considered foolhardy. But sensitivity to tax treatment was nearly a religion for many investors.

Unfortunately, the existence of federal and state taxation on securities gains remains a stumbling block for some investors after the distinction between long and short term has been eliminated. Granted no one likes to pay taxes, but paying capital gains taxes is a reality for all investors. The objection to paying taxes on a gain is just another rationalization for not making a sale decision. Ignore taxes and sell when the time is right; it is self-defeating to avoid cashing in on a profitable stock because of your unwillingness to pay taxes.

> **INSIGHT**
>
> It's better to pay capital gains taxes on the earnings you've made investing in the stock market than to take a capital gains loss because you've lost money in the market.

WHY HOLDING FEELS GOOD

When you own a good stock, holding keeps you in more of a comfort zone than if you were to take action and change your circumstances by selling. Holding keeps you close to your past, to memories and cherished feelings. Many investors hold stock in companies whose fortunes peaked years or even decades ago and cannot seem to explain why they resist selling despite dim prospects for the stock's future recovery.

Maybe grandfather worked for the company or you grew up in a town where the company was a major employer or sponsored the softball team. Perhaps years ago you made a profit, or at least had a good paper profit for a while. Or, your parents always spoke well of the company and confided they had made money buying and selling shares. These nostalgic feelings surround the stock and make it difficult to sell.

Our positive association with a particular stock creates a bonded feeling. If the stock is held for a number of years, it virtually gets adopted as a family member. Thus, our primary inclination is to not sever ties or terminate this comfortable relationship. Why end a good thing? Being with, rather than without that stock represents staying in one's comfort zone. Selling means deliberately walking outside that zone, which represents taking a risk

In a fast-moving world where technology both amazes and scares us, we are all looking for any anchor against pending storms. Great companies whose stocks have treated us well frequently act as a psychological bedrock to set our anchor. We therefore strongly resist any suggestion or motivation to sell.

It doesn't matter that the stock has become grossly overvalued, or has lost its fundamental greatness, or is having trouble making profit projections. We tend to cling to our old favorites no matter what their current merit. From the late 1980s into the early 1990s, computer stocks like IBM held a mystical power over their shareowners despite the rapid changes that were occurring in the computer industry. Investors held IBM as a matter of nearly religious conviction due to its past merits, even when the company's earnings started declining in 1986. In late 1993, the stock bottomed below $40, down some 75 percent. This is a good example of why it's important to battle against nostalgia and the tendency to cling onto old lighthouses.

IF THERE'S SMOKE, DON'T PANIC

When there's smoke in the stock market, and the bears are in charge, follow along with what the experts are doing and focus on the long term. Shop around for good buys on quality stocks because where there's smoke, there are bargains. Sell your loser so that you have money to buy winners at bargain prices.

As uncertain as investing in stocks may seem, there are still many certainties in the market. One is that no matter how robust the economy or the market may seem, the next correction is always just around the corner. A correction is a substantial drop in stock prices that occurs when the market gets too high. There's a fine line between a correction and a crash, but most analysts consider a market decline of 5 to 20 percent to be a correction, and more than 20 percent to be a crash.

> **WARNING**
> Don't blame external forces or events for your losses on a bad trade. Denial won't turn a bad trade into a winner and it will destroy your confidence in making a good trade next time.

In the past century, there have been hundreds of market corrections. Each time the press and the TV talk shows always treat the occasion like the second coming of the 1929 market crash. They talk in dire terms about the possible consequences of this unexpected bombshell, striking fear into the hearts of novice investors.

Veteran investors know that corrections are no reason for panic. They see them as a natural part of the stock market process. But the media frenzy that accompanies the more severe corrections tends to spook inexperienced investors into selling their holdings in a classic "buy high, sell low" fashion. Experienced investors will wait patiently for these corrections to pass and coolly add to their holdings by taking advantage of bargain prices.

TAKE PROFITS EVERY CHANCE YOU CAN

An old Wall Street adage is you can't lose money making a profit. Even with your best stocks, it sometimes pays to sell, take the profit to the bank, and move money into other investments. Top money manager Lee Kopp says he sometimes sells out a portion of his holdings in his best stocks for no other reason than to add more balance to his portfolio.

When one of your stocks rises quickly, it can suddenly account for a disproportionately high percentage of your portfolio's assets. During a correction, it may be prudent to pare back your winners. But do it carefully because it's hard to find the big winners. If a large share of your investment dollars are in one stock and the prospects for that stock suddenly change, you should sell.

> **POINTER**
>
> By practicing good money management habits and making the stock market's trend your friend, you will position yourself for bigger gains and smaller losses.

Pull the sell trigger every chance you get to make a profit. Buying and selling is where the money is made. No one makes any money standing on the sidelines. Develop a game plan and get in the game when market conditions are favorable. This will give the confidence to enter and exit trades more quickly and with razor-like precision.

WATCH OUT FOR COCKROACHES

Beware of the lowly cockroach, the losing company, because there may be others hiding in the cupboards. They're the most feared creature on Wall Street. When a company reports disappointing earnings, get out quickly. According to the cockroach theory, when you see one, there are probably others coming. William Berger, founder of the Berger Funds, prefers to get out of a stock when a company has disappointing earnings. He says, "We think one surprise may beget another surprise, so we get rid of the stock." Parkstone Fund Manager Roger Stamper takes the same tack when one of his stocks takes a turn for the worse. "Even if we have to take a 30 percent loss, we'll get out," says Stamper. "It's the cockroach theory. I've seen too many times when you wait around a quarter or two to see if the company improves, and it just gets worse."

George Vanderheiden, manager of the Fidelity Advisor Growth Fund also confesses to a fear of cockroaches: "As soon as I see the first crack in a stock with cockroaches coming out of it, I get out," says Vanderheiden. "I want to sell my mistakes quickly. If I buy a stock thinking the company's new concept will do well, and it doesn't work out, I'll sell. Usually the first piece of bad news is not the last piece of bad news." If many of Wall Street's finest managers have all reached the same conclusion, it's probably a strategy you should consider as well. The cockroach theory is particularly relevant to smaller growth stocks that can be volatile.

WATCH OUT FOR EXCUSES

Most corporate managers try to keep a strong profile for their company. When weaknesses occur, they try to minimize the damage, sometimes reporting only part of the problem in hopes that things will turn around in the ensuing quarters. Most of the time, the problems persist and earnings continue to dip, pushing the stock price down even further. So when bad news breaks for one of your stocks, bail-out. Otherwise you too may face an army of cockroaches.

DON'T FILL YOUR PORTFOLIO WITH LOSERS

Two thoughts cross our minds when we plunge into the stock market. We'd like to make a big profit, and avoid a huge loss. Achieving both objectives has a lot to do with how well you build your position. Let's face it, we all have a tendency to dwell on our successes and keep quiet about out failures. The following story illustrates my point.

My friend Jack jumped into the market and bought six stocks that his brother-in-law, who knew less about the market than he did, told him were "hot stocks." After a couple of months, three of the stocks were up and three were down.

Jack promptly sold the winners and bragged to anyone who would listen to him about how he had made a killing in the market. He kept the three losers in the hopes that they too would go up some day, and used profits from his winners to buy three more "hot stocks" recommended by a friend. Two of these went up, and he promptly sold them but held onto his loser, and bragged to his friends about how well he was doing in the market.

CUT YOUR LOSSES SHORT

If the trade goes against you, get out. Don't be afraid to take small losses because if you wait, your losses will grow to disruptive levels. Don't let your losers run. If the trend has changed and is dragging your stock down with it or if news impacts the viability of your stock, get out.

By repeating this process, Jack ended up with portfolio filled with losers. If he had done the opposite and sold his losers, he would have built up a portfolio of winners. He could also have taken the tax break when he dumped the losers. Your ultimate investment goal should be to build a great portfolio of winning stocks and funds. You don't do that by selling your winners. Cut your losses by selling your losers, replace them with winners, and let your winners run.

Unfortunately, many investors are reluctant to sell because they're convinced the stock will recover and take off. After all, now that the stock has fallen 8 percent, it has to bounce back, right? Wrong. Wall Street is littered with stocks that may take years to regain their former glory. Every 50 percent crash in the price of a stock starts out as a small 8 percent loss. There's no sure way to tell the difference. Even well-known stocks may continue to fall, shrinking your capital. Goodyear

Tire & Rubber, J.C. Penney, and Xerox are all big-cap stocks that have lost two-thirds of their value in recent years. No one likes to sell a losing stock. It means admitting you made a mistake. But everyone, including the best professional investors, makes mistakes. The goal is to learn from your miscues and keep losses as small as possible.

A selling strategy while losses are small is a lot like buying an insurance policy. You may feel foolish selling a stock for a loss and downright embarrassed if it recovers. But you're protecting yourself from devastating losses. Once you've sold, your capital is safe. If you cut your losses, it's relatively easy to bounce back. An 8 percent loss on a stock takes only an 8 percent gain on the next purchase to break even. But a 25 percent loss requires a 33 percent gain and you'll need a 100 percent winner to repair the damage of a 50 percent loser.

If you don't stop the bleeding in your portfolio quickly, small price declines can hemorrhage into massive losses. That is especially true if you're investing in a bad market. You're losing money and the stock isn't working. You don't need to look for any other reason to pull the plug. Cutting your losses by 8 to 10 percent is cheap protection when you consider how many mighty corporations like Microsoft have plunged 50 to 70 percent or more in the past. The 8 to 10 percent sell rule is in our opinion a maximum. You may choose a lower percentage that's more suitable to your tolerance or lack of tolerance for risk.

NEVER BUY DOWN

Never buy a stock on the way down and always sell on the way up. Momentum is one of the strongest forces of the stock market. When stocks catch fire, they can climb far beyond reasonable levels. And when they drop, they can also drop beyond all common reason or expectations. The historical chart of Amazon.com in figure 7-1 illustrates our point. The stock peaked at $85 a share in the beginning of

FIGURE 7-1 Amazon.com's Stock Chart

the year 2000. If you had bought and sold somewhere near the peak, you would have been in good shape. But look what would have happened if you still owned the stock when it started to drift down in March. It continued to tumble throughout the remainder of the year. At year-end, shares were selling for $15, a whopping 82 percent decrease in value in less than 12 months.

When you sell a stock on the way up, hoping to time your move at the peak, you risk missing out on even greater growth. Imagine investors who sold out their Wal-Mart stock in 1969 after a nice run up. If they had held onto the stock instead, $1,000 worth of Wal-Mart stock would have grown to more than $1 million 25 years later. When you try to time a buy on the way down, hoping to catch it at the bottom before it turns around, you could be in for a long unexpected drop.

BUYING AND SELLING CHECKLISTS

The questions below have been designed to help you focus on selling strategies. Evaluate your answers to these questions to fine-tune your strategies. Photocopy the pages with the questions and refer to them when you're thinking about selling a stock.

Each stock should have its own separate checklist that you should keep in a notebook. Over time, you will create a highly useful record that reveals recurring patterns of selling strengths and weaknesses. Here's what to include in your buy checklist:

1. Date stock bought.

2. Price paid per share and number of shares. For reference, record the DJIA and Nasdaq level on the buy date.

3. What is your target sell price and why?

4. What is your target sell date and why?

5. What events or market changes will make the stock go up or down?

6. Did you enter a stop-loss order and if so, at what price?

An example of what a checklist looks like for San Juan Basin (NYSE-SJT) is shown in figure 7-2. Notice that a chart of SJT's stock performance is included on the checklist form for reference purposes. At the top of the form, we show relevant trading information on the day in which SJT was added to our portfolio. Use this or your own form to give you instant access to key information about every stock that's in your portfolio.

In addition to the "buy" checklist, here are important questions to ask yourself when you're considering selling or holding a stock. They should trigger answers that will help you arrive at a sell or hold decision. When you review each stock in your portfolio, ask yourself the same set of questions so that you consistently review all of your holdings.

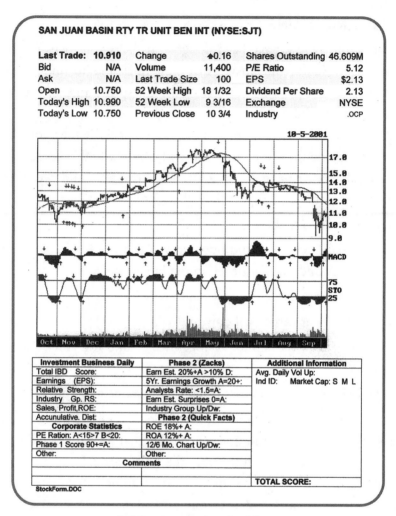

FIGURE 7-2 LNCR Checklist

- Are you currently more or less excited about each stock that's in your portfolio than you were when you first bought it?

- Has the expected good news for any of your stocks played out yet? If not, is there still a chance it will? If yes, did the stock go up at all on the related or partial news? Did it reach your price objective?

- What is each stock's price now and how much has it gone up or down since you bought it?

- What is expected to happen fundamentally now with each stock in your portfolio? If you had the money, would you buy more shares today?

- Where do you expect the price of each stock to go over the next eight weeks? Will it go up or down and why?

- What is the revised estimated annualized percent of return for each stock and does it still meet your short- and long-term expectations?

- What is the downside price risk from the current prices of your stocks if the market turns down?

- Where are the DJIA and Nasdaq now and how are the market averages affecting the prices of your stocks?

- Have there been negative surprises from the company or its industry since your purchase date?

- Since purchase, did you almost decide to sell, only to hold on a little longer? Was a mental or actual stop-loss price set or revised?

- Given your current knowledge, would you buy this stock again right now at today's price?

- Have significantly better opportunities been identified for purchases right now over any stock in your portfolio?

Written responses to these questions are recommended for two reasons: They reinforce the discipline of thinking through the exercises in detail and they provide an archival notebook record that can be used for future reference. Create a tickler file in which you review each stock in your portfolio. If your review results in a hold decision, file the page for review at a later date. Our questionnaire will help to impose closure on situations that are not working out as expected. A decision to hold should be every bit as active as a decision to buy or sell.

DON'T STOP YOUR WINNERS

Peter Lynch once said, "Never jump off a fast moving train or a winning racehorse. If you get out of a stock too soon, you can miss on big multiples of appreciation." That lesson was driven home in the late '80s when Lynch sold Magellan's position in Toys "R" Us, which had returned a lot of money to the Magellan Fund. Lynch recalls, "I bought the stock early, before there was really any competition in toy retailing. When I saw Milton Petrie buying up 20 percent of the company, I figured that the stock would back off because that was probably all that Petrie would buy. So I sold Magellan's position and guess what happened? The stock went up four-fold over the next 12 months." The mistake that Lynch made was ignoring the stock's fundamental values. If it's a growth company, and not just a cyclical stock, stick with it.

Winning stocks go through three stages: discovery, accumulation, and distribution. At the discovery stage, quality mutual funds and other big investors ferret out the best new companies at the forefront of a dynamic industry. For example, top-rated funds spotted companies such as Cisco Systems, Dell Computer, and EMC Corp very early. After finding great new companies, the big institutions start building positions. These heavy hitters can't buy all the shares they want at the drop of a hat. They have to buy thousands of shares day after day, month after month.

After a series of bases and advances, a stock becomes well known to the general public. The CEO shows up on the covers of business magazines, while analysts tout the stock on TV. Ordinary investors go into a buying spree because everybody knows the stock is going up. Of course, when it's obvious to everyone, there's usually something wrong. Mutual funds may see the company faces slower growth or more competition down the road. So they begin selling out, which takes a long time.

How many times have you concluded a stock's best days are behind it, only to watch it soar as you stand on the sidelines? This assumption often comes back to haunt investors. In reality, the stocks that are doing best tend to keep doing well, while those that are slumping usually continue to do poorly. Why? The great companies manifest their strength through superior performance in terms of earnings, sales, profit margins, and even the performance of their stock.

A study of the greatest stock market winners found that all-star stocks had, on average, outperformed 87 percent of the market before they began their most dramatic price advances. In other words, they were already in leadership positions. This concept is contrary to the popular bargain-hunting mentality, but is based on historical facts. You can draw a rough parallel to the real estate market. Homes that are structurally sound and have all the amenities will sell for higher prices and appreciate more over time than those that are structurally inferior. In either market, you get what you pay for.

If you want to find next year's winning stocks, look at the better-performing ones. Remember, the biggest winning stocks have historically been, on average, in the top 13 percent of stocks at the time they began their major advances. To help you identify today's leaders, *Investor's Business Daily* developed the Relative Price Strength, or RS Rating. This rating compares the price performance of each stock to help you identify the strongest. Each stock is rated on a scale of 1 to 99, with 99 representing the top 1 percent in terms of price movement over the last 12 months. An RS Rating of 85 means that stock is outperforming 85 percent of all stocks in terms of price. An RS Rating of 25 means the stock is being outperformed by 75 percent of the market and should be avoided.

A good starting point for selecting winning stocks is to identify those with the highest RS Rating in an industry group that's leading the overall market. You can find every stock's RS Rating in *Investment*

Business Daily, available at most newsstands that sell *The Wall Street Journal*.

WATCH FOR BREAKOUTS

Champion thoroughbreds burst out of the gate as they race for the finish line. But it takes more than a good start to win the race. Market leading stocks are much the same way. They burst out of sound price bases in heavy volume. But don't even think about relaxing after you buy a stock and it breaks out of its base. The first days and weeks after a breakout are critical. Many stocks will pull back a day or two after a breakout, which is normal as long as they don't crash back into their bases. Affiliated Computer Systems (ACS) offers a classic example of a company that broke out of a solid base (see figure 7-3). Notice how the stock formed a relatively flat base from May through July and then took off on a rapid acceleration and consistently climbed above its 50-day moving average line. The price of the stock jumped from $35 to $70 over the next six months.

You can also manage a winning stock by buying more shares as the price of the stock rises. If executed properly, averaging up in price leverages your gains and minimizes potential losses. Here's how you do it. After deciding how large a dollar position you want to own in a quality stock, invest half that amount just as it breaks out of a sound price base in heavy trading volume. Then begin buying smaller dollar amounts as the stock moves up. Buying up means you're buying a stock that's working. It's a confirmation your first purchase was sound.

If a stock's line stays on an up-trend, it shows the stock is keeping ahead of the overall market, acting as a confirmation of the stock's up-trend. If a stock's relative strength line fails to follow along with a new high in price, that's a warning signal. This shows the overall market is moving up faster than the stock. This may signal the stock is weakening, though the price may not reflect it immediately.

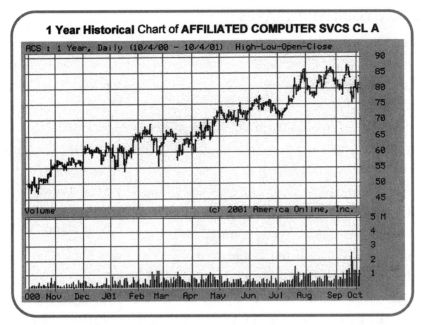

1 Year Historical Chart of AFFILIATED COMPUTER SVCS CL A

ACS : 1 Year, Daily (10/4/00 - 10/4/01) High-Low-Open-Close

(c) 2001 America Online, Inc.

FIGURE 7-3   ACS Breakout Graph

A winner always exerts pressure over its rival. With stocks, that special edge can take many forms. It might be the first company to go to market with a much-needed product or service. As a result, sales and profits surge, taking the stock along for the ride. The same is true for management shake-ups. Old ways of doing business are swept aside to make room for new, more profitable methods. Or a company may benefit from a big industry shift.

Whatever form the changes take, they can generate profits for astute investors. For many travelers, a plane's takeoff is the most nerve-rattling part of a trip. Once it's over, they can sit back and enjoy the ride. Investors face a similar dilemma with stocks. When a stock shoots up after a breakout, it may be tempting to sell and take a quick profit. But you'll often receive a bigger reward if you hold on. That initial jump could signal the start of a long advance.

REVIEW YOUR PAST TRADES

All investors make mistakes, but most don't learn from them. A review of your past trades is critical to improving your stock's prowess. It also helps you spot your weaknesses. Once you've identified a problem, you've done half the work of solving it. Keep a spreadsheet listing the stocks you've purchased, along with the dates and prices at which you bought and sold them. Allow sufficient time to pass to be objective about your dealings. Then analyze your winners and your losers.

Always be on the lookout for a fresh face. Once in a while you may come across a stock with a good base and strong fundamentals. If you've never heard of the company and don't know exactly what it does, conduct some fundamental research to find out. That should pique your interest. If you find winning stocks before they become widely known, you can get in on the ground floor.

POINTER

No investor should pick stocks based on a single factor. At a minimum, weigh the full picture, including a company's earnings, industry group performance, institutional sponsorship, and chart patterns.

WHAT GOES UP MUST COME DOWN

As fast as stocks advance during rallies, the retreats come even faster. If you don't spot market tops quickly, your hard-earned profits can vanish in a few days. So keep a close eye on the major market averages and the prices of leading stocks. You can also get a confirmation that a market is about to top out from the market's leading stocks. The leaders will be rolling over during the first couple of distribution days. Their tops may take the form of a climax run, where their prices move into record territory during the day, only to close near the low of the day.

Yahoo offers a classic example of how complacency with this great stock could have cost you plenty in the long run. It's stock price surged

FIGURE 7-4   Yahoo Stock Chart

458 percent in seven months starting September 1998. Right before this phenomenal move, Yahoo reported three quarters of earnings growth of 400, 500, and 800 percent respectively, which were clear indications Yahoo was building a strong track record and poised for further growth.

Figure 7-4 shows how well Yahoo was trading as we entered the new millennium filled with the promise of the good investment times we enjoyed in the late '90s. Yahoo was consistently trading at well over $90 a share in the fall of 2000. In September, many of the tech stocks started to run into trouble as massive sell-offs began to dilute their share value. Even great tech stocks can't sustain a weak industry forever. Yahoo plunged to $12 in March 2001. If you owned Yahoo and weren't watching what was happening, you could have lost 90 percent of your investment.

WHAT DRIVES BIG GAINS IN STOCKS?

Research shows that earnings growth is the single most important indicator of a stock's potential to make a big price move. The companies with the best earnings growth are the ones that will in fact continue to grow. There is absolutely no reason for a stock to go anywhere if the current earnings are poor. How many times have you kicked yourself for passing up a great stock like Microsoft or Home Depot? There were telltale signs that these winners were about to make major moves before they became household names. There were also lots of telltale signs when they fell out of favor in 2001.

Earnings, also called profits or net income, are what a company makes after paying all its obligations. Companies often conclude their quarters at the end of March, June, September, and December, though some companies end their quarters in different months. There are two ways of reporting earnings: a bottom-line total and a per-share amount. The per-share figure is calculated by dividing total earnings by the number of shares outstanding. For example, if XYZ Corporation has 45 million shares of stock outstanding and reports earnings of $35.8 million, its earnings per share would be 80 cents ($35.8 million/40 million). The per-share amount is most relevant for investors.

> **INSIGHT**
> Always try to rub up against money, for if you rub up against money long enough, some of it will rub off on you.

A study of the greatest stock market winners dating back to 1953 looked at all the biggest winning stocks that doubled, tripled, or went up even more in value. This comprehensive study analyzed every fundamental and technical variable in each stock studied. What emerged were common earnings characteristics among the big winners.

Three out of four companies averaged earnings increases of 70 percent or more in the quarter right before their stock started to take off.

Three-quarters of these top stocks averaged annual earnings advances of at least 30 percent in the three years before their major price move.

Earnings research continues today and consistently confirms the original findings about the significance of strong earnings growth. It also reinforces that selecting stocks based on outstanding earnings performance still works today when searching for winning stocks. When it comes to investing, look at a company's quarterly and annual earnings record. If you find a winning stock with great earnings potential, buy it but don't get complacent. Watch it closely and be prepared to sell if the situation changes as it did with Yahoo.

PUTTING IT ALL TOGETHER

We've covered some of the conscious and subconscious reasons why investors become complacent and as a result, prefer holding over selling their stocks. Recognizing and understanding these hidden drivers of your thinking will help you become a more successful investor. If you see some aspects of your own behavior that prevents you from selling, you'll know where they come from and be better equipped to deal with them. Success in investing is a battle, and selling is a more challenging arena than buying. Keep in mind that the capital losses resulting from holding too long include opportunity costs. Selling a stock that's going nowhere and replacing it with a stock that has a better chance of increasing in value is smart investing.

If you want to make money in the stock market, stocks must not only be bought at the right time, but also sold at the right time. Until a sale occurs, the outcome is only a temporary paper result. A handsome profit can melt away at any moment until you actually sell a stock. The questions we've asked should be used as a reminder, guide, and prompting tool to sharpen your sale execution skills. Formalize your stock review process along the lines we've covered.

Write everything down so that you not only track where you have been, but where you are going. And do it on a regular basis.

CHAPTER-RELATED WEB SITES

Best Calls (www.bestcalls.com) provides access to companies' quarterly earnings press conferences.

Zacks Investment Research (www.zacks.com) reports on what analysts are saying about most of the stocks on the U.S. exchanges.

Worth magazine columnists are second to none, including Peter Lynch, and its regular features are dynamite. For subscription information, call 800-777-1851.

CBS Market Watch (www.marketwatch.com) offers feature articles on the market and breaking news targeted at investors.

Company Sleuth (www.companysleuth.com) will send you news updates each day on companies you're following via e-mail.

Investor's Business Daily is a great financial newspaper that publishes important information to help determine the value of a stock. For subscription information, call 800-831-2525 or visit their Web site at www.investors.com.

PC Quote (www.pcquote.com) offers current stock prices, a portfolio tracker, company profiles, and broker recommendations.

Cruise the International Market to Heaven

"I think global investing means buying stock in Taco Bell."

—MITCH WOLF

ACCORDING TO INTERSEC RESEARCH, WHICH TRACKS FOREIGN INVEST-ment opportunities, Americans have a trillion dollars invested abroad. But much of that was put there in the 1980s, when international stocks far outperformed domestic stocks. During the '80s, Japan, Hong Kong, and Germany consistently outperformed the U.S. markets and provided diversification to U.S. investors at the same time. However, all of that dramatically changed in the 1990s.

Although Europe produced a respectable average annual gain of 12 percent during this period, the Japanese market fell into negative returns. The emerging markets took investors on a roller coaster ride, plummeting in 1994 after Mexico suddenly devalued the peso, then again in 1998 when the Asian financial flu gripped markets around the world. For many investors, the international ride seemed far too bumpy for average returns of just 4 percent for the decade. The U.S. market climbed so fast in the 1990s (the S&P's 500 stock index appreciated 316 percent) that it left the rest of the world's stocks comparatively undervalued. They were up only 68 percent over the same period.

However, as we turned the corner and entered into the new millennium, there was a growing consensus that the overseas stock markets were poised to outperform those in the United States. Asia was rebounding and even Japan was coming out of its long financial slump. The time is now right for you to consider investing a portion of your portfolio in the international market.

INTERNATIONAL INVESTING IS EASY

True revolutions know no borders. This is the case with the online international investor revolution. Today, online investors can easily invest in stocks in every part of the globe. In many cases, it is no different than buying U.S. stocks. You don't need a broker in Singapore, Hong Kong, or London to fulfill your order. In fact, as we'll discuss later, you don't need a broker at all to invest overseas.

Investors are often surprised to discover that many products and services they use every day are produced and sold by overseas companies. Furthermore, by virtue of using certain products, you probably know more about some foreign companies than you think. Table 8-1 lists several familiar brand names that are produced by foreign companies. Furthermore,

> **INSIGHT**
>
> Make sure the odds are in your favor when you invest in an international stock (i.e., sentiment, trend, volume, and news). Don't trade just to trade. If there isn't a clear reason for putting on the trade, pass on it.

TABLE 8-1   International Companies With a Major Presence in the U.S.

Product or Service	Parent Company and Country of Origin
Pillsbury food products, Burger King restaurants	Diageo (United Kingdom)
Nokia cellular phones	Nokia (Finland)
Wisk detergent, Dove soap	Unilever NV (Netherlands)
Hard Rock Café	Rank Group (United Kingdom)
Stop and Shop stores, Giant supermarkets	Ahold (Netherlands)
Seven-Up soft drinks	Cadbury Schweppes (United Kingdom)
Fila footwear	Fila (Italy)
Luxottica eyewear, Lens Crafters outlets	Luxottica (Italy)
Tagamet antiulcer medication, SmithKline laboratory outlets	SmithKline Beecham (United Kingdom)
Novolin insulin	Novo-Nordisk (Denmark)
TDK cassette tapes	TDK (Japan)
Eureka and Frigidaire home appliances	Electrolux (Sweden)

these companies allow U.S. investors to buy their stocks online. And the information on foreign companies is more plentiful than ever.

Many market experts will tell you that the benefits of going global with your portfolio are illusory and a virtual minefield if you don't know what you're doing. Given the past performance of international stocks, it would be difficult to argue to the contrary. However, Wall Street is famous for its short-term memory. In the late 1980s and early '90s, investing in international stocks was the rage, with investors making huge returns on stocks in emerging countries. The bottom line is that real benefits exist for investors who include overseas investments in their portfolio.

THE NUMBERS ARE CHANGING

Patient investors will benefit from the long, gradual strengthening of global economic performance. They are the ones who will make the money. Although many investors believe the investing world doesn't extend beyond U.S. borders, the facts point in the opposite direction. Over three-quarters of the world's companies are listed on foreign stock exchanges. Non-U.S. companies already account for over 60 percent of the world's stock market size, and their share is expected to exceed 70 percent in less than ten years.

The fact is that a plethora of investment opportunities exist outside the U.S. and many of these investments have turned in stellar results over the years. One reason is because of the fast-growing economies in many foreign countries. For example, the Gross Domestic Products (GDPs) of over 16 countries have grown faster than the U.S. GDP in the past two years. Economic activity in developing countries is, on average, growing at rates well above those of developed countries.

To ignore such economic growth is to ignore the investment opportunities that accompany it. Even if you don't buy into the diversification benefits of investing abroad, it still makes sense to include selected foreign investments in your portfolio. In many cases, their growth opportunities will exceed those of many U.S. based corporations. In addition to fast-growing foreign economies, several other factors point to higher stock prices abroad in the coming years.

- *Values relative to U.S. stock.* International stocks as a group have lagged behind U.S. equities in the past few years. This underperformance has created excellent values in many international markets relative to U.S. equities. Although value doesn't always equate to immediate price rises, patience and a long-term focus are necessary when investing overseas.

- *Fall of communism.* The fall of communism has led to a worldwide shift toward free markets. Countries are seeing the wisdom of shifting the control of corporations from the government to the private sector. Of course, adjustments to new economic systems don't occur overnight and many countries will see their economies worsen before they improve under free markets. Still, over the long term, the shift toward more capitalistic societies will be positive for investors in foreign equities.

- *Global competition.* The increasing cost-consciousness of U.S. companies and the continued paring of corporate fat have not gone unnoticed overseas. U.S. companies have become even more formidable competitors in the global marketplace. Foreign companies now understand that in order to be successful in the global market, they have to cut costs, shed losing operations, and improve productivity to attract investors.

- *Increased flow of U.S. pension dollars.* According to *The Wall Street Journal*, U.S. pension funds have increased their international holdings over the past five years at a 30 percent average annual rate. U.S. pension funds could have 14 percent of their total assets in non-U.S. investments within the next five years, up from 11 percent in 2001.

- *Changing attitudes.* Many countries are seeing slow but steady progress in changing investors' attitudes toward their stocks. For example, changing regulations should fuel greater equity participation in countries such as Japan. More and more pension funds are investing in foreign stock markets.

- *Global merger activity.* Investors have reaped the benefits of massive merger activities that have occurred in U.S. markets in recent years. As global markets develop, this merger activity will expand beyond our borders. International mergers are already taking place in utilities, steel, health care, and financial services. It will be commonplace in every industry sector in the next couple of years. International mergers could accelerate even more if relative valuations between U.S. and international companies persist and U.S. companies find it cheaper to merge rather than build abroad.

Today, many less-advanced nations are enjoying strong increases in personal income as they begin to discover excellent markets for their goods and services in wealthier nations. They're also installing American-style investor protection programs into their stock exchanges by combining standardized accounting practices with public disclosure to make their stocks safer, and therefore more attractive to international investors. Due to these factors and others, the odds are good that many foreign stock markets will outperform U.S. markets.

GLOBAL MUTUAL FUNDS

There are now 1,700 international mutual funds that actively invest in multinational companies compared to 120 in 1990. They hire thousands of analysts to closely follow foreign stocks. During the past ten years, only 10 percent of U.S. mutual fund managers outperformed the S&P 500-stock index, whereas 31 percent of the global funds outperformed the MSCI Europe index and 51 percent beat the MSCI Emerging Markets index.

Many investment advisers believe that mutual funds represent the safest way for investors to venture into foreign markets. International funds have professional managers who have special expertise in navigating international investment waters. Funds provide the necessary diversification when investing in potentially volatile markets and also take care of tax problems that can arise when investing overseas.

A well-diversified international mutual fund offers an excellent way to invest overseas, providing expenses are not too high, and you don't have the inclination to pick individual stocks. However, be aware of the fact that not all international funds are alike. Some focus exclusively on a specific country, while others target a particular region. Many global funds invest in both U.S. and foreign stocks. So make sure you know what you are buying when you consider an international fund.

If you already have ample U.S. stock holdings in your portfolio, a global fund with large U.S. holdings may not be the best choice. Also, a fund that claims it's diversified across the world, but in reality has 40 percent of its assets in the Pacific Rim, may not offer you the diversification you're looking for. Finally, an international mutual fund may focus on small-capitalization foreign companies, which can increase not only the fund's expected return but also its risk. Make sure you understand the investment objectives and holdings of international funds before you buy.

Morningstar (www.morningstar.com) estimates that the average annual expense ratio of an international fund is roughly 2 percent versus about 1 percent for most U.S. funds. In other words, for every $50,000 in the typical international equity fund, an investor pays $1,000 per year in "carrying fees." And fees are only part of the costs. International mutual funds can create unwanted tax liabilities every time the fund distributes capital gains to fund holders.

CLOSED-END VERSUS OPEN-END INTERNATIONAL FUNDS

Closed-end international funds are similar to open-end funds in that they permit investment in a basket of stocks selected and managed by an investment company. However, open-end funds continually sell new shares to the public and redeem shares at the fund's net asset value, which is the market value of the firm's portfolio of stocks, minus short-term liabilities. Closed-end funds sell only a certain number of shares at their initial public offering, just like a stock. Once the shares are sold, the fund is "closed" and new money is not accepted.

Closed-end funds trade on the stock exchanges, while open-end funds do not. Because closed-end funds are publicly traded, their prices are set by supply and demand just like common stocks. How do you know if a closed-end fund is trading at a discount or premium? Such information is given regularly in *The Wall Street Journal* and *Barron's*.

TWO GREAT INTERNATIONAL FUNDS

Most major no-load fund families offer international funds. Two funds to consider are the T. Rowe Price International Stock Fund (800-638-5660), a diversified international fund, and Acorn International Fund (800-922-6769), an international small-cap fund.

A number of closed-end funds focus on international investments. These funds include both international bond and stock funds. Just because an international closed-end fund trades at a discount does not make it a good investment.

It's important to determine if the fund meets your investment objective and fits in with the rest of your portfolio. For example, if your only international investment is a closed-end fund, it probably isn't a good idea to buy a single-country closed-end fund. You may want to consider buying a regional or truly global fund that invests in several countries. If you're an online investor who prefers to pick your own stocks, several foreign stocks are listed on U.S. exchanges. That means the companies issuing them have agreed to conform to SEC regulations and U.S. accounting standards. This enables investors to buy and sell their international stock holdings with the same ease they enjoy with domestic stocks.

AMERICAN DEPOSITORY RECEIPTS (ADRS)

One of the easiest ways to invest in specific overseas companies is through American Depository Receipts (ADRs), which are securities that trade on U.S. exchanges and represent ownership in shares of foreign companies. ADRs are issued by U.S. banks against actual stock shares of foreign companies held in trust by a correspondent institution. Often, ADRs are not issued on a share-for-share basis. Instead, one ADR can be the equivalent of five or ten of a company's stock.

ADRs have become increasingly popular in recent years. Today, there are over 1600. One reason for the growing popularity of ADRs is convenience. Investors can buy and sell them just like they buy and sell any stock in a U.S. company. ADRs are also quoted and pay dividends in U.S. dollars. Some investors who buy well-known foreign companies, such as Sony or Royal Dutch Petroleum, don't even know they're actually buying an ADR rather than common stock. That's because the difference between an ADR and a stock is transparent to the investor.

> **WARNING**
>
> Don't try to be a "Jack of All Trades and Master of None." Apply yourself and master one or two strategies when investing in the international market. As you increase your expertise, add other strategies as needed.

Over 150 ADRs offer direct-purchase programs where investors can purchase directly from the company's U.S. agents. Shares are purchased in the same way as shares in U.S. companies, through direct purchase plans (see table 8-2 for a partial listing of participating companies). To get into the program, call or write the company that interests you, and request a prospectus of their plan and an enrollment form. Fill out the enrollment form and return it with a check for the number of shares you want to purchase. The minimum initial investment in all ADR direct-purchase plans is $250. Once the initial investment has been made, you can make subsequent purchases directly. The plan makes it easy for investors with limited funds to buy quality ADRs and build a diversified international stock portfolio over time.

TABLE 8-2   Sample of Foreign Stocks Listed on U.S. Exchanges Offering Direct Purchase Plans

Company	Country	Stock Symbol	Exchange
Aegon	Netherlands	AEG	NYSE
Alcatel	France	ALA	NYSE

TABLE 8-2   continued

Company	Country	Stock Symbol	Exchange
Astra	Sweden	A	NYSE
Banco de Galicia Buenos Aires	Argentina	BGALY	Nasdaq
British Steel	UK	BST	NYSE
British Telecommunications	UK	TEF	NYSE
CANTV-National Telephonos de Chile	Chile	VNT	NYSE
CBT Group	Ireland	CBTSY	Nasdaq
Compania de Telecom de Chile	Chile	CTC	NYSE
Elan Corporation	Ireland	ELN	NYSE
Elf Aquitaine	France	ELF	NYSE
Fila Holdings	Italy	FLH	NYSE
Gallaher Group	UK	GLH	NYSE
Grupo Televisa	Mexico	TV	NYSE
Imperial Chemical Industries	UK	ICI	NYSE
News Corporation	Australia	NWS	NYSE
Petroleum Geo-Services	Norway	PGO	NYSE
Repsol S.A.	Spain	REP	NYSE
Rhone Poulenc	France	RP	NYSE
Saville Systems	Ireland	SAVLY	NYSE
SGS Thompson Micro-electronics	Netherlands	STM	NYSE
Shell Transport & Trading Co.	UK	SC	NYSE
Sony Corp.	Japan	SNE	NYSE
Telecom Argentina	Argentina	TEO	NYSE
Telefonica de Espana	Spain	TEF	NYSE
Telefonica de Peru	Peru	TDP	NYSE
Unibanco-Uniao de Bancos Brasileiros	Brazil	UBB	NYSE
Vodaphone Group	UK	VOD	NYSE

THE J.P. MORGAN PLAN

In 1996, the J.P. Morgan Company became a major administrator of ADRs when it announced its Shareholder Services Program. The program allows investors to make initial investments in many foreign companies whose ADRs are administered by J.P. Morgan. This is summarized as follows:

- Initial purchases are available to investors in all 50 states.
- Minimum initial purchase is $250.
- Subsequent purchases can range from $50 to $100,000 per year and are made at least weekly.
- There is a one-time enrollment fee of $15.
- Per-transaction fees are $5 plus 12 cents per share.
- Investors are charged a proportion of approximately 12 cents per share to reinvest dividends.
- Automatic monthly investments via electronic debit of a bank account are available.
- Shares can be sold via the telephone.

Bank of New York's Global Buy Direct Plan

An index that tracks the performance of ADRs is now available from the Bank of New York. The bank's ADR Index consists of 431 companies from 36 countries and contains a composite index with four regional indices: The Europe ADR Index, the Asia ADR Index, the Latin America ADR Index, and the Emerging Market ADR Index. The intricacies of American Depository Receipts are fully explained by a specialist from The Bank of New York, which issues ADRs for companies in more than 50 countries. For more information, visit their Web site at www.bankofny.com/adr.

The site also includes an excellent primer on ADRs, what they are, how they work, where they trade, and the benefits of investing in them.

You'll find profiles of companies whose ADRs are listed on U.S. exchanges along with links to their Web sites. Following Morgan's lead, Bank of New York offered its Global BuyDIRECT program for ADR clients in 1997. The following are the terms of Bank of New York's ADR direct-purchase plan:

- Initial purchases are available to investors in all 50 states.
- Minimum initial purchase is $200.
- Subsequent purchases can range from $50 to $250,000 per transaction.
- Shares are purchased at least weekly, and daily if practical.
- There is a one-time enrollment fee of $10.
- Per-transaction fees are $5 plus 10 cents per share.
- Reinvestment fee is 10 cents plus 5 percent of the amount of reinvested dividends ($5 maximum).
- Automatic monthly investment services are available.
- Shares can be sold via the telephone.

Citicorp's International Direct Investment Program

Not to be outdone, Citicorp launched its International Direct Investment Program for ADR clients in 1998. Here are the terms of the plan:

- Initial purchases can be made by investors in all 50 states.
- Minimum initial investment is $250.
- Subsequent investments can range from $50 to $100,000 per year.
- There is a $10 enrollment fee.
- Purchasing fees are $5 plus 10 cents per share.
- Selling fees are $10 plus 10 cents per share.

- Sell instructions must be submitted in writing. All sell instructions are processed no later than five business days after the order is received.

- There is no charge to reinvest dividends other than a brokerage charge of 10 cents per share.

- Automatic monthly investment services are available.

ADR direct-purchase plans offer a cost-effective way to diversify when compared to the typical international mutual fund, especially if you are investing for the long term. You don't necessarily have to own 50 ADRs to be "properly diversified." An investor can have adequate portfolio diversification with 13 to 20 U.S. and foreign stocks. Just by adding a few ADRs to a stock portfolio, an investor should enjoy the benefits of investing overseas.

WHAT FOREIGN MARKETS ARE BEST FOR YOU?

The areas that stand out as solid investments over the next couple of years are Europe and Latin America. Europe is still the safest place to invest and it's benefiting from many of the same factors that have fueled corporate profits in the U.S., such as restructuring and cost cutting. The environment for investing is improving with the development of the European Common Market and increased merger activities. Although Eastern Europe is still encountering economic and stability problems, countries like Poland are well ahead of the curve in the region.

> **INSIGHT**
>
> Trading in the international market should be effortless. If it's a strain or causes stress, don't make it a part of your game plan.

Latin America has always promised big things, but ill-advised economic policies seem to short-circuit companies in this region. Still, certain countries like Mexico offer good potential. Mexico is dramatically raising its standards of living and the emerging middle class is helping consumer-oriented firms grow significantly. Chile is another up and coming country with lots of exciting opportunities.

For aggressive investors, check out Asia and the Pacific Rim countries. In the past, news coming from this region has been bad. Japan's financial markets have been stuck in low gear and other Pacific Rim countries have been experiencing difficult economic times. In the long term, the Pacific Rim poses perhaps the biggest challenge to more aggressive investors. Many analysts believe that China offers the biggest investment opportunities if you're patient.

INTERNATIONAL DIVERSIFICATION

If you're interested in diversifying your investments, you should definitely consider adding an international component to your portfolio. The consensus is that you should have between 10 and 20 percent of your holdings in the international market. A long-time argument for investing overseas is that international investments enhance a portfolio's diversification because the returns on these investments are not closely correlated with U.S. stock returns.

The essence of portfolio diversification is a correlation of returns among the portfolio's holdings. A portfolio in which all investments move in the same direction and magnitude is not a diversified portfolio. A diversified portfolio has assets that are not closely correlated. In that way, when one group of investments is doing poorly, other investments in the same portfolio are picking up the slack.

Because of advances in communications and computer technology, the world is becoming a much smaller place. The interdependence of world economies is causing a convergence among market returns across countries. In short, the movements of the U.S. markets are becoming much more correlated with movements in international markets. As convergence of worldwide markets continues at an accelerated pace, the diversification benefits increase.

In the last few years, when U.S. markets have outpaced international markets dramatically, you would have been better off investing solely in U.S. stocks rather than mixing U.S. and foreign investments. However, remember that diversification means investing in assets that are not closely correlated. For example, a company like Sony understands that every U.S. investor who owns Sony represents a lifetime Sony customer. Direct-purchase plans provide a way for foreign-based companies to build brand-name recognition and consumer goodwill in the U.S. Direct-purchase plans also provide a way for foreign companies to diversify their shareholder base geographically.

ADD AN INTERNATIONAL COMPONENT TO YOUR RETIREMENT ACCOUNT

In many cases, the biggest pool of money investors control is in their IRA and 401(k) plans. If this situation applies to you, it is imperative that you consider diversifying your account by adding an international investment component. How do you do that? Check with your IRA or 401(k) plan administrator to see if foreign stock funds are one of your investment options. If so, check out the record of the fund by visiting Morningstar's excellent Web site at www.morningstar.com. Your plan's administrator should have performance reports on the fund as well. Make sure you compare the fund's performance relative to other foreign funds pursuing a similar investment approach. How has the fund performed over the last one, three, and five years? If the performance is acceptable, you might want to move some of your 401(k) or IRA money into the fund.

You should feel comfortable investing at least 10 percent of your retirement assets in international funds. If you have a choice among funds, choose the one with the broadest geographic exposure. In an

IRA, you can invest in both international mutual funds and stocks. If you prefer funds, focus on quality ones with moderate expenses like Acorn International and T. Rowe Price International Stock Funds.

If you prefer to invest in international stocks, focus on ADRs like AEGON (insurance/financial services), Ahold (supermarkets), Baan (software), British Airways (airline), Dassault Systemes (computer-aided design systems), Elan (pharmaceuticals), New Holland (farm equipment), Nokia (cellular telephones), Novo-Nordisk (drugs/chemicals), Royal Dutch Petroleum (oil), Reuters Group (financial-information services), Unilever NV or PLC (consumer products), Saville Systems (billing systems), and Vimpel Communications (cellular telephone services).

FOREIGN INVESTMENT PITFALLS

Although investing in foreign stocks offers plenty of pluses for investors, there are also several pitfalls. One of the biggest potential problems is currency fluctuations that can impact the performance of international investments. When local currencies weaken against the U.S. dollar, foreign investment returns suffer. Conversely, if you own shares in a country whose stock market is rising and whose currency is strengthening against the dollar, you'll get a double-powered boost to your portfolio.

One of the common arguments against investing overseas is that individual investors do not have the necessary expertise to make informed foreign investment choices. Other considerations include accounting standards that are not uniform and make it difficult to analyze a foreign company. Although these are important

POINTER

The Internet is a rich source of information on foreign companies. Three particularly useful Web sites are www.bankofny.com, www.jpmorgan.com, and www.global-investor.com.

concerns, they should not prevent you from considering investing overseas. As far as obtaining financial information on most foreign companies, annual and quarterly reports are readily available by contacting the company's U.S. agent. Value Line and S&P's Stock Guide provide ample coverage of international firms and tell who to contact for more information.

A final potential pitfall is the political and economic instability of many foreign countries. Volatile political and economic systems can create major shocks, such as rampant inflation, oppressive regulations, and currency devaluations, all of which negatively impact stock prices. For that reason, diversify your investments across a number of regions, especially when investing in emerging countries.

PUTTING IT ALL TOGETHER

Just a few years ago, many financial pundits were sounding a death bell for international investments. At the time, emerging stock markets from Asia to Russia to Brazil were in shambles. Fortunately, over the past few years, we have seen a broad recovery in the world economy. Foreign stock markets as a group have delivered higher total returns than many U.S. equities.

Globalization is alive and well and there are several good reasons why you should consider participating in this phenomenon. More than 95 percent of the world's population lives outside the U.S. The global dispersal of technology has dramatically increased manufacturing productivity in less-developed nations, which has led to higher economic growth rates. And Europe and Japan continue to deregulate their industries to make them more competitive.

In order to maximize portfolio profits in the future, you cannot ignore investment opportunities outside the U.S. Fortunately, the online investor revolution has created an environment in which it is as easy to invest overseas as it is in the U.S. No-load international mutual funds, closed-end international funds, and ADR direct-purchase programs all provide investors with access to foreign markets that far surpass what was available a few years ago. We've summarized the international investment options covered in this chapter in table 8-3.

TABLE 8-3   Summary of Foreign Investment Options

Investment Vehicle	How They Work	Advantages	Disadvantages
American Depository Receipts (ADRs)	Tracks shares of foreign companies but trade on U.S. exchanges.	Trade as easily as U.S. stocks: Issues must comply with SEC rules, which are tighter than those in most foreign countries.	ADRs often move in correlation with U.S. markets, so they offer limited portfolio diversification.
Foreign Stocks	Some are listed on U.S. exchanges. Others can be bought through U.S. brokers.	Can help diversify a portfolio and offer access to fast-growing markets.	Often difficult and expensive to buy and sell. Only limited information is available on many companies.
U.S.-Based Multinational Companies	Listed on U.S. exchanges.	Easily bought and sold.	Offer little or no diversification because most follow the U.S. markets.
Global Mutual Funds	Worldwide portfolios that include U.S. stocks.	Allows fund managers to be totally flexible and pick stocks anywhere in the world.	Because of their U.S. holdings, they may provide less diversification than a pure foreign fund.
International Mutual Funds	Invest only in non-U.S. companies.	Offer an easy way to diversify.	Expenses are often higher than those of domestic funds.
Regional Mutual Funds	Invest in individual countries or regions such as Latin America.	By focusing their investments, they sometimes produce huge annual returns.	These are high-risk funds.

CHAPTER-RELATED WEB SITES

The Intelligent Asset Allocator (www.efficientfrontier.com) offers comprehensive information on how to build a diversified portfolio.

Find a Fund (www.findafund.com) publishes a list of the weekly top-performing funds and lots of other fund selection information.

Mutual Fund magazine (www.mfmag.com) offers feature articles and tools for selecting funds that are right for you.

Mutual Funds Interactive (www.fundsinteractive.com/profiles.html) provides recommendations, analysis tools, and profiles of many of the top funds.

Smart Money (www.smartmoney.com) offers an excellent "search and find" tool for quickly finding the "Top 25 International Funds."

Diversify Everything in Your Portfolio

"If you manage to amass two nickels to invest, it's a good idea to keep them in separate pockets and not in the same pants."

—BEN FRANKLIN

THE IDEA OF DIVERSIFYING YOUR INVESTMENTS HAS BEEN AROUND FOR centuries. In Shakespeare's 16th-century play *The Merchant of Venice*, merchant Antonio explains that his "ventures are not in one bottom trusted, nor in one place." That translates to "I don't put all of my eggs in one basket or rather, one boat." Asset diversification is all about not putting your eggs in one basket. It's the ultimate protection should things go wrong in one investment sector, as is sometimes the case.

Unfortunately, many investors have come to believe that asset diversification is as outdated as Shakespeare's prose. They're quick to remind you that anyone who threw their money into a S&P 500 index fund ten years ago did better than the prudent investor who was intent on diversifying their investments among large- and small-cap stocks, foreign stocks, and bonds. In this chapter, we will show you why investment diversification is critical to the success of your long-term investment strategy. You'll learn how to allocate your assets and adjust your diversification plan to keep up with changing times.

WHAT IS INVESTMENT DIVERSIFICATION?

Many investors spend sleepless nights worrying about which stocks to buy and sell, which funds to own or dump, or whether to get into bonds and money market accounts. All of these are legitimate concerns because if their overall investment diversification plan is weak, they could sustain substantial losses. Investment diversification means investing in different asset classes of investments, like stocks and mutual funds, from different sectors, bonds, and money market accounts to help minimize the gyrations in the market.

Studies show that asset diversification is the single greatest determinant of solid investment performance. Unfortunately, many investors blithely sink money into the market without ever formulating an investment diversification plan. Yet implementing a good investment diversification plan is the first thing a good financial advisor recommends to new clients. We'll show you how to set up a plan later in the chapter.

WHAT IF YOU DON'T DIVERSIFY?

Let's suppose all of your money is invested in high-tech stocks. Then imagine that something happens to the tech market, as it did in March 2000 when millions of investors suddenly decided tech stocks were overpriced. As a result, there was a huge sell-off that caused the Nasdaq to fall more than 50 percent. If you were heavily invested in the tech sector and didn't get immediately out, you probably got hurt. Or, you put your money into bonds and quickly discovered that the bond market was also having its up and downs. If you got disgusted with bonds and put your money in a money market account, you didn't make much either.

Historically, a bad year in the stock market shows up later as nothing more than an insignificant blip. That's because the stock market is the best long-term investment vehicle there is; it has delivered an average return of more than ten percent over the past ten years. In the short term, the stock market is more volatile than other investments. Consequently, investors with less risk tolerance, like those who are close to retirement, should put less money into the stock market than younger investors, and invest a significantly greater percentage of their assets in bonds.

An individual's risk tolerance and goals for returns on their investments are dominant factors influencing what percentage of their investments should be put into different investment categories. Making these choices wisely delivers the maximum return within a person's comfort zone for risk, and enables them to reach realistic financial goals without losing sleep. Here's an overview of important points you should consider when diversifying your portfolio:

- *Time is on your side.* Investors with more years until retirement can afford to put a greater percentage of their assets in the stock market.

- *Stocks mean risk with higher returns.* Investors with a higher tolerance for volatility should put more money in the stock market than those in the same age group who have a lower tolerance.

- *Education funds need stocks.* If you're investing for your kids' education, consider putting a greater percentage into stocks than you put into your retirement investments, especially if your kids are young.

- *Get professional advice.* The best way to develop an effective asset diversification plan is to consult a qualified financial planner or knowledgeable friend.

- *Make diversification a key goal.* Studies show that asset diversification is the single most important factor in determining solid returns from investing.

- *Consider including mutual funds in your plan.* Check out mutual funds that invest in specialized sectors like foreign stocks and municipal bonds.

Always remember that it's never too late to revamp or revise an asset diversification plan because things will change. In fact, if you don't do it at least once a year, you are probably not monitoring your investments as much as you should.

WHAT'S THE RIGHT MIX FOR YOU?

Your goals, risk tolerance, and time horizon are the key to determining the right mix in your investment portfolio. For example, your ultimate financial goal may be to retire in style. How soon you retire and in what style can significantly affect your decisions on how you allocate your assets earlier in life. In accounting for risk when diversifying your portfolio, it's more productive to think in terms of your tolerance for volatility. This is because one of the greatest investment risks is to do nothing and subsequently miss out on superior returns.

If you're planning to retire in 15 years and have a high tolerance for volatility, you may want to invest as much as 70 percent of your holdings in the stock market, 25 percent in bonds, and only 5 percent in money markets. If you're retiring in 25 years, consider increasing your securities holdings to 80 percent. If you're retiring in 15 years but with less stomach for volatility, keep 50 percent in stocks, 40 percent in bonds, and the rest in money market accounts.

Near-term retirees are faced with the daunting task of diversifying their assets for maximum return without betting the farm. A nasty market dip could occur immediately before retirement and eliminate most of their savings. If you're close to retirement and can tolerate high volatility, you may want to put all of your holdings in stocks, weighted mainly in large-cap stocks that are more dependable than mid-cap and small-caps stocks. If you can't take the heat, put 50 percent in bonds, 10 percent in money market accounts, and 40 percent in stocks.

> **POINTER**
>
> There are several excellent Web site tools you can use to create a diversification plan that's right for you. They're listed under "Diversification Plans" in the Appendix II.

If one of your investment goals is putting your kids through college, consider putting more in the stock market when your kids are young. For example, those with high volatility tolerance might put 80 percent in stocks, while those who sleep more fitfully might limit their securities investments to 65 percent or even less in the stock market. Achieving the right mix of investments, which might include small-, mid-, and large-cap stocks and short-, medium-, or long-term bonds to achieve maximum return for your volatility tolerance while maintaining adequate diversification is a tricky business. So you may want to consider consulting a qualified financial planner for advice.

HOW DIVERSIFIED ARE YOUR TODAY?

Before you actually invest in accordance with your diversification plan, make sure you know what you already own. Many investors don't know if their investments are diversified because of the mutual funds that are in their portfolios. If this applies to you, find out exactly what your funds invest in. For example, some funds call themselves small-cap. But, given the less-than-stellar performance of small-cap stocks over the past few

INSIGHT

Sometimes your best investments are the ones you don't make. There's nothing wrong with sitting on the sidelines until you're ready to get back into the game.

years, these same funds may have veered off into large-cap territory to boost their returns. Call them or read their latest prospectus to find out what's in your portfolio. Without this knowledge, you could be under the false assumption that your stocks are diversified across companies by size.

You should also know what types of stocks your funds are buying by sector (i.e., industry). If your fund is tech-heavy, that's okay, as long as you don't have too much in this fund and are sufficiently diversified with stocks from more traditional sectors like manufacturing, which tend to rise when techs fall. Similarly, don't take your short-term bond fund's word that its holdings are all short term. Find out what they think is short, mid, and long term to determine what they actually own.

DIVERSIFYING WITH MUTUAL FUNDS

Mutual funds have become a fast food for investors. They're easy to get into and feature diversification opportunities that allow you to buy into several equities without the hassle of pouring over stock tables and thumbing through annual stock reports. If you ignore the option of investing in mutual funds, you're missing out on an excellent opportunity to diversify your portfolio.

However, finding a good fund can be frustrating since there are over 8,000 funds to choose from. That's nearly four times the number of stocks on the New York Stock Exchange. And,

INSIGHT

Although growth funds often dominate the market, value funds have a better long-term record. Since the late 1920s, value stocks have gained an average of 13 percent as compared to 10 percent for growth stocks.

despite a fund's professional management team, diversification, and finely tuned trading strategies, the vast majority of funds have lagged behind the stock market over the past ten years. Fortunately, there are a few exceptions that rise above the crowd.

When you invest in a mutual fund, you become a shareholder in a portfolio of dozens or hundreds of different stocks. You don't have to worry about the volatility of a single stock since your investment is spread across several stocks and industries. Additional advantages of owning mutual funds include:

- *Professional management.* A professional portfolio manager handles all buying and selling of stocks in the fund, as well as all the other day-to-day responsibilities, leaving you to do other things like playing golf.

- *Low fees.* About half of the 8,000 mutual funds on the market are known as "no-load funds" because you pay no fee to buy or sell shares. You are assessed a small annual management fee of about 1 to 2 percent of your holdings to cover fund expenses. "Load" funds charge a front-end fee ranging from 3 to 8 percent when you buy the fund. Some also charge a "back-end" fee when you sell. In most cases, buy no-load funds. Studies show that the no-loads perform just as well as load funds, so why not save on fees?

- *Variety.* You can invest in a wide variety of stocks and bonds through mutual funds. There are funds that specialize in small stocks, large stocks, specialty sectors, high yielding stocks, international stocks, and a whole range of bonds and balanced stock and bond portfolios. You can have a strong

> **POINTER**
>
> In an era in which there are more mutual funds than listed stocks, it becomes important to do you homework before investing in any fund.

position in nearly every type of stock, both foreign and domestic, just by buying a handful of mutual funds.

Types of Funds to Consider

Over the years as fund groups have grown in number, they have become more and more specialized in their investments. Here are some examples of the specialization mutual fund investment categories available today:

- *Sector funds.* Sector funds do what their name implies: they restrict investments to a particular segment or sector of the economy. For example, a fund like Northern Technology only buys tech companies for its portfolio. Munder NetNet cuts it even finer by holding only Internet-related tech stocks. Fidelity has a whole stable of sector funds from Fidelity Select Insurance to Fidelity Select Automotive. The idea is to allow investors to place bets on specific industries or sectors whenever they think that industry might heat up.

- *Blend funds.* These can go across the board. They might invest in both high-growth tech stocks and cheaply priced automotive companies. They are difficult to classify in terms of risk. The Vanguard 500 Index fund invests in every company in the S&P 500 and could therefore qualify as a blend fund.

- *Value funds.* Value funds like to invest in companies that the market has overlooked. They search for stocks that have become "undervalued" or priced low relative to their earnings potential. Sometimes a stock has run into short-term problems that will eventually be resolved.

- *Growth funds.* As their name implies, growth funds tend to look for the fastest-growing companies on the market. Growth managers are willing to take more risk and pay a premium for their stocks in an effort to build a portfolio of companies with above average momentum or price appreciation.

- *Micro-cap funds.* Micro-cap funds look for companies with market values below $250 million. These funds tend to look for either start-ups or companies about to exploit new markets. With stocks this small, the risk is always extremely high, but the growth potential is exceptional.

- *Mid-cap funds.* These funds fall in the middle of the capital value range. They invest in companies with market values in the $1 to $6 billion range. The stocks in the lower end of their range are likely to exhibit the growth characteristics of smaller companies and therefore add some volatility to these funds.

- *Small-cap funds.* A small-cap fund focuses on companies with a market value below $1 billion. Their volatility often depends on the aggressiveness of their manager. Aggressive small-cap managers will buy hot growth companies and take high risks in hopes of high rewards. More conservative managers will look for companies that have been beaten down temporarily. Value funds aren't as risky as the hot growth funds but they can still be volatile.

> **INSIGHT**
> The fund industry has gone on a rampage in recent years trying to attract customers with every type of market segmentation fund imaginable. Between 1993 and 2001, the number of funds has grown from 2,600 to over 8,000 funds.

- *Index funds.* For many investors, index funds are by far the easiest, most effective way to go. If your goal is long-term growth without having to pay much attention, these workhorse funds are the best solution. They simply buy all the stocks or bonds in a chosen index with the goal of matching that group's performance.

Mutual funds offer you a convenient way to diversify the equities in your portfolio. Look for funds that have performed well over the last several years and fit with a risk level you're comfortable with. When you buy a fund, watch its performance just as you would an individual stock in your portfolio. If it's not performing to your expectations, get rid of it. In most cases, you can do that online.

How to Find Winning Funds

If you build a portfolio that includes strong mutual funds, you'll enjoy excellent returns over time. With more than 8,000 mutual funds on the market, the most difficult aspect of mutual fund investing is deciding which funds are best for you. There's a wide range of books and magazines that rate mutual funds, including *Money*, *Mutual Funds*, *Forbes*, *Barron's*, *Consumer Reports*, and *Bloomberg Personal Finance*. Most are available at your library or local newsstands. Here are several key factors you should consider in deciding which funds are right for you:

- *Five-year track record.* Rarely do the best funds lead the market every year. It's a mistake to choose a fund based on its performance over just one year. Instead, compare fund performances over a three- to five-year period. Look for funds that have been top performers in their category over several years (three to five years) and have done well relative to the market year in and year out.

- *Same fund manager.* The success of any mutual fund is a reflection of the fund's manager. Before you select a fund based on its great performance, be sure the person who established that record is still managing the fund. If they've moved on, so should you.

- *Fees.* All other factors being equal, you should select the fund with the lowest fees. Choose no-load funds over similarly performing load funds. There are plenty of great no-load funds from which to choose.

Smart Money offers an excellent "search and find" tool for quickly finding top performing mutual funds on their Web site at www.smart money.com (see figure 9-1). Under the "Best & Worst" column of their funds menu, go to the "Top 25 Funds" option. Two "pull down"

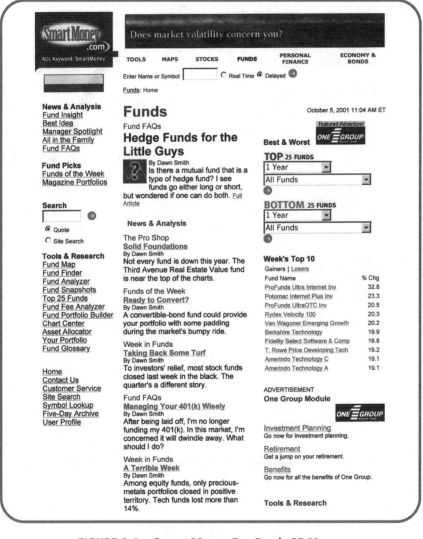

FIGURE 9-1 *Smart Money* Top Funds 25 Menu

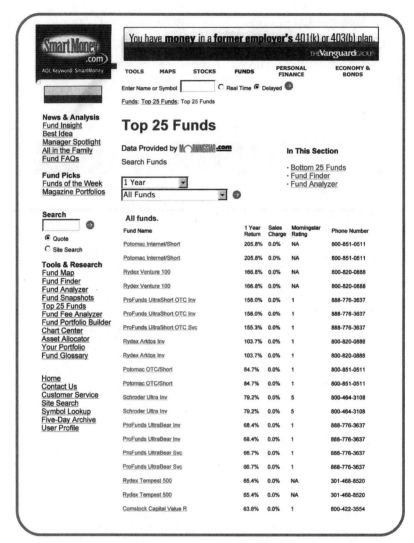

FIGURE 9-2 *Smart Money* List of Top 25 Funds

menus are used to select the top 25 funds that interest you. The first menu is the time option. The example in figure 9-1 shows "One Year." If you select this option, *Smart Money* will show you the top 25 funds based on their returns over the past 12 months. You have the option of selecting other time zones like the top 25 funds over the last two, three, or five years or even 13 weeks if you're looking for near-term results.

Staying with our example, let's assume that you're interested in reviewing the top 25 performing funds over the past 12 months. Directly below the time option menu is the menu for the type of fund that interests you. Figure 9-2 shows that we have selected "All Funds." However, there are over 50 different categories of funds (e.g., international fund groups, different bond funds, and domestic stock funds) that you can select if you want to refine your search to the "Top 25 Funds" in a specific area. Buy selecting "One Year" and "All Funds" we end up with a great list of the top 25 mutual funds that are worth considering (see figure 9-2).

> **POINTER**
>
> Check out fund company Web sites like Fidelity.com, Vanguard.com, and Troweprice.com to learn more about their funds. There are five excellent general information sites listed under "Mutual Fund Resources" in the Appendix II.

BIG IS NOT NECESSARILY GOOD

With a little research, you can accumulate a portfolio of all-star funds managed by some of the ablest managers in the investment business. The more successful a fund becomes, the faster its assets grow through its net asset value (NAV). In fact, not only does it grow from within through the

> **BUZZWORD**
>
> **Net Asset Value,** or NAV is a mutual fund's portfolio value per share. For example, a fund with $100 million in assets with five million shareholders would have a NAV value of $20 per share. The NAV then becomes the price per share you pay on a given day to acquire one share of a fund.

fund's savvy investments, it also grows from without through the inevitable flood of new investors attracted to its sterling track record. Once lean and mean, many popular funds quickly become obese and are no longer able to maneuver lightly through the market. That's why many funds close their doors to new investors after their assets reach a certain level.

Oversized funds face several drawbacks not the least of which is a dwindling universe of investment choices. First, they will limit their holdings of individual equities in their portfolio to 2 to 5 percent to maintain proper diversification. Second, they are usually unwilling to hold positions representing more than 5 to 10 percent of a firm's outstanding shares to ensure adequate liquidity should the fund wish to sell shares.

Together, these constraints sharply limit the number of companies available for investment to large funds. A fund with $1 billion in assets and a 2 percent maximum holding in any individual stock could invest in about 2,650 stocks if it is willing to hold 10 percent of the company's capitalization, and 1,825 stocks if the limit is set at 5 percent. But for a fund that has grown to $20 billion, the comparable numbers are 352 and 176 companies. In other words, growing from one to $20 billion in size can reduce the number of securities available for them to purchase by as much as 90 percent.

Trading is another drawback to size. Moving substantial blocks of securities around affects market prices. If a fund tries to unload a large block of stock they own, they may be forced to liquidate their position only at a discount. What does that mean for mutual fund investors? Look for funds with stellar track records, but favor funds with smaller, more manageable asset bases. There are plenty of good funds with solid track records that have asset bases under $1 billion.

How to Get Started in Funds

There are several ways to buy mutual funds. Most funds can be purchased directly from the funds' group. For example, you can buy all of

Fidelity's funds through Fidelity (www.fidelity.com). If you don't have an online account, call the fund's group and they'll send you an application along with a prospectus. Toll-free phone numbers of groups with more than two funds are listed in *Investor's Business Daily's* mutual fund tables. The Investment Company Institute also publishes a directory of fund groups (202-326-5872). The 100 Percent No-Load Mutual Fund Council publishes a directory (call 212-768-2477, fax 212-768-2476, or visit their Web site at www.networth.galt.com/council). The Mutual Fund Education Alliance has a directory of mutual funds (816-471-1454).

Many load funds are sold through brokers who charge a commission. Load structures vary. Some have front-end loads, where the investor pays 1 percent to 5 percent of the amount they buy in commissions. For example, if you're investing $2,000 into a fund, you would pay a $100 commission if the broker was charging 5 percent front-end load.

DIVERSIFICATION TOOLS

Smart Money offers a free asset diversification worksheet on their Web site (www.smartmoney.com) that helps you build a customized diversification portfolio. You enter key variables such as your age, income, net worth, spending needs, risk tolerance, and expectations about the future to determine an asset diversification that's best for you (see figure 9-3). Generally, the younger you are, the more you can afford the short-term volatility of investment options. As your age or spending needs increase, you'll need to protect your principal by shifting money toward less volatile investment options like bonds.

Smart Money's asset-diversification system helps balance your risk tolerance and economic outlook. It also helps you create a well-diversified investment program that takes into account the historical relationships between stocks, bonds, and cash. Here we're more concerned with how much time and interest you plan to devote to your portfolio. That's the

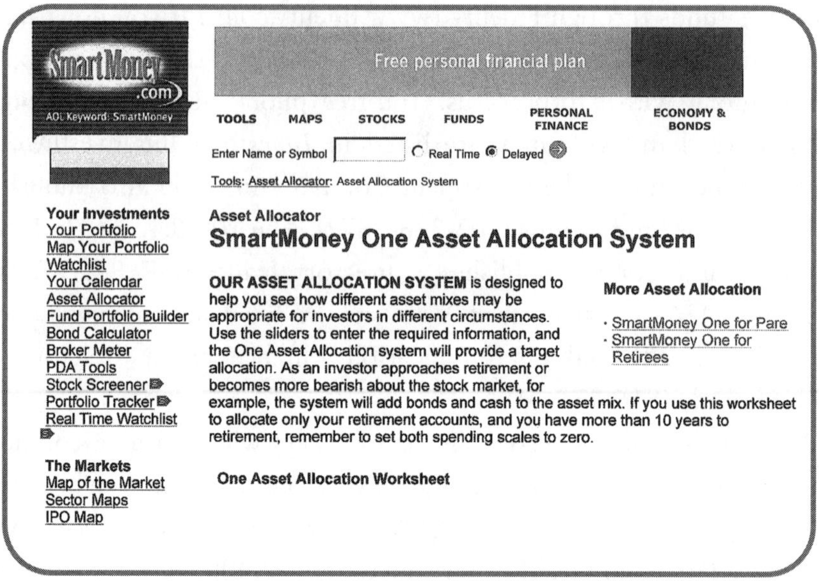

FIGURE 9-3 *Smart Money* Asset Allocate

biggest factor in choosing specific stocks and bonds to meet your diversification objectives. The more work you're willing to put in, the greater your potential returns. Portfolios that have greater portions of individual stocks generally require a lot more attention than fund-laden portfolios.

PUTTING IT ALL TOGETHER

Yogi Berra once said, "When you come to a fork in the road, take it." Asset diversification is the key to successful long-term investing. When you come to a fork in the road and have a decision to make between investing in two equally qualifying stocks, consider going both ways. Buy shares in each and fill your portfolio with as broad a selection of stocks as possible. Some investors think they're diversified when they own five or six stocks. But you're not diversified if some of those stocks are in the same industry group.

Investment diversification is easy if you follow the advice we've offered. Since uneven price movements can upset the balance over time, adjust your diversification plan at least once a year. This has the added benefit of lending a vital measure of discipline to your investing. It prods you to take the appropriate amount of risk when you're feeling overly cautious. It reins you in during those times when the sky seems to be the limit.

Make sure the diversification system you choose is designed to help you meet both your short- and long-term investment goals. Money already earmarked for short-term goals might include savings for a down payment on a new house or college tuition that's just a few years away. Because you have no time to make up a short-term down-turn in the stock market, those kinds of savings demand a more conservative approach.

CHAPTER-RELATED WEB SITES

□ Legg Mason's Web site (www.leggmason.com) provides an online questionnaire to help you develop a diversification plan.

□ Frank Russell Company (www.russell.com) features a "Comfort Quiz" to help you allocate your investments.

□ Fidelity's Asset Diversification Planner (www.fidelity.com) offers diversification advice, a risk questionnaire, and five model portfolios.

□ The Intelligent Asset Allocator (www.efficientfrontier.com) offers comprehensive information on how to build a diversified portfolio.

□ Invest-O-Rama (www.investorama.com) is an extensive, well-organized site that lists fund-related Web links.

□ Morningstar (www.morningstar.com) is a premier site providing all kinds of information about mutual funds.

CHAPTER-RELATED WEB SITES, continued

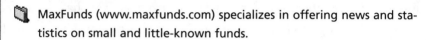 MaxFunds (www.maxfunds.com) specializes in offering news and statistics on small and little-known funds.

CBS Market Watch (www.marketwatch.com) provides articles, news, and market data on funds. Click the "Super Fund" icon to see the fund information.

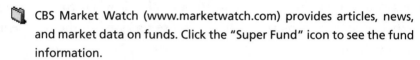 Find a Fund (www.findafund.com) publishes a list of the weekly top performing funds and lots of other fund selection information.

Beware of the Margin Game

"The margin-debt hole is deeper than you think. How long can you hold your breath?"

—GERRI DETWEILER

TIM NELSON KNEW ALL ABOUT TAKING RISKS. HE'D SURVIVED FIVE years in a Vietnam prison camp and went on over 50 covert secret missions before he finally retired from the Marines. He had an iron stomach for anything and decided to make a fortune investing in the stock market with $50,000 he'd saved for that purpose. He opened an online account with a margin option that allowed him to borrow up to 75 percent of his account balance.

Tim felt he had nothing to lose. With $50,000 in his online account, his broker was eager to lend him another $37,500 on margin, secured by the value of his portfolio. Tim could now almost double his gambling chips. At first, he made small buys in blue chips like Cisco and Dell. As his profits grew, so did his confidence.

When the market is rocketing upward, all investors think they're geniuses, especially those who use margins to propel the rocket like Tim did. But when the market turns south and the rocket comes back to earth, it can be a different story. Tim had loaded up on tech stocks using his margin account, only to lose it all in the great tech sell-off that started to occur in 2000. If you plan to play in the margin game, you better know exactly what you're doing or you'll get burned.

WHAT ARE MARGIN ACCOUNTS?

You have a choice of two types of online brokerage accounts to open: cash account or margin. A cash account is a simple one you use to buy and sell securities with the cash you deposit in your account (i.e., just like a checking account). You pay for each trade transaction with cash. A margin account is a credit account. You pay a certain percentage of the purchase price of your marginable securities and borrow the remainder from the brokerage firm.

A margin account lets you borrow money from your broker to buy securities. You are in effect taking out a secured loan against your own portfolio. The advantage is that you don't have to sell any of the equities in your portfolio to obtain the cash and you have no repayment schedule. You're free to repay the loan at anytime, unless your collateral falls below the required amount. While many investors' use borrowed cash to buy additional securities, you can use it for any purpose. However, the wholly owned securities in your portfolio are collateral for the loan. You'll also need a margin account if you are engaging in short sales, which we'll cover later in the chapter.

When opening a margin account, you sign a margin agreement form that outlines the rules for using the account. Once your securities are in the account, you can borrow on margin anytime without having to complete any other forms. To buy on margin, you must have an account that's backed by collateral in the form of cash or securities. The initial margin is the smallest amount that the investor must pledge at purchase. The minimum that must stay in your account is the maintenance margin. When the balance falls below this amount and if the margined securities drop in value, you'll get a margin call, which is a demand that the account be brought back up to its maintenance margin.

A margin call is a demand by your broker for you to deposit cash or fully marginable securities. If the value of your collateral falls below the broker's minimum requirement (usually about 30 percent of the loan), you will receive a margin call by letter, telephone, email, or other means to request additional collateral in the form of cash or fully marginable securities to meet the requirement.

However, only a percentage of a security's market value can be used to meet your margin call. If you fail to meet the call, your broker is authorized by the margin agreement form you sign to sell the margined securities and any other collateral needed to repay the loan, interest, and commissions. You're responsible for any deficit that may remain after your assets (i.e., stocks) are sold.

If you cannot meet the margin call, the broker can sell any and all of your margined securities and other assets to meet the call. Nasdaq requires a maintenance margin on equities of 25 percent. However, your online broker may impose higher margin maintenance requirements.

MARGIN ACCOUNT LIMITATIONS

The board of governors of the Federal Reserve Board (FRB) or Fed as it is called applies restrictions on margin lending practices. For example, you can't borrow the full amount of your portfolio. The Fed regulates the amount of credit brokers can extend to its customers. Currently, you can borrow up to 50 percent of the value of your marginable stocks to make a new purchase. In the past, it has varied between 40 and 100 percent. The NYSE minimum initial equity requirement holds that your equity be at least $2,000 whenever you enter into a new margin account transaction. The NYSE Minimum Maintenance Rule requires that the equities in your account be at least 25 percent of the current market value of margined securities.

All of these requirements are minimums and can be increased or decreased at any time by your online brokerage firm or by the regulatory agencies of the securities industry. Not all securities are fully marginable. Your brokerage firm may have its own requirements and they can tell you which ones would not apply. Online brokers like any other stockbrokers charge interest on margin loans at varying rates depending on the amount you borrow.

You cannot have shares registered in your name and sent out to you when you've purchased shares on margin. They must remain in the margin account in "the street name." You'll receive credit in your account for any dividends they pay. You may remove the shares from the margin account only after you have repaid the amount you borrowed on margin to purchase these shares. If the value of your collateral rises, you can withdraw the amount over your minimum requirement or use it for additional investments.

WHY OPEN A MARGIN ACCOUNT?

Margin accounts let you magnify your gains if you choose wisely. They'll also magnify your losses if you choose unwisely. You benefit from using margin only if the stocks you purchase rise in price. If they stay the same, or worse, drop in price, you lose and must pay interest on the margin whether your stock rises or not. For example, suppose you purchase 500 shares, at $11 a share, for a total of $5,500. A year later, you sell the stock for $33 per share and receive $16,300 before commissions on your $5,500 investment, or a 296 percent return. Not bad. However, you could have used your margin account to earn an even higher rate of return.

Suppose you bought on margin 500 shares of stock for $11 a share. You put up 50 percent of the stock's purchase price ($2,750) and borrowed the other 50 percent from the brokerage firm to complete the transaction. Next year, the stock is valued at $33 per share. If you sell the stock and repay the broker, you are left with $13,450 ($16,300 from stock sale less $2,750 plus interest for the margin loan). That's a whopping 489 percent return on your money ($13,450 / $2,750).

However, what if your stock had dropped in price to $8 dollars a share? In the cash transaction, you would receive about $4,000 back excluding commissions from your original $5,500 investment. In the margin transaction, you would receive $4,000, repay the $2,750 you borrowed from your broker, and be left with $1,250 of your original $5,500, excluding commissions and interest. That's almost an 80 percent loss.

Before you rush out and open a margin account, let's review the main points of margin accounts. It's essentially a collateralized line of credit. You may use proceeds from a margin account for other investments and other purposes. You pay interest on money borrowed from a margin account. If you use the margin to buy securities, you must meet certain minimum margin requirements and maintain the appropriate amount of collateral. If the collateral level falls, you can expect a margin call.

WHEN TO BUY ON MARGIN

Here's an example of when you might want to buy a stock on margin. Suppose you believe that a particular stock will rise in price. It's currently trading at $15 per share and you believe it will soon hit $20. You only have $3,000 in cash to buy 200 shares. You borrow $3,000 on margin and buy another 200 shares with the $6,000 you have (i.e., total of 400 shares). The stock hits $20, and you sell, adding $8,000 to your cash account. You pay back the $3,000 you borrowed plus $100 interest, leaving you with a tidy gain of $1,900 ($8,000 – $3,000 –$3,100). If you had not used your margin account and only bought 200 shares, your gain would have only been $1,000 ($4,000 – $3,000). The chance to magnify your earnings is what buying on margin is all about.

However, if the stock declined to $10 a share and you sold, your losses would have been $2,100 ($6,100 – $4,000). Buying on margin is a strategy for the short term, since holding on to borrowed money too long could result in a loss. You are responsible for meeting all margin calls promptly and repaying all funds borrowed on margin, even if this amount exceeds the value of your account.

As with all investing, there is risk in buying on margin. One of the biggest reasons people lost fortunes in the stock market crash of 1929 was that they bought too much stock on margin and couldn't pay it back. The government stepped in soon after to create margin limits. The board of governors of the Fed publishes a list of marginable securities. Most brokerages will extend margin on the following types of securities:

- Listed common and preferred stocks
- Municipal bonds
- Federal government bonds, notes, and bills
- Nasdaq Securities
- Convertible bonds (if convertible into a marginable security)
- Corporate bonds (if rated Baa or higher by Moody's)

Check with your online brokerage firm to determine if a security is marginable and if a higher maintenance requirement is imposed on it. Some securities are marginable only up to a certain value of the security while others are not eligible for margin. Most Initial Public

Offerings (IPOs) have to wait at least 30 days after being traded before they can become marginable. Certain mutual funds and all options may not be bought on margin or used as collateral in a margin account. Buying on margin is a simple process but it's also risky. If you buy a security on margin and it nose-dives in value, you cannot rescue it with more margin buying.

SELLING SHORT

Margin accounts are not just used for buying. You can also use them to sell securities, which is called selling short. Selling short involves borrowing securities you believe will decline in value and then selling them. You are selling securities you do not own. Looked at another way, short selling is about selling high and then buying low, just the opposite of regular trading. Once you have sold your securities, you hope that the price falls, in which case you buy shares back at a lower price. If the price rises, you may be forced to buy shares at the higher price, losing money on the transaction. Remember, you have to buy them back because you must return them to the brokerage firm.

A short sale occurs when you "borrow" a security from your broker and sell it with the intent of repurchasing it in the future to repay the loan of the security. You might sell short if you believed the price of a security was going to drop and you could repurchase it at a price significantly below the price for which you sold it.

You may have a "long" or "short" position in a security. When you have a long position in a stock or bond, you actually own the security in your account. On the other hand, sometimes you may want to take advantage of a price movement in a security you don't own. When you do this, you may take a short position by borrowing the security. Here's a summary of how selling short works:

- You borrow a security from your broker.
- You sell the security at its current price.

- You buy the security back when you believe the price has fallen sufficiently or the broker calls for it (which ever comes first).

- You return the security back to the broker.

Here's how selling short works. Let's say you believe that XYZ, Inc., which is trading at $10 a share, is going to fall fast. You borrow 100 shares of XYZ from your broker and sell them for $1,000 ($10 x 100). Soon afterward, the stock drops to $4 a share and you buy the 100 shares back for $400, which you return to your broker. Remember, you borrowed them initially to set-up a short transaction. You come out $600 ($1,000 – $400) ahead before commission and interest.

However, if XYZ, Inc., becomes a hit and its price rises, you'll take a loss. Let's say it rises to $15 by the time you must repay the shares. It will cost you $1,500 to buy those 100 shares back. You therefore must pay $1,500 to replace the shares you sold for $1,000 plus commission and interest costs. Dividends or interest earned on the shorted security belong to the person from whom you borrowed it. The broker can also demand that you return the shares at any time regardless of whether the price is up or down.

Rewards and Risks of Selling Short

Investors use short sales to make gains in a declining market or to hedge against losses in an investment. If you sell short and buy back at a lower price, you stand to make larger gains than if you had a long position in a security that declines in value. For example: you borrow 100 shares from a corporation, which has a market price of $35. You sell the 100 shares for $3,500. The price later falls to $25. You buy back 100 shares for $2,500. You have made a profit of $1,000 ($3,500 – $2,500).

As with any investment strategy, there's a downside. If you're incorrect, you may have to repurchase the borrowed security at a price higher than you sold it. In our previous example, if the price of the stock increases from $35 to $40 and you have to buy the shares back, you have to pay

$4,000 and lose $500. When you have a "short position" in a security, you are responsible for paying any dividends or interest it distributed to the investor you borrowed it from even though you did not receive it. The security can be called at anytime by your broker and you must return it immediately regardless of the market price.

An important thing to remember when selling short is that you have only a limited amount of money you can make if you're correct. However, your potential to lose money has no limits. This is true because the money you can make is restricted to the difference between the stock's current market price and the floor price for all securities or $0.00. Whereas, a security can hypothetically appreciate indefinitely. This means that when you sell short, your losses could accrue indefinitely if you do not close out the position.

You need a special brokerage account to take advantage of selling short. All orders to sell a security short must be placed in a short account. You must have margin privileges with your brokerage firm in order to have a short account. Since selling short requires that you borrow from your broker, you will need to establish credit with your broker and abide by the rules for borrowing against your account.

PUTTING IT ALL TOGETHER

The core objective of any investment program has to be the preservation of capital. Assets need to increase, not decrease in value. If they are used wisely, margin accounts can help you substantially increase the value of your portfolio. Here are a few thoughts to point you in the right direction:

- *Invest in companies with good earnings.* Stock prices almost always follow earnings. It's a "no brainer." If earnings are up, the price of a stock goes up. If earnings are down, the price of a stock goes down. If earnings show significant operational losses, watch out if you're holding onto that stock.

- *Be cautious of companies that are betting on the future.* Yes, they may take off but they may not and they're not worth betting margined money on. Make sure the news you read is "real" news and not "maybe" news.

- *Be careful of the "hot tips" you get and never bet margined money on a tip that you haven't thoroughly checked out.* Although most of them are given with good intentions, they are usually worthless.

- *When in doubt, don't touch your margin money.* Buy only when there is the highest likelihood that a stock will go up. Constantly look for opportunities to buy.

Using margin accounts to leverage your investment returns can make you a lot of money if you're careful and know what you're doing. Conversely, you can lose a lot of money if you buy on margin and the market crashes. For this reason, it is vitally important that you put stop-loss transactions in place on any stock that you buy on margin.

CHAPTER-RELATED WEB SITES

- Invest Wisely (www.sec.gov/consumer/inws.htm) is a feature educational article for new investors from the SEC.

- Investing Basics (www.aaii.com/invbas) offers feature articles about how to start successful investment programs, pick winning stocks, and how to evaluate your options.

- Money and Investing (www.eldernet.com/money.htm) offers tutorials and advice on investing in stocks, mutual funds, and bonds.

- For a crash investment course, take the interactive Money 101 investment seminar at www.money.com.

CHAPTER-RELATED WEB SITES, continued

 Morningstar's University (www.morningstar.com) offers a comprehensive investment education program.

 Money Central (www.investor.com) allows you to download information on stocks that you're interested in buying on margin. You can create your own screens that weed out stocks that don't meet your requirements.

Summary
and
Conclusions

THE MOONLIGHTER'S ONLINE TRADING BIBLE HAS PROVIDED YOU with lots of ideals and tools to help you become a successful online investor. In the beginning chapters, we emphasized the planning part of the process and what you need to know to make money in trading stocks online, one of the most exciting revelations of our time. We showed you how to find a quality low-cost online broker that you could trust to help get the job done.

Even when armed with all the tools and ideas that are in this book, you can still lose if your stock and fund selections perform poorly. That's why most of the chapters focused on how to find outstanding stocks and mutual funds that would make you lots of money. We showed you how to diversify your portfolio and suggested you consider international investment opportunities. You learned how margin accounts can be used to accelerate your returns if you know what you're doing.

INVEST ONLY IN WINNERS

There are thousands of ways to consistently make money in the stock market. One of the best ways is to only invest in top-performing stocks. Buy stocks that have low PE ratios, and that are financially rock solid, and have consistently risen in price. Great stocks typically rank in the top 10 percentile of their industries, and as industry leaders, they enjoy strong sales growth because their respective products and services are considered outstanding.

Don't rush out and buy the cheapest stock you can find. Owning 1,000 shares of Igotu.com at a dollar a share is not the same as owning ten shares of IBM at $100 a share. Although it may give you bragging power when you tell your friends you own 1,000 of shares of "this great company," you'll get it in the end. Focus first on quality stocks rather than price. A proven quality company is one that has performed well over time and has a strong leadership position in a growing industry.

HARNESS YOUR TIME

Always remember that the most significant success factor in any investment program is time. Get into an online stock investment game as soon as possible. Even a chimpanzee throwing darts at the Wall Street Journal to select stocks to buy would have averaged a ten percent return over the past ten years. If you wait to get started, you'll diminish the one factor (i.e., time) that can help you get ahead.

And, just because you're trading online doesn't mean you have to act like a "day trader" who's moving in and out of multiple stocks several times a day. Successful investing is a marathon and not a sprint. Conversely, the odds are that you'll make money if you buy value stocks today and hold on to them as long as they continue to show promise.

NEVER BE AFRAID TO SELL

If you're afraid to sell, you will end up with a bunch of losers in your portfolio, hoping that they will some day bounce back to what you once paid for the them. That way, you won't have to admit you made a mistake. However, your mistake is compounded by the fact that you have money tied up in negative returning assets and are therefore unable to take advantage of investing in profitable stocks. It's a double-edged sword.

Conversely, if you buy into a winning stock and based on your analysis, believe it has topped out, sell it and take your profits to the bank. Pat yourself on the shoulder. If it continues to climb after you sold it, so be it. Nobody, including every expert in the game, knows how to sell stock at its absolute peak. And, as Warren Buffet would say, "An investor who can always take profits to the bank will never go broke."

PAY ATTENTION TO DIVIDENDS

Ask your friends how they compute a stock's total return and they will almost always tell you it's based on the stock's price over a period of time. A stock that goes from $5 to $10 has a total return of 100 percent, right? Wrong. A stock's total return has two components: price appreciation and dividends. Dividends are often the forgotten heroes of many portfolios.

Dividends not only enhance a portfolio's return but serve as a hedge against bear markets. For example, if you buy a stock with a 6 percent dividend yield (there are plenty of them out there), you have already locked in a return that in many cases beats the bond market. Also, consider the fact that if a stock is paying a strong dividend yield, it is probably in a strong financial position.

I sincerely hope you enjoyed the book and wish you the best as an online trader. I hope you make a fortune. Make sure you have lots of fun along the way and never stop learning. Feel free to email me at any time (westpubs@cs.com) and share your thoughts about the exciting world of online trading.

—David E. Rye

The What Do You Know Quiz

TAKE THE "WHAT DO YOU KNOW" QUIZ TO HELP YOU DETERMINE what you know and may not know about investing in the stock market. That will allow you to concentrate on specific areas to not only improve your overall knowledge of the market, but to become a better trader as well.

1. Which of the following would you check out to track the performance of small-company stocks?
   a. The Wiltshire 5000 index
   b. The Russell 2000 index
   c. CBN Moneyline

2. A downward-sloping advance/decline line means:
   a. The market has bad breadth and more stocks are declining than advancing
   b. The market has good breadth because more stocks are advancing than declining
   c. The market has halitosis and needs a swig of Listerine

3. Diversifying your portfolio among a variety of different assets that don't all move in lockstep:
   a. Allows you to achieve a better balance between risk and reward
   b. Decreases the odds that your investments will all tank at once
   c. Both of the above

4. A bear market is typically defined as:
   a. A decline of 10 percent or more in the market value of a major stock index such as S&P's 500
   b. A decline of 20 percent or more in the market value of a major stock index such as S&P's 500
   c. What happens just after you move your money into stocks

5 An inverted yield curve is often a sign that:
   a. The economy is headed for a recession
   b. The economy is poised for robust growth
   c. Damn kids have been fooling around with the traffic signs

6. A tax-efficient fund is one that:
   a. Delivers its gains in dividend and capital-gains distributions
   b. Delivers its gains in share-price appreciation
   c. Delivers its gains without blabbing to the IRS

7. A study of more than 66,000 households with discount brokerage accounts found that investors who traded most frequently earned:
   a. The highest returns
   b. Average returns
   c. The lowest returns
   d. The undying affection of their brokerage firms

8. The statistical gauge that measures the degree to which two assets move in sync is:
   a. Coefficient of correlation
   b. Duration
   c. Moving average

9. When the price/earnings ratio for a stock is way above its historical average, it's a sign that:
   a. Investors are optimistic about the stock's prospects
   b. The market is going to crash soon
   c. Alan Greenspan is about to make another "irrational exuberance" speech

10. If a stock is trading at $10.50 a share but you want to buy it for $10.25 or less, you would give your broker a:
    a. Stop order
    b. Limit order
    c. Market order
    d. Restraining order

11. Value investors often look for stocks that trade:
    a. At high price/earnings ratios
    b. At low price/book value ratios

12. If the Investor Intelligence Sentiment index shows that 55 percent or more of investment advisers are bullish, it's a sign that:
    a. Stock prices are likely to surge to new highs
    b. Stock prices are likely to stagnate or even fall
    c. The other 45 percent of advisers are just being jerks

13. What is typically the main cause of a bear market?
    a. Bloated stock prices
    b. Rising interest rates
    c. Right-wing conspiracy

14. To get a sense of whether an advance or decline in a stock index is the beginning of a significant move, a breed of market watchers known as technical analysts will often:
    a. Plot the index against its moving average
    b. Pore over the annual reports of companies in the index
    c. Consult a Ouija board

15. Standard deviation is:
    a. The amount by which stock returns usually deviate from bond returns
    b. A measure of volatility that tells how much an investment's returns bounce around its average return
    c. An oxymoron. How can something be both standard and a deviation?

16. You can effectively build your own tax shelter by:
    a. Buying and holding growth stocks that pay dividends
    b. Buying and holding growth stocks that pay no dividends
    c. Buying a tax-shelter kit at Home Depot

17. Which of the following is often used to gauge the value of companies with large non-cash expenses such as depreciation?
    a. Price/earnings ratio
    b. Price/cash-flow ratio
    c. Price/book-value ratio

18. If a bond has a call feature, then:
    a. The issuer has the right to repay the bond's principal before its stated maturity date.
    b. The issuer has the right to extend the bond's maturity date.
    c. You have the right to call the issuer and complain if the bond goes into default.

19. S&P 500 stock index contains:
    a. The 500 U.S. stocks with the highest market values
    b. The 500 top-performing stocks in the U.S.

20. Interest and dividends earned by municipal bonds are exempt from federal income tax.
    a. True
    b. False

21. All else being equal, the lower a bond fund's average credit quality, the higher its yield.

a. True

b. False

22. Index funds:

a. Seek to track the investment returns of a specified stock or bond benchmark.

b. Try to beat the investment return of a specified stock or bond benchmark.

c. Buy only stocks in S&P's 500-stock index.

d. Seek to invest in the best performing sectors of the stock market

23. If interest rates declined, the price of a bond or bond fund generally would:

a. Increase

b. Decrease

c. Stay about the same

d. Interest rates have no effect on bond prices

24. Dollar-cost averaging is:

a. A strategy that entails buying low and selling high

b. A way to sell fund shares to minimize capital gains

c. An approach in which you invest the same amount of money in a stock or mutual fund at regular intervals

d. None of the above

25. If you own only U.S. stocks in your investment portfolio, you will reduce your overall risk by adding international stocks.

a. True

b. False

26. Which market benchmark or stock exchange is the best gauge of the performance of the entire U.S. stock market?

a. S&P 500 index market index

b. Wilshire 5000

c. Dow Jones industrial average

d. Nasdaq composite index

27. If you invest in a 401(k) plan at work, you are not eligible to contribute to an IRA.
    a. True
    b. False

28. How long must you hold a stock or mutual fund to receive the lowest capital-gains tax rate?
    a. More than one month
    b. More than six months
    c. More than one year
    d. More than five years

29. The long-term historical return on U.S. stocks has averaged:
    a. 5 percent a year
    b. 10 percent a year
    c. 19 percent a year
    d. 28 percent a year

30. Which of the following is not an attribute of mutual funds?
    a. Diversification
    b. Professional management
    c. Guaranteed return
    d. None of the above

31. If your investment returned 10 percent last year and inflation was 3 percent, your "real" return was:
    a. 3.3 percent
    b. 7 percent
    c. 13 percent
    d. 30 percent

32. A mutual fund that invests in government securities is guaranteed not to lose money.
    a. True
    b. False

33. The average stock mutual fund charges an annual expense ratio rang-
    ing from:
    a. 0.5 to 0.99 percent
    b. 1 to 1.49 percent
    c. 1.5 to 1.99 percent
    d. More than 2 percent

34. Contributions to a Roth IRA are tax deductible.
    a. True
    b. False

ANSWERS TO THE QUIZ

1. (b) consulting firm Frank Russell Co. tracks the small-cap market.

2. (a) The advance/decline line is a running tally of the difference
   between the number of stocks with price gains and those with losses.
   When falling stocks outnumber risers, the line points downward,
   which is considered a negative sign for the market.

3. (c) Diversification decreases the odds that your holdings will get clobbered all at once, and helps you get the maximum reward for the level
   of risk you're willing to take.

4. (b) A decline of 20 percent or more is a bear market. A drop of more
   than 10 percent, but less than 20 percent is considered a correction.

5. (a) An inverted yield curve, which is what you have when short-term
   treasury securities yield more than long-term ones. This usually occurs
   when the Federal Reserve pushes up short-term rates to slow the economy and stem inflation. That strategy can lead to recession.

6. (b) Unlike dividend and capital gains distributions, which are taxed
   yearly, share-price appreciation isn't taxed until you sell the fund.
   As a result, funds whose gains come from share-price buildup generate fewer tax bills, making them more tax-efficient.

7. (c) Researchers found that the most active traders earned seven percentage points a year less than the least active.

8. (a) The higher the correlation between two assets, the more they zig and zag in unison. So, for example, large-cap stocks have a higher correlation with small-cap stocks than with bonds.

9. (a) Above-average PE ratios indicate that investors are willing to pay more than usual for future corporate earnings, which means they're optimistic about stocks' prospects.

10. (b) A limit order may get you a stock below the prevailing price. But if no one meets your limit price, you won't get the stock at all.

11. (b) Price/book value is calculated by dividing a company's share price by its book value (assets minus liabilities) per share. The lower this ratio, the more assets you're getting for your buck.

12. (b) When 55 percent or more of advisers are bullish, market watchers take it as a sign that stock prices will likely fall. The theory is that a high percentage of bulls means most people have already put their money in stocks, leaving less cash on the sidelines that can drive up prices.

13. (b) Rising interest rates cause bear markets by raising borrowing costs for businesses (which hurts profits) and making interest-paying investments like bonds more attractive relative to stocks.

14. (a) A moving average is designed to dampen the effect of daily fluctuations in stock prices and help analysts get a fix on where the market is heading.

15. (b) Standard deviation measures volatility of returns. If a fund has a 12 percent average annual return and a standard deviation of 20 percent, two-thirds of its annual returns will fall between 32 percent and 8 percent, or 20 percentage points above or below the average.

16. (b) Growth stocks that pay no dividends offer a superior tax shelter since taxes can be as high as 39.6 percent on dividends, but no higher than 20 percent on long-term capital gains.

17. (b) Since non-cash expenses depress reported earnings, analysts often look to cash flow (earnings before deducting non-cash charges) to gauge the earning power of a company with large non-cash expenses.

18. (a) A call feature gives the issuer the right to repay, or call, the bond on certain dates prior to maturity.

19. (b) The S&P index committee chooses stocks they judge to be leading companies in leading industries and not necessarily the biggest or top performing.

20. (a) True

21. (a) True

22. (b) True

23. (a) Increase

24. (c) Strategy of investing the same amount at regular intervals

25. (a) True

26. (b) Wilshire 5000

27. (b) False

28. (c) More than one year

29. (b) 10 percent a year

30. (c) Guaranteed return

31. (b) 7 percent

32. (b) False

33. (c) 1.5 to 1.99 percent

34. (b) False

How Did You Score?

Give yourself three points for each correct answer and total your score to see how you measure up on the scale below.

96–102: Wow, you really know this stuff. Maybe you should be writing this book instead of reading it.

85–95: Terrific score. You've managed to learn quite a bit about investing. If it weren't for those questions on standard deviation and correlation, I bet you would have aced this quiz.

70–84: You've built a solid foundation of investing knowledge. But until you fill in a few remaining gaps, I suggest you exercise caution when making investment decisions.

50–69: You're obviously no Warren Buffet, but you still managed to answer at least half of the questions correctly. Work on the topics that tripped you up and you'll be in good shape.

Below 50: I'm not going to sugarcoat it. You flunked, but don't despair. Re-read this book and I'm sure you'll move up in the rankings. According to the SEC's Office of Investor Education and Assistance, an investors' ability to trade online, or offline for that matter, requires that you've done the necessary homework. Otherwise, you are flying blind.

Comprehensive Online Directory

ANNUAL REPORTS AND COMPANY PROFILES

To get a company's investment package, call them. You can get their phone number from Value Line, a magazine article, the Internet, or directory assistance. On the Web, try typing www.name of company.com to find the company's site. For instance, you'll find IBM at www.ibm.com and Ford at www.ford.com.

- Companies Online (www.companiesonline.com) provides links to more than 100,000 corporations with online presence. You enter the company's name and the search engine will find its Web site.

- Thompson Investor Net (www.thompsoninvest.com) covers over 7,000 indepth company reports that are updated twice a month.

- Best Calls (www.bestcalls.com) provides access to companies' quarterly earnings press conferences.

- Wall Research Net (www.wsrn.com) provides annual reports for more than 16,000 publicly traded companies.

- Investor's Relations Information Network (www.irin.com) offers over 2,500 company annual reports online.

- Public Register's Annual Report Service (www.prars.com) offers both online and hard copy annual reports.

ANALYSTS EVALUATIONS

Finding out what analysts are saying about a stock you're considering can help you determine if it's the right time to buy. Here are several sites that will get you the information you need:

- S&P Advisor Insight (www.advisorinsight.com) allows you to review S&P reports for the major stocks.

- Zacks Investment Research (www.zacks.com) reports on what analysts are saying about most of the stocks on the U.S. exchanges.

ASSOCIATIONS

Unfortunately, there are not many good national investment associations that cater to online investors. Here are two good ones to check out.

- The National Association of Investors Corporation (NAIC) is a national association with local chapters throughout the country. Its goal is to help investors develop a disciplined approach to successful investing. For more information, visit their Web site at www.investing.org.

- American Association of Individual Investors (www.aaii.org) offers a variety of valuable services to members, including local chapter meetings in the major metropolitan areas.

BONDS

Although we talked only briefly about bonds in the book, they can be an attractive investment alternative to stocks. Here are several sites that can get you started in the bond market:

- The Bond Market (www.bondcan.com) specializes in investing in Canadian bonds.

- Bonds Online (www.bondsonline.com) provides charts and historical data that compare the various bond market sectors.

- The Bond Market Association (www.bondmarkets.com) is loaded with information about thousands of bonds and their respective trading history.

BROKERS (ONLINE)

- Accutrade (www.accutrade.com) 800-494-8939

- American Express (www.americanexpress.com) 800-658-4677

- Ameritrade (www.ameritrade.com) 800-454-9272

- Brown & Co. (www.brownco.com) 800-822-2021

- CSFBdirect (www.CSFBdirect.com) 877-355-5557

- Datek (www.datek.com) 888-463-2835

- Discover Brokerage (www.discoverbrokerage.com) 800-688-3462

- E*Trade (www.etrade.com) 800-387-2331

- Fidelity (www.fidelity.com) 800-544-8666

- Muriel Siebert (www.msiebert.com) 800-872-0444

- National Discount Brokers (www.ndb.com) 800-888-3999

- Net Investor (www.netinvestor.com) 800-638-4250

- Quick & Reilly (www.quickwaynet.com) 800-837-7220

- Schwab (www.schwab.com) 800-435-4000

- Suretrade (www.suretrade.com) 800-394-1452

- Wall Street Access (www.wsaccess.com) 800-925-5782

- Waterhouse (www.tdwaterhouse.com) 800-934-4448

CHARTS AND COMPANY PROFILES

Always remember that a stock's chart is your friend and that a picture is worth 10,000 words. At a quick glance, a stock's chart can tell you not only where it has been historically but probably where it's going.

- *Smart Money* (www.smartmoney.com) offers free charts and quotes on all U.S. stocks and most funds. The Web site features company profile articles and timely comments on market trends.

- *Money* magazine's Web site (www.money.com) offers an excellent fund and stock charting service.

- Hoover's Online (www.stockscreener.com) provides information on over 8,000 companies.

- *Research Magazine* (www.researchmag.com) offers both a charting and company profile service.

DIRECT PUBLIC OFFERINGS

Direct public offers (DPOs) are programs where a company agrees to offer its stock directly to the public when it initially issues stock (IPO). The advantage to the shareholder is that they pay no broker fees. Check out these Web sites to learn more about DPOS.

- Direct Stock Market (www.dsm.com) provides information about companies that offer direct public offerings.

- Netstock Direct (www.netstockdirect.com) is an online source for purchasing stocks directly from a company.

DIVERSIFIED PLANNING

Diversifying your portfolio is the best way to insure you're covered when the segments of the market fluctuate in different directions. The following sites will help you put together a diversification plan that's right for you:

- Legg Mason (www.leggmason.com) provides an online questionnaire to help you develop a diversification plan.

- Frank Russell Company (www.russell.com) features a "Comfort Quiz" to help you allocate your investments.

- Fidelity's Asset Diversification Planner (www.fidelity.com) offers diversification advice, a risk questionnaire, and five model portfolios.

- The Intelligent Asset Allocator (www.efficientfrontier.com) offers comprehensive information on how to build a diversified portfolio.

DIVIDEND REINVESTMENT PROGRAMS

Dividend reinvestment programs (DRIPs) allow you to purchase shares of stock directly from participating companies without having to pay broker fees.

- DRIP Advisor (www.dripadvisor.com) lists most of the companies that offer DRIP programs.

- Netstock Direct (www.netstock.com) not only lists companies that offer DRIPs but its search engine will allow you to find companies within industries that interest you.

- Stock One (www.stock1.com) offers advice and suggestions on how to get started in DRIPs.

EARNINGS ESTIMATES

How do you find out what the experts estimate the earnings will be for a company that you want to invest in? The following Web site will help you find the answer:

- Zacks Investment Research (www.zacks.com) provides estimated earnings based on broker opinions.

ECONOMIC INFORMATION AND TRENDS

To find out how the economy is doing today and what it is projected to do in the future, check out these Web sites:

- Census Bureau (www.census.gov) provides information about industry statistics and general business conditions.

- STAT-USA (www.stat-usa.gov) is sponsored by the U.S. Department of Commerce and provides financial information about economic indicators, statistics, and economic news.

- The Bureau of Economic Analysis (www.bea.doc.gov) calculates and displays in its site economic indicators such as the gross domestic product and other regional, national, and international data.

EDUCATION

Over the past few years, significant improvements have been made in the online education investment field. It's still not great, but it's getting better. Check out these sites:

- Invest Wisely (www.sec.gov/consumer/inws.htm) is a feature educational article for new investors from the SEC.

- Investing Basics (www.aaii.com/invbas) offers feature articles about how to start successful investment programs, pick winning stocks, and how to evaluate your options.

- Money and Investing (www.eldernet.com/money.htm) offers tutorials and advice on investing in stocks, mutual funds, and bonds.

- Vanguard (www.vanguard.com) offers online courses that cover the fundamentals of investing in mutual funds.

- Bloomberg Personal Finance (www.bloomberg.com) offers online training when you click on the Bloomberg University module.

- For a crash investment course, take the interactive "Money 101" investment seminar at www.money.com.

- Morningstar's University (www.morningstar.com) offers a comprehensive investment education program.

- The Motley Fools at www.fool.com offer an investment seminar.

- The American Association of Individual Investors offers advice on funds and portfolio management at www.aaii.com.

- The Mutual Fund Education Alliance (www.mfea.com) is the trade association for no-load funds and offers advice on how to select funds.

- Investor Guide (www.investorguide.com) features over 1,000 answers to frequently asked questions.

EXCHANGES

Both the Nasdaq and New York Stock Exchange offer a wide variety of appealing investment features.

- American Stock Exchange (www.amex.com).

- The National Association of Securities Dealers (www.nasdaq.com).

- The New York Stock Exchange (www.nyse.com).

EXPERTS ADVICE

In-depth research and savvy advice from the Wall Street experts are available to you at no charge if you know where to look. Here are several great sites to get you started:

- Merrill Lynch (www.ml.com) allows you to download research reports by such well-known experts as Merrill's chief economist Bruce Steinberg. Click on the research tab at the right of the main menu to find the reports.

- Morgan Stanley (www.morganstanley.com) provides free advice from the firm's top names like Barton Biggs, Byron Wien, and Stephen Roach. Click on the "Global Strategy Bulletin."

- Paine Webber (www.painewebber.com) provides specific analytical reports by company even if you're not a customer. The firm's top-ranked strategists produce the reports.

- Raymond James (www.raymondjames.com) was recently named by *The Wall Street Journal* as one of the top stock pickers in the country. A weekly commentary about the market and the economic outlet plus other great features are available at his site.

FINANCIAL TOOLS AND CALCULATORS

The Web sites listed in this section offer a multitude of solution-oriented features.

- Altamira Resource Center's Net Worth Calculator (www.altramira.com) helps you determine your current net worth and track changes over time.

- The Financial Center (www.financialcenter.com) has a "Savings" icon. Click on it and then click the calculator titled, "What will it take to become a millionaire?" Enter the required data and click "Calculate." The results show how much you need to invest today to be a millionaire in the future.

- Charles Schwab (www.schwab.com) helps you develop a financial plan with his online calculators, tools, and advice.

FUNDAMENTAL ANALYSIS

Visit the following Web sites to find the fundamental data you need before buying a stock.

- J&E Research (www.jeresearch.com) specializes in financial modeling, research, and analysis. Their stock analysis program has an Excel spreadsheet that you can use to complete the fundamental analysis of any stock.

- Financial Engines (www.financialengines.com) is a site developed by Nobel prize-winning economist William Sharpe.

- 411 Stocks (www.411stocks.com) offers simple one-stop shopping with lots of fundamental information about stocks including pricing data, news, charting, financial statements, and more.

THE MOONLIGHTER'S SHORT-TERM TRADING BIBLE

GAMES

If you're interested in testing your skills as an online trader with Monopoly money, check out these adult investment game sites:

- Hedge Hog Competition (www.marketplayer.com) allows participants to build on a $1 million stock portfolio as they compete against other contestants.

- Virtual Stock Exchange (www.virtualstockexchange.com) is a stock simulation game that allows you to trade shares just as you would in a real brokerage account.

INDEXED FUNDS

There are literally hundreds of mutual funds that index every segment of the market. Here are two of the better ones to consider:

- Fidelity Spartan Market Index Fund mirrors the S&P 500 index (800-544-8888).

- T. Rowe Price Equity Index Fund mirrors the S&P 500 (800-638-5660).

INDUSTRY INFORMATION

These sites allow you to compare the performance of investment candidates to their industry.

- ABC News (www.abcnews.com) features articles on current industry news and market expert commentary.

- Hovers (www.stockscreen.com) offers excellent information on industries at their Web site.

- *Research Magazine* (www.researchmag.com) features "Industry Spotlights" with indepth industry analysis.

- American Society of Association Executives (www.asaenet.org) provides high-quality industry overviews including briefing on industry trends.

INTERNATIONAL INVESTING

The Internet is a rich source of information on foreign companies. Three particularly useful Web sites are www.bankofny.com, www.jpmorgan.com, and www.global-investor.com. Here are two additional sites to visit:

- Worldly Investor (www.worldlyinvestor.com) is the international investor's forum. They featured a daily column along with international trends in stocks, mutual funds, and bonds.

- FT Market Watch (www.ftmarketwatch.com) provides up-to-the minute news on offshore companies and foreign markets.

INVESTMENT STRATEGIES

Developing an investment strategy that's right for you is a critical component in your overall investment strategy. Here are two sites that will help you get started:

- Investor Home at (www.investorhome.com) provides information about the investment process and how to bulletproof your portfolio.

- Bank of America (www.bankamerica.com) offers a 12 question survey. Enter your answers and the online calculator suggests an investment strategy that suits your current needs and situation.

MAGAZINES

Several excellent investment magazines on the market cover everything from expert advice to hot stock and mutual fund tips. Most of the better magazines also support Web sites that you can review before you subscribe.

- *Forbes* (www.forbes.com) features articles on personal finance, investing, and special market reports as well as stock and fund quotes.

- *Newsweek Online* (www.newsweek.com) not only covers general news but also the latest news about the stock market.

- *Smart Money* is the "Wall Street Journal Magazine of Personal Business" and it's excellent. For subscription information, call 800-444-4204 or subscribe online (www.smartmoney.com).

- *Worth* magazine columnists are second to none, including Peter Lynch's column, and the magazines regular features are dynamite. For subscription information, call 800-777-1851.

- *Kiplinger's* magazine (www.kiplinger.com) has a broader scope than either *Smart Money* or *Worth*. Instead of talking just about investing, *Kiplinger's* moves into other issues of personal business such as credit card spending, loans, college tuition, and vacation planning. For subscription information, call 800-544-0155.

- *Money* (www.money.com) magazine does an excellent job of keeping its readers informed about what's happening in the mutual fund market. You can subscribe online.

- *Business Week* (www.businessweek.com) is available online to all of its subscribers.

MARKET INDEXES

Market indexes are relied upon by financial analysts and investors alike to gauge the direction of a particular market segment. The following are the most popular indexes:

- Dow Jones Industrial Average (Dow) is one of the most closely followed indexes that's made up of 30 premier companies on the New York Stock Exchange. The sum of their respective stock prices is reported throughout the day to reflect on the state of the overall market.

- The S&P 500 index contains 500 of the largest companies' stocks from the New York, Nasdaq, and American exchanges. The index is derived from the market capitalization of its component stocks rather than price, which is the case with the Dow.

- S&P 400 and S&P 600 are two indexes that were designed to track smaller companies than those in the S&P 500.

- New York Stock Exchange Composite Index tracks all stocks traded on the NYSE. Check out the exchange's Web site at www.nyse.com.

- American Stock Exchange Market Value Index tracks roughly 800 companies that trade on the American Stock Exchange. See the exchange's Web site at www.amex.com.

MUTUAL FUNDS: GENERAL INFORMATION

There are almost as many mutual funds to choose from as there are stocks. The following Web sites will help you find the best ones.

- Invest-O-Rama (www.investorama.com) is an extensive, well-organized site that lists fund-related web links.

- Morningstar (www.morningstar.com) is a premier site providing all kinds of information about mutual funds.

- MaxFunds (www.maxfunds.com) specializes in offering news and statistics on small and little-known funds.

- CBS Market Watch (www.marketwatch.com) provides articles, news, and market data on funds. Click the Super Fund icon to see the fund information.

MUTUAL FUNDS: SCREENING

There are an infinite number of ways to screen through the mass of mutual funds that are on the market to find the one fund that's right for you. Checkout the Web sites that we cover in this section to learn how to "fine tune" your screening criteria.

- Find a Fund (www.findafund.com) publishes a list of the weekly top performing funds and lots of other fund selection information.

- *Mutual Fund Magazine* (www.mfmag.com) offers feature articles and tools for selecting funds that are right for you.

- Mutual Funds Interactive (www.fundsinteractive.com/ profiles.html) provides recommendations, analysis tools, and profiles of many of the top funds.

- Morningstar (www.morningstar.net) evaluates and ranks over 7,000 funds.

- Quicken (www.quicken.com) offers a mutual fund screener. Click on the Mutual Fund Finder to get there.

- Quote.com Mutual Fund Screen (www.quote.com/screening) offers a fund screener where you can also find out how different funds did in bull or bear markets.

- *Research Magazine* (www.researchmag.com) allows you to search for funds based on 40 search variables.

- *Smart Money* magazine (www.smartmoney.com) provides an easy search tool for finding the top 25 funds in specialty areas.

MUTUAL FUNDS: ORDERING ONLINE

Most of the major funds allow you to order their funds online or over the phone. Obviously, you will need to set-up an account before you can do that. Here are several Web sites to review:

- Fidelity (www.fidelity.com) offers direct purchase options online for their funds and their competitors' funds.

- Vanguard (www.Vanguard.com) offers direct purchase plans for their funds.

- T. Rowe Price (www.Troweprice.com) offers direct purchase plans for their funds.

- Mutual Funds Online (www.mfmag.com) provides access to fund family guides, performance rankings, and a weekly email newsletter.

- Strong Automatic Investment Plan (www.strongfunds.com/ strong/learningcenter/aipbroch.htm) has an automatic investment program for many of their funds.

- Janus (www.janus.com) has a family of no-load funds that you can purchase or apply for online.

- Vanguard (www.vanguard.com) has over 80 funds that you can purchase direct from the company.

NEWS ONLINE

One of the biggest advantages of getting your news online is that you can go to the specific news sector (i.e., Market Watch) without having to thumb through a bunch of paper to get there. Here are several excellent sites to try:

- ABC News (www.abcnews.com) features business and industry news and market commentary.

- Bloomberg Personal Finance (www.bloomberg.com) is loaded with timely business news, data, and an analysis of the market.

- CBS Market Watch (www.marketwatch.com) offers feature articles on the market and breaking news targeted at investors.

- Company Sleuth (www.companysleuth.com) will send you news updates each day on companies you're following via e-mail.

NEWSLETTERS

If you're short on time and willing to pay someone else to search for great stock bargains, then subscribing to a newsletter may be for you. Most of them will send you a free copy to check out before you subscribe.

- Newsletter Access (www.newsletteraccess.com/subject/invest.html) offers a searchable directory for specific types of newsletters.

- First Capital Corporation (www.firstcap.com) offers two free newsletters. *Market Timing* presents a short-term technical approach for the stock and bond markets. *Global Viewpoint* provides a weekly technical analysis of world markets.

- *Dick Davis Digest* is full of information. Companies covered in each issue are listed alphabetically on the first page, making it easy for you to monitor the latest on stocks you own or are watching. For subscription information, call 800-654-1514.

- *John Dessauer's Investor's World* is a good general-purpose newsletter that discusses global investment issues and stock recommendations. For subscription information, call 301-424-3700.

- *Louis Navellier's MPT Review* publishes performance numbers on hot stocks. It is one of the top-performing newsletters around, listing hundreds of volatile growth stocks from which to choose. For subscription information, call 800-454-1395.

- *The Neat Sheet* lists hot stocks to watch and caters to people who do not have a lot of time to research and monitor stocks. Subscribers also receive a straight-shooting annual report. For subscription information, call 800-339-5671 or visit their Web site at www.neatmoney.com.

- *Louis Rukeyser's Wall Street* is one of the best investment newsletters around. It's a good balance between Dessauer's conversational letters and the hard data contained in other newsletters. For subscription information, call 800-892-9702.

- Standard & Poor's publishes the *Outlook* weekly. It is one of the most widely read investment newsletters. For subscription information, call 800-852-1641.

- *Outstanding Investor Digest* is a collection of the best ideas from the most successful investors. For subscription information, call 212-777-3330.

- *The Red Chip Review* is a comprehensive small-cap investment publication. For more information, call 800-733-2447 or visit their Web site at www.redchip.com.

- Value Line publishes the premier stock-research tool, *The Value Line Investment Survey* covering over 1,700 companies. Almost everything you could want to know about each company is condensed to a single page. For information, call 800-634-3583.

- Standard & Poor's Stock Guide is a professional publication that lists vital information about stocks. For more information, call 800-221-5277.

NEWSPAPERS

Financial newspapers are still a way of life in the stock market's paper-oriented world, although some of them are beginning to migrate over to the online world. Here's a rundown of the best papers:

- *The Wall Street Journal* is the Big Kahuna among investment newspapers, although its authority isn't as unquestioned as it used to be. For subscription information, call 800-778-0840 or visit their Web site at www.wsj.com.

- *Investor's Business Daily* is a great financial newspaper that publishes important information to help determine the value of a stock. For subscription information, call 800-831-2525 or visit their Web site at www.investors.com.

- *Financial Times* (www.ft.com) provides special reports on the market and the different industry sectors.

- *News Page* (www.newspage.com) allows you to customize daily news abstracts it sends to your e-mail address.

- *The New York Times* (www.nytimes.com) provides a business section that includes quotes and charts, a portfolio management tool, and breaking business news.

- *USA Today* (www.usatoday.com) features a money section that includes investment articles and news, economic information, and information on industry groups.

PORTFOLIO MANAGEMENT TOOLS

There are several portfolio management tools available at the following Web sites:

- Morningstar (www.Morningstar.com) provides a portfolio setup menu that is easy to use.

- Quicken (www.Quicken.com) offers a variety of financial tools including an excellent portfolio management program.

- Reuters Money Net (www.moneynet.com/home/moneynet/homepage/homepage.asp) has a wealth of financial data and one of the best portfolio management programs on the Web.

- Stock Point (www.stockpoint.com) offers a free personal portfolio-tracking program.

- Financial Portfolio (www.finportfolio.com) tells you how to construct your portfolio to meet your financial goals and evaluates your investments to determine how much you should buy to keep your portfolio in balance.

QUOTES (STOCKS AND MUTUAL FUNDS)

The Internet provides several quote servers that provide real-time and delayed quotes on stocks, mutual funds, and bonds.

- Individual Investor Online (www.iionline.com) offers delayed quotes, stock prospecting tools and screens, portfolio management tools, and financial news.

- Microsoft Investor (www.investor.msn.com) has a free stock ticker that you can personalize along with portfolio tracking tools.

- Personal Wealth (www.personalwealth.com) features quotes and research along with expert advice.

- Data Broadcasting Online (www.dbc.com) can retrieve up to several ticker symbols at one time.

- PC Quote (www.pcquote.com) provides current stock prices, a portfolio tracker, company profiles, and broker recommendations.

- American Stock Exchange (www.amex.com) offers quoting services on their Web site for stocks that are traded on its exchange.

- The National Association of Securities Dealers (www.nasdaq.com) offers quoting services for stocks that are traded on its exchange.

- The New York Stock Exchange (www.nyse.com) offers quoting services on their Web site for stocks that are traded on its exchange.

RETIREMENT PLANNING

To bone up on the basics of retirement planning, consult these Web sites:

- Hovers (www.stockscreen.com) provides a special module for retirement planning.

- Money Central (www.moneycentral.com) walks you through the process of setting up a retirement plan, including calculating your living expenses and determining your income requirements.

- Schwab Investor Profile (www.schwab.com) offers an investor's profile questionnaire that matches you to one of six retirement-oriented portfolios.

SEARCH AND SCREENING TOOLS

There are over 18,000 stocks and mutual funds to choose from, a number that is overwhelming to most investors. Fortunately, there are several excellent tools on the Internet that will help you substantially cut that number down to get at the few stocks and funds that are of interest to you.

- *Smart Money* magazine (www.smartmoney.com) offers an excellent "search and find" tool for quickly finding the "Top 25 Funds."

- Hover's Stock Screener (www.stockscreener.com) allows you to enter up to 20 variables for selecting stocks. The results are then sorted and displayed alphabetically.

- Daily Stocks (www.dailystocks.net) has an advance stock screen that allows you to enter important criteria to select stocks that meet your needs.

- Vector Quest (www.eduvest.com) features a database to help you find stocks that meet your selection criteria.

- Market Guide (www.marketguide.com) allows you to screen for stocks by using any of 20 variables.

- IQ Net Basic Stock Scan (www.siliconinvestor.com/help/iqc/) allows you to use 12 variables to screen for stocks.

- MSN Investors (www.investor.msn.com) shows you how to use 12 pre-built stock screens and how to set-up your own screens.

- American Association of Individual Investors (www.aaii.org) has a downloadable library of stock screening software for members.

- Quicken (www.quicken.excite.com/investments/stocks/search/) has pre-built screens for stock searches.

- Money Central (www.investor.com) allows you to download information on stocks that you're interested in buying. You can create your own screens that weed out stocks you have no interest in owning.

TAX ASSISTANCE

If you're struggling with taxes and the preparation of your return, theses sites can help:

- Internal Revenue Service (www.fourmilab.ch/ustax/ustax.html) enables you to access the complete text of the U.S. Internal Revenue Code.

- Secure Tax (www.irs.ustreas.gov) is a well-organized tax guide that allows you to print out tax forms.

TECHNICAL ANALYSIS

Technical analysis is what you use to determine when to buy and when to sell based on a stock's indicators. Here are several Web sites to help you get through the process:

- Quicken (www.quicken.com/investments) has an extensive investment section that covers stocks, mutual funds, and bonds.

- Flex Trader (www.flextrader.com) is one of the best sites to get a quick look at a stock's technical outlook. It provides you with a rundown on a variety of indicators.

- Stock Trader (www.stocktrader.com) is an online brokerage firm with excellent technical analysis tools.

- Equis International (www.equis.com) offers an excellent technical analysis program that you purchase. Check out their latest prices and see a demo of their system on their Web site.

● ● ●

The author wishes to thank the following companies that allowed us to feature their Web screens throughout this book:

- Compuserve (www.compuserve.com)

- Online Investors (www.investortoolbox.com)

- *Smart Money* Magazine (www.smartmoney.com)

- *Money* Magazine (www.money.com)

- Investors Business Daily (www.investors.com)

- Fidelity Investments (www.fidelity.com)

Glossary
of
Terms

American Stock Exchange (AMEX). A stock exchange whose companies are generally smaller than those traded on the New York Stock Exchange. The American Stock Exchange is located in downtown Manhattan.

Ask Price. The price at which a security is being offered for sale. If you are buying, you want to know the asked price.

Asset Allocation. The process of deciding how to divide your money among the three types of asset classes: stocks, bonds, and cash equivalents. How you make this decision is determined by your tolerance for risk and your time horizon.

Asset Allocation Fund. A mutual fund that features a mix of stocks, bonds, and cash equivalents to meet a specific growth objective.

Automatic Investment Plan (AIP). An agreement between you and a brokerage firm in which you authorize regular investments to be made through payroll deductions or automatic transfers from your checking account.

Automatic Reinvestment. An agreement by which all dividends produced by your investments are reinvested into your account and used to buy more shares of the same or another investment.

Back-End Load. A charge for redeeming your shares within the first few years. It is also called a contingent deferred sales charge because it's reduced with each passing year.

Balanced Fund. A mutual fund that attempts to produce both income and growth from a mix of stocks, bonds, and cash equivalents.

Bear Market. A declining market, in which prices are falling because more people want sell than to buy.

Beta Coefficient. The ratio between the volatility of a stock or mutual fund's price and the volatility of the market in general. If the beta of a stock is greater than one, the stock is expected to rise or fall more than the market. If the beta is below one, the stock typically moves up and down less than the market as a whole. The S&P 500 index has a beta of one. Conservative investors typically consider investing in stocks that have a beta lower than one.

Bid and Ask. The buy and sell prices for securities, representing the spread in the market. You buy at the ask, and sell at the bid.

Bid Price. The highest price anyone is willing to pay for the security at a given time. This is important to know when you are selling.

Big-Cap Stock. A stock with a large number of shares outstanding. Microsoft, IBM, and AT&T are considered big-cap stocks.

Blue-Chip Stock. A nationally known, public company that has a longstanding reputation for quality and good fundamentals, such as earnings and profitability.

Bond. An IOU that represents a loan agreement between the issuer as borrower and the investor as lender. Specified interest is paid periodically and the principal amount is repaid at final maturity.

Bonds (Government). A bond issued by the U.S. Treasury or other agency. Everyone views U.S. government securities as the safest investments.

Bond Maturity. The lifetime of a bond, concluding when the final payment of that obligation is due.

Broker Dealer. A securities firm that sells mutual funds or other securities.

Brokerage Account. An account with a brokerage firm that allows you to buy and sell securities.

Bull Market. A rising market, in which prices are going up because more people want to buy than sell. A bullish investor believes that prices are going up and buys aggressively in anticipation of a market advance.

Business Cycle. A recurring pattern of economic expansion (recovery) and contraction (recession) with effects on inflation, growth, and employment.

Buy-and-Hold. An investing strategy that encourages investing for the long term by buying and then holding, rather than selling based on the market's day-to-day ups and downs. Buying and then trying to sell based on the movement of the market is the opposite investment strategy and is called market timing.

Capital Appreciation. The growth of the principal of your investments.

Capital Gain. The profit you receive when you sell an investment for more than you paid for it. Capital gains are taxable income and must be reported to the IRS on your tax return.

Capital Gains Distribution. A payment you receive when your mutual fund makes a profit by selling some of the securities in its portfolio. Capital gains distributions are usually made annually.

Capital Growth. An increase in the market value of a security, as reflected by the appreciation of the security's net asset value per share. Capital growth and income are the two major long-term goals of mutual funds.

Capital Loss. The amount of money you lose when you sell an investment for less than you paid. Capital losses may be deducted from your annual income and must be reported on your tax return.

Capital Return. The capital gain or loss realized from the market appreciation or depreciation of your investment. For example, if you purchased stock for $1,000 and sold it for $ 1,500, your capital gain would be $500.

Capitalization. For a specific company, capitalization is the total stock market value of all shares of that company's stock.

Cash Account. A brokerage account in which transactions are settled on a cash basis.

Certificate of Deposit (CD). A type of investment made with a financial institution, such as a bank or savings and loan. You deposit a specified amount for a specified period of time, at a preset, fixed interest rate. CDs are FDIC insured.

Channel Lines. On a stock chart, channel lines are determined by drawing a straight line connecting three of the price peaks and a somewhat parallel line connecting three of the price lows during the same period, usually covering a couple of months to help determine how a stock has performed over time.

Closed-End Mutual Fund. A mutual fund that distributes a fixed number of shares that trade much like stocks. They are usually listed on a major exchange, and they may trade in the market at a premium or discount to net asset value (NAV).

Commission. The fee paid to a brokerage firm for executing a trade.

Commodities. Goods such as agricultural products like wheat or pork bellies, or metals, are traded on a separate commodities exchange. Commodity contracts state a future date of delivery or receipt of a certain amount of the product. Speculators generally invest in these contracts at a price that they hope they can turn into a profit when the actual commodities are delivered.

Common Stock. Securities that represent an ownership interest in a corporation. The difference between common and preferred stock is that holders of preferred stock usually receive preferential treatment. For example, dividends must be paid on preferred stock, while dividend payment on common stock is optional.

Commission. The fee paid to a broker for purchasing or selling on your behalf.

Compounding. The growth that results from income being reinvested. Compound growth has a snowball effect because both the original investment and the income from that investment are reinvested.

Consumer Price Index. The measurement of change in consumer prices calculated monthly by the U.S. Bureau of Labor Statistics.

Contrarian Indicators. Specific psychological indicators used by investors who subscribe to contrarian strategies. Historically, when these indicators reach one extreme or another, they overshadow contrary market activity.

Cost Basis. An investment's original cost. This number, which is used for tax purposes, includes any dividends that have been reinvested and any capital gains distributions.

Country Risk. The potential for fluctuation in the price of a stock sold in a foreign country. Fluctuations may happen for a variety of reasons such as political or financial events.

Credit Rating. Evaluation of debt securities' credit risk, or likelihood of default determined by rating services such as Moody's Investors Service and Standard & Poor's Corporation.

Credit Risk. The possibility that the issuer of a bond (the borrower) will fail to repay the principal or interest owed on a bond, either at the agreed-upon time or at all (default).

Currency Risk. The possibility that the price in dollars of an international stock may fluctuate as a result of changing currency exchange rates.

Current Yield. The amount of annual interest on a bond divided by the amount paid for it, expressed as a percentage. For example, if you receive $80 a year from a bond that has a current price of $900, the current yield is 8.9 percent ($80 divided by $900).

Custodial Account. An account set up and managed by an adult for the benefit of a minor. It is set up in the name of a child, with a parent or trustee as custodian. Assets placed in the account are considered an irrevocable gift and belong solely to the child.

Day Order. An order to buy or sell a security that remains valid until executed or canceled by the customer. At the day's market close, if the order has not been executed or canceled, it is canceled automatically.

Default. Failure of a bond issuer to make timely payments of interest and principal as they come due.

Defined Benefit Plan. A company retirement plan in which the employee, after retirement, receives a fixed amount of money on a regular basis from the employer (i.e., a pension).

Defined Contribution Plan. A company retirement plan in which an individual's retirement benefit is based on the amount contributed to the employee and the employer. Defined contribution plans include 401(k) or 403(b) plans, in which the employee elects to defer salary into the plan.

Discount Broker. A brokerage firm that executes orders to buy and sell at commission rates that are lower than those of a full commission brokerage firm.

Diversification. The allocation of investment money among multiple investments to spread risk so that you own a mixture of different securities. Diversification is important to help cushion you against an unexpected price decline of any one or a few of your investments.

Dividend. The part of the income earned by a company issuing stock that is distributed to shareholders.

Dividend Reinvestment Program (DRP). The automatic reinvestment of your dividends from a stock into more shares of that stock.

Dollar Cost Averaging. An installment-purchase technique that involves investing a fixed amount of money in stocks or mutual fund shares at regular intervals (i.e., monthly or quarterly), rather than all at once. The objective is to buy fewer shares when prices are high and more shares when they are low.

Dow Jones Industrial Average. One of the most commonly used measurements of the U.S. stock market. The Dow Jones Industrial Average was created by Charles Dow and Eddie Jones, who started publishing *The Wall Street Journal* in 1889.

Earnings. A company's revenue after related costs and expenses have been deducted.

Earnings Per Share (EPS). A company's net income, minus preferred dividends, divided by its number of common shares outstanding.

EDGAR. An acronym for Electronic Data Gathering Analysis and Retrieval, an online service of the SEC (wwwsec.gov). It offers information about specific companies, including financial sheets that show net income, gross profit, debt, and acquisitions.

Emerging Markets Fund. A mutual fund that invests chiefly in developing economies. These funds are often volatile, and their values can fluctuate substantially.

Employee Stock Ownership Plan (ESOP). A company retirement plan that invests in and pays benefits in the form of company stock instead of cash contributions.

Equity. Another name for stock. Also, the money value of a property or of an interest in a property in excess of all claims or liens against it.

Equity Income Fund. A mutual fund that pursues current income by investing at least 65 percent of its assets in dividend-paying equity securities.

Ex-Dividend. For stocks, the period between the announcement of a dividend and payment of that dividend. When a stock is trading ex-dividend, new buyers do not receive the dividend.

Exhaustion Gap. A technical term describing how a stock's price opens up on a gap from the prior day's high close. This usually indicates the last stage of a stock's move after the stock has had an extended price advance over several months.

Expense Ratio. For mutual funds, the percentage of a fund's average net assets that are used to pay fund expenses. This percentage accounts for management and administrative fees.

Face Value. The value appearing on the face of a bond, indicating the principal amount that the issuer will pay when the bond matures and the amount on which interest is calculated. Face value is not an indication of market value.

Family of Funds. Group of mutual funds operated by a single investment management company or brokerage house. Shareholders in one of the funds can usually switch their money into any of the family's other funds, sometimes at no charge.

FDIC. An acronym for the Federal Deposit Insurance Corporation, a U.S. government agency that insures cash deposits, including certificates of deposit that have been placed in member institutions, for up to $100,000 per institution.

Fixed-Income Investment. An investment that produces a constant rate of interest income, even if the market value of the principal amount changes. Most fixed-income securities produce a steady stream of semiannual interest payments.

403(b) Plan. A qualified retirement plan designed for nonprofit organizations. Employers can match some or all employee contributions.

Front-End Load. A sales commission, or load, that you pay when you purchase shares of some mutual funds. It can be as high as 8.5 percent of the purchase amount ($85 on a $1,000 buy-in) but is more typically 4 to 6 percent.

Fund Family. A group of mutual funds from the same organization. Investing in funds from the same fund family usually gives you exchange privileges between the funds, and you receive one statement for all of the funds in the family.

Fundamental Analysis. The numbers and statistics behind each stock. Fundamental analysis evaluates a company's earnings, sales, return on equity, profit margins, balance sheet, and share of market as well as a company's products, management, and industry conditions. Fundamental analysis determines the quality and attractiveness of a stock.

Futures Trading. A highly speculative and risky endeavor that should not be undertaken without a solid understanding of the marketplace and strong money management techniques. Futures are contracts betting on the future delivery of a specific product at a certain time and price.

Gap (in Price). Denotes a day where the stock opens and trades several points above or below the previous day's trading range. It can be identified on a daily chart of a stock's price changes.

Ginnie Mae. The nickname for the federally backed debt securities issued by the Government National Mortgage Association. Ginnie Maes represent a pool of mortgages, and investors receive the homeowners' payments of interest and principal.

Global Fund. A mutual fund that invests in both U.S. and non-U.S. companies. Typically 20 to 50 percent of the money is in U.S. equities. By contrast, an international fund invests only in foreign companies.

Good-Till-Canceled (GTC). A limit order that a customer places with a brokerage firm to buy or sell stock; it remains valid until executed or canceled by the customer.

Gross National Product (GNP). The total value of goods and services produced in the U. S. economy over a given period. The GNP growth rate is a key indicator of the status of the economy.

Growth and Income Fund. A mutual fund that seeks both capital appreciation (growth) and current income. Stocks are selected based on both their appreciation potential and their ability to pay dividends.

Growth Fund. A fund whose main objective is capital appreciation rather than income. Growth funds buy mostly stocks that are expected to increase steadily in value over time. Current income is a secondary concern, if a concern at all.

Growth Stock. The stock of a company that has previously seen rapid growth in revenue or earnings and is expected to see similar growth beyond the short term. Growth stocks generally pay relatively low dividends and sell at a relatively high price, considering their earnings and book value.

Hedge. A defensive investment strategy often involving the buying or selling of options, to offset possible losses and thereby reduce risk.

Income Fund. A mutual fund that seeks current income over capital growth, often by investing in bonds and high-yielding stocks.

Index. A group of securities considered yardsticks of market behavior. Well-known market indexes include the S&P 500 Index, the Dow Jones Industrial Average, and the Schwab 1000.

Index Mutual Fund. A mutual fund that seeks to replicate the performance of an established index. Investing in an index fund gives you a way to participate in an overall market while diversifying your portfolio.

Inflation Risk. The possibility that increased inflation will increase the cost of living, and reduce or eliminate a specific investment's returns.

Institutional Investors. Mutual funds, banks, pension funds, and insurance companies engaged in investing. They are responsible for most of the trading that occurs in the market and their impact on both an individual stock's price movement as well as the movement of the general market is tremendous.

Institutional Sponsorship. Refers to the shares of a company owned by an institution. The largest sources of demand for stocks are mutual funds and other institutional buyers. It is important to have institutional support behind the stock you're thinking about purchasing.

Interest. Payments made to compensate an investment at a fixed percentage rate during each year the investment is owned. For bonds, payments are usually made semiannually.

International Fund. A mutual fund that invests only in foreign companies and holds no stock in U.S. companies (as opposed to a global fund, which invests in both U.S. and non-U.S. companies, with typically 20 to 50 percent of the money in U.S. equities).

Intra-Day High and Low Price. This represents a day's price action in terms of three variables. The top of the bar signifies the highest price the stock traded for the day; this is the intra-day high price. The bottom of the bar marks the low price of the day; this is the intra-day low price. The horizontal intersecting slash shows where the stock closed for the day.

IPO (Initial Public Offering). A private company whose shares are being offered to the public for the first time. Also called a "new issue."

IRA (Individual Retirement Account). A retirement account that provides tax benefits. The money you invest in an IRA is tax-deferred, meaning that you don't pay taxes on it until you withdraw it during your retirement.

IRA Rollover. A tax-free transfer of assets from one qualified plan to another. Also called a "conduit IRA."

Keogh Plan. An employer-sponsored retirement plan for self-employed people. It requires significantly more paperwork than an IRA and is more complex to understand and manage. You may want to meet with a financial adviser to discuss Keogh plans in detail.

Large Capitalization Stock. The stock of a company with a market value of over $10 billion. Large-cap companies are well established, with solid track records of steady growth and dividend payments.

Limit Order. An order to buy or sell a security at a specified price or better. A limit order to buy sets a maximum purchase price. A limit order to sell sets a minimum sale price.

Liquid Investment. An investment that can be easily converted to cash. How quickly you can convert an investment into cash is called liquidity.

Load. Commission or sales charge for buying fund shares through a broker, financial planner, or insurance agent. Some funds that sell directly to the public also charge loads. Funds that do not are called no-load funds. A charge imposed when you sell shares is called a back-end load or exit fee.

Load Fund. A mutual fund that assesses a sales charge or commission.

Long-term Capital Gain. A profit you make after selling a stock or mutual fund that you have owned for more than one year.

Management Fee. Charge against investor assets for managing the portfolio of a mutual fund. The fee is a fixed percentage of the fund's asset value, typically 2 percent or less per year, and is disclosed in the fund's prospectus.

Management Ownership. Percent of common stock which is owned by the company's management; a higher percentage generally assumes an increased level of commitment.

Margin Account. A brokerage trading account that allows you to use borrowed money from the brokerage firm when purchasing stocks.

Market Bottom. Phase that refers to the overall general market making a low point and then turning around for a period of improvement.

Market Timing. A strategy of buying or selling securities, including mutual fund shares, to take advantage of or reduce one's exposure to anticipated changes in market conditions. For example, fund shareholders might switch from a stock fund to a short-term bond or money-market fund when they think the stock market is about to fail.

Money Managers. Professionals that manage portfolios for institutions (i.e., mutual funds, banks, pension funds, or insurance companies).

Money Market Fund. One that invests in short-term government securities, bank certificates of deposit, and other low risk, low-return securities. These funds pay money market interest rates and withdrawals from them can be made anytime at a predictable per-share value.

Municipal Bond. Bonds issued by state or local governments. In most cases, the interest paid is exempt from federal taxes and, if the bondholder lives in the state where the bond was issued, from state and local taxes too.

Mutual Fund. An investment company that pools the money of many investors and buys various securities such as shares of stock in many companies or various bonds. Investors who own shares of the mutual fund automatically achieve the safety of a diversified portfolio without having to buy the individual investments themselves.

Nasdaq. An acronym for National Association of Securities Dealers Automated Quotations, a computerized system for reporting current price quotations on active over-the-counter securities. The system provides price quotations and permits execution of small customer orders. Large orders are executed by separate negotiations.

National Association of Investors Corporation (NAIC). An organization that provides information and support for both new and experienced investors. It has over 390,000 members and has been operating since 1941.

Net Asset Value (NAV). The market value of a single share of a mutual fund. It is calculated at the end of each business day by adding up the value of all the securities in the fund's portfolio, subtracting expenses, and dividing the sum by the number of shares outstanding.

Net Profit. The remaining profit on an investment once you've deducted all expenses.

Net Worth. The total value of all of the assets you own once outstanding debts have been deducted.

New Highs. Refers to a stock attaining a new price high when compared to its old price high of the last 52 weeks.

New York Stock Exchange (NYSE). Founded in 1792, the oldest and largest exchange in the U.S. where buyers and sellers meet via their brokers to execute buy and sell orders. It is located on Wall Street in New York City.

No-Load Mutual Fund. A mutual fund that charges no dealer or underwriting fee or commission, either at the time of purchase or at the time of sale. Its shares are sold at the fund's net asset value.

Offering Price. The purchase price per share of a mutual fund. This is determined by adding any sales charges that apply to the fund's net asset value per share (also called ask price).

Open-End Mutual Fund. A mutual fund that continuously sells its shares to the general public without the need for fixed capitalization.

Open Order. A buy or sell order that has not yet been executed or canceled.

Option. An agreement that gives the buyer the right to buy (call option) or sell (put option) in shares of a particular stock or stock index at a fixed price during a preset period. An option produces income, called a premium, for the seller, who gives up ownership of the securities if the option buyer exercises his right. For example, a call option buyer hopes the stock will rise in price by an amount that exceeds the premium paid for the option, while a put option seller hopes the stock will remain stable, rise, or drop by an amount less than his or her profit on the premium.

Over the Counter. A transaction involving securities that are not listed and traded on a central exchange. Trading in these securities is conducted through the National Association of Securities Dealers Automated Quotation system (NASDAQ), which is a computer-linked network of broker-dealers who stand ready to buy or sell certain stocks and bonds for their own account.

Paper Trading. Tracking "pretend" buys and sells on a piece of paper as a way of getting your feet wet in the market without actually being in it and trading with real money.

Par. For common stocks, the dollar value assigned to the stock when the stock is issued.

Penny Stock. A low-priced stock, generally selling below one dollar per share. The SEC has defined penny stocks as those with a value of less than five dollars and that do not meet certain asset or other requirements.

Point. A one-dollar change in a stock's market price. If a stock is up ten points, its price has increased by $10.

Portfolio. The securities owned by an investor such as stocks, bonds, mutual funds, and cash equivalents.

Portfolio Management. The money management techniques one employs to hopefully increase the value of their portfolio over time.

Portfolio Manager. The person in charge of managing a mutual fund's holdings.

Post-Analysis. Vital process of evaluating your successes and mistakes in the stock market by posting all previous buys and sells on charts for a specified time frame and separating out those that made money from those that were losses. Allows investors a way to improve their future performance by learning from past decisions.

Preferred Stock. A class of stock that has a claim on the company's earnings before payment is made on the common stock if the company declares a dividend.

Price/Earnings Ratio (PE). A stock's current price divided by its earnings of the past year. A stock's PE is an indicator of the market's expectations about that stock. A higher PE means higher expectations for the company's growth in earnings.

Prime Rate. The interest rate charged by banks for their customers they deem most creditworthy or prime.

Principal. The amount of money that is financed, borrowed, or invested.

Prospectus. A legal statement that describes the objectives of a specific investment. Every mutual fund is required to publish a prospectus and to give investors a copy, free of charge. To get one, just call the fund itself.

Proxy. A shareholder's written authorization giving someone else the authority to cast his or her vote at a shareholder meeting.

Rally (and False Rally). An attempt by a stock or the general market to turn and advance in price after a period of decline. Successful rallies are usually identified by more consistent price increases on greater than normal volume. False rallies are generally signified by increases in price but a lack of big or increased volume, indicating absence of large buying in the market. False rallies frequently either do not last as long or do not recover as much in price.

Rating. An evaluation of a bond issuer's creditworthiness and risk of default by a rating service. Moody's and Standard & Poor's are two well-known rating services.

Real Estate Investment Trusts (REIT). An investment company, usually traded publicly, that manages a portfolio of real estate in order to earn profits for shareholders. Modeled after mutual funds, REIT'S invest in properties that range from shopping centers and office buildings to apartment complexes and hotels.

Relative Strength Line. Available in most good charting services, relative strength line compares a stock's price performance with the overall market. If a relative strength line is trending up, the stock is outperforming the broader market (S&P 500). If it is trending downward, it is lagging the general market. It is normally wise to avoid stocks showing an overall down trend in their relative strength lines.

Retirement Plan Distribution. A withdrawal of funds from a retirement plan.

Return on Equity (ROE). An indicator of a company's financial performance. It measures how efficient a company is with its money.

Rollover. A transfer of assets from one retirement plan to another.

Round Lot. The basic unit of trading for a particular security. Most frequently, a round lot is 100 shares.

Sales Growth. A company's annual and quarterly rate of increase in revenues (sales). A measure of growth and success as long as it is accompanied by an equally strong rate of increase in earnings per share. You want to see both in a potential investment.

Secondary Market. A market where previously issued securities are traded (usually a stock exchange or the over-the-counter market).

Sector Fund. A mutual fund that seeks growth by investing in a specific sector of the economy, such as communications, finance, health, natural resources, precious metals, real estate, technology, or utilities.

Securities and Exchange Commission (SEC). The federal government agency, established by Congress, regulates and protects investors against malpractice in the securities markets.

Selling Long. Selling a security that you own, which is also called a long investment.

Selling Short. Selling a security that you do not own. You borrow the security from your broker and repurchase or deliver the security to pay back your broker.

SEP-IRA (Simplified Employee Pension Plan-IRA). A SEP-IRA is a tax-deferred retirement account designed for self-employed individuals.

Settlement. The close of a securities transaction when you pay your brokerage firm for the securities you've purchased, or when you deliver securities you've sold and receive the proceeds from the sale.

Settlement Date. In a securities transaction, the date when payment is due either to the customer or to the broker and the date when the certificates must be in the broker's possession.

Shakeout. A sharp pullback or correction in the price of a stock that scares people out, and then turns around and advances.

Share. The ownership in a company represented by a stock certificate that specifies the company and the shareholder. For mutual funds, a unit of ownership in the fund.

Short Sellers (or Selling Short). Investors that borrow shares of a stock from their brokerage firm and then sell the shares of the stock hoping it will go down in price. They must later purchase the borrowed shares on the open market (presumably for less than they sold them for previously), making money between the initial sale and the subsequent buy back at a lower price. Short selling is difficult and not recommended for new or inexperienced investors.

Short-Term Capital Gain. A profit on the sale of a stock or mutual fund that the investor owned for less than one year.

Simple 401(k) Plan. A retirement savings plan, similar to a 401(k) plan, but tailored to the needs of small employers, specifically those with fewer than 100 employees.

Simple IRA Plan. An employer-sponsored salary reduction retirement plan available only to companies with 100 or less eligible employees.

Small Capitalization Stock. The stock of a company that has a market value of under $500 million. Small capitalization (small cap) companies tend to grow more rapidly than larger companies, and they tend to reinvest their profits toward company growth rather than paying dividends. They also tend to be more volatile than larger companies.

Small Company Fund. A mutual fund that seeks capital appreciation by investing in stocks or companies with market capitalization of less than $1 billion.

Social Security. Money paid out by the U.S. government's social insurance program of the same name, especially during an individual's retirement.

Social Security calculates the amount of the monthly benefit that you receive using a formula that's based on the contributions you've made and the age at which you retire.

Spousal IRA. An IRA established for a nonworking spouse or a married couple with only one spouse working outside the home who may contribute on behalf of their spouse.

Stalling of Price. A term indicating a type of price activity occurring on one of the market indices like the Dow, S&P 500, or Nasdaq composite. It occurs when the index price closes barely up, unchanged, or slightly down on increased volume from the day before after having advanced noticeably for several days. This indicates distribution or selling in the index at that point.

Standard & Poor's 500 (S&P 500). An index of 500 major companies broken down as follows. 400 industrial firms, 20 transportation firms, 40 utilities, and 40 financial firms.

Statement. An individual's monthly record of their trading activity from the brokerage. Your statement is one of the most important documents you'll receive from your brokerage, so take time to understand its sections and explanations.

Stock Split. A technique where a company's board of directors can increase the total number of outstanding shares of its stock by authorizing the exchange of a current share for more shares. For example, a two for one stock split exchanges 2 shares of stock for every one share a stockowner owns. The purpose is often to reduce the price per share of a high-priced stock, making it easier to trade.

Stop-Limit Order. An order to buy or sell a security at a specified price or better (the stop-limit price), but only after a given stop price has been reached or passed. There is no guarantee of execution.

Stop Order. An order to buy or sell a security once it reaches or trades through a set market price, called the stop price. Stop orders automatically become market orders once the set price is reached. Stop prices are not guaranteed. A stop order to buy must be placed at a price higher than the current market price. A stop order to sell must be placed at a price lower than the current market price.

Stock. A type of security that represents part ownership of a company.

Stock Certificate. A certificate of ownership of one or more specified shares of a company's stock. You cannot buy or sell stock without the certificate, which includes information such as your name or the name of your brokerage firm, the number of shares, the name of the issuer, and the stock's par value.

Stock Dividend. An investor's share of the income earned by a company issuing stock.

Takeover. A change in the controlling interest of a corporation through a friendly acquisition, a merger, or an unfriendly bid that the management of the target company opposes.

Tax Deferral. The postponement of a tax obligation until sometime in the future.

Technical Analysis. Study of a stock or general market's price and volume movement, mainly by using charts to analyze buying and selling in the market.

Ticker Symbol. An abbreviation of a security's name that is used to identify it for trading purposes and in newspaper financial pages and price quotations.

Total Return. The dividends, interest, and capital gains and price appreciation that a mutual fund achieves in a given period. A total-return fund is one that pursues both growth and income by investing in a mix of growth stocks, high-dividend stocks, and bonds.

Trade Date. The actual date on which a security is bought or sold. The purchase price is determined by the closing net asset value on this date. The trade date also determines whether you are eligible for dividends.

Treasury Bill (T-bill), Note, or Bond. A security issued by the U.S. government.

Turnaround Stock. Company that has been doing poorly for some time but is now turning its sales and earnings back up, usually due to new management, new products, or a major improvement in industry conditions.

Turnover Rate. The number of shares traded per year as a percentage of shares held by a mutual fund. An indicator of a fund's trading activity. Many aggressive growth funds have higher turnover rates.

Value Investing. An investing strategy that focuses on companies believed to be undervalued. Value stocks are typically viewed as being bargain-priced and a good value. This strategy focuses on fundamentals and less on technicals. A value fund is a mutual fund that invests in undervalued stocks.

Volatility. A measure of the degree of fluctuation in a stock's price. Volatility is exemplified by large, frequent price swings up and down.

Zero-Coupon Bond. A bond that makes no periodic interest payments but instead is sold at a discount from its face value. The buyer of a zero receives the rate of return by the gradual appreciation of the bond, which is redeemable at face value on its maturity date.

Index